BECKETT
REMEMBERING
REMEMBERING
BECKETT

BECKETT

REMEMBERING

REMEMBERING

BECKETT

A CENTENARY CELEBRATION

EDITED BY JAMES AND ELIZABETH KNOWLSON

ARCADE PUBLISHING
NEW YORK

FIRST ENGLISH–LANGUAGE EDITION

Library of Congress Cataloging-in-Publication Data

Beckett remembering, remembering Beckett : a centenary celebration / edited by James and Elizabeth Knowlson. —1st English-language ed.
    p. cm.
  The first half is comprised of interviews with Samuel Beckett. The second half is reflections on him by various people.
  Includes bibliographical references.
  ISBN 1-55970-772-0
1. Beckett, Samuel, 1906– —Interviews. 2. Beckett, Samuel, 1906– —Friends and associates. 3. Authors, Irish—20th century— Interviews. 4. Authors, French—20th century—Interviews. 5. Beckett, Samuel, 1906– —Stage history. 6. Irish—France— Interviews. I. Beckett, Samuel, 1906– II. Knowlson, James. III. Knowlson, Elizabeth.

  PR6003.E282Z57188 2005
  848'.91409—dc22   2005010308

Published in the United States by Arcade Publishing, Inc., New York
Distributed by Time Warner Book Group

Visit our Web site at www.arcadepub.com

10 9 8 7 6 5 4 3 2 1

Designed by Hewer Text U.K., Ltd., Edinburgh

EB

PRINTED IN THE UNITED STATES OF AMERICA

CONTENTS

Part II Remembering Beckett

Chapter 4 Post-war Success:
   The French Novels and *En attendant Godot*

Chapter 5 Growing Fame

Chapter 6 Beckett as Director

Chapter 7 Memories of Beckett in London and Berlin

ACKNOWLEDGEMENTS

Our first and most important debt in this volume published for the centenary of Samuel Beckett's birth in 1906 is to Beckett himself for the many personal interviews which he granted to James Knowlson in 1989 and which are collected here for the first time. Beckett imposed no restrictions on the use of any of this material and the interviews are collected and printed by permission of the Samuel Beckett Estate, which owns the copyright to Beckett's words.

The book could not have been realized, however, without the ready consent and full, enthusiastic cooperation of the many interviewees or their heirs and without the input of Beckett's friends, some of whom have written pieces especially for it.

We thank most warmly all the contributors and their heirs, who are listed below.

Certain photographers waived their professional rights and kindly provided a photograph as their gift to this volume in memory of Beckett and we thank them for their generosity: Beppe Arvidsson; John Haynes; Sandra Lousada; Lütfi Özkök; Albert Maysles; Wolfgang Suschitzy; the William MacQuitty Estate. We also wish to acknowledge the kindness of those who have provided photographs, some of which were previously unknown, to add to the more familiar ones of Beckett and his family.

A few very short extracts are reprinted from interviews with or essays by Peter Brook; Emil Cioran; Eugène Ionesco; B. S. Johnson; Jay Levy; John Montague; Edna O'Brien; Robert Pinget; Tom Stoppard. All references to the books in which these extracts originally appeared are fully listed in the chapter entitled *In brief*.

Finally, we should make clear here exactly what is being published in the appendix on 'Beckett on Racine'. This consists of Mrs

Grace West's (née McKinley) student notes on two of Samuel Beckett's lectures to her class. These are, of course, her own words, as can be seen by contrasting her version of the lectures with those by Rachel Burrows (née Dobbin) and Leslie Daiken, which are held in Trinity College, Dublin and the University of Reading archives respectively. As such they do not constitute a new Beckett text and should be approached with some degree of caution. But the notes are clear and coherent and offer a fascinating insight into the early encounter of one writer of genius with a dramatist whom he much admired.

Institutions

Campbell College Archive, Belfast; Dartmouth College Library, Hanover, New Hampshire; The Deutsches Theatermuseum, Munich; Getty Images; the Historisches Archiv, Stuttgart; The Heinz Köster Archiv; The Board of Trinity College, Dublin and the Alumni Office there; The Beckett International Foundation, the University of Reading; *Journal of Beckett Studies*; the Library of Syracuse University; Ullstein Bild; the Nobel Foundation; University College, London Library; the McFarlin Library of the University of Tulsa; The Morris Library, Southern Illinois University, Carbondale.

The following private individuals:

Edward Albee and the Albee Foundation; Avigdor Arikha; Walter Asmus; Anne Atik; the late Fernand Aude; Paul Auster; Patrick Bailly-Cowell; the late Boleslaw Barlog; the late Ann Beckett; Edward Beckett; John Beckett; Georges Belmont (Pelorson); Horst Bollmann; the late Patrick Bowles; Enoch Brater; Peter Brook; the late Brenda Bruce; Professor Mary Bryden; the late Dr Robert Burkitt and Robin Burkitt; the late Rachel Burrows (née Dobbin); the late Dr Gottfried Büttner and Dr Marie-Renate Büttner; Meta Buttnick (née Bloom); James Campbell; Pierre Célice; the late E. M. Cioran; Rick Cluchey; Jonathan Coe; Professor Ruby Cohn; Cathy Courtney; Professor Thomas Cousineau; the late Gervase Cowell (SOE adviser); the late Hume Cronyn; Susan Cooper-Cronyn; the late William Cunningham; Nancy Cunningham; Lori Curtis (University of Tulsa); the late Emile Delavenay; Zoe Dominic Photography; Christel Dormagen; Annika Ekdahl (The Nobel Foundation); Geoffrey Elborn; the late Martin Esslin and Monica Esslin; Margaret Farrington (the Thomas MacGreevy Estate); Raymond Federman; Martha Fehsenfeld; Casey Flynn; Daniel Fogel; Gilian Furlong (University College, London Library); Phyllis Gaffney; Sir Herbert Gamble; Julian Garforth; Grainne Gaynor; S. E. Gontarski; the late Evelyn Nora Goodbody (née Strong); Ursula Greenwood; Edward Gretton (the Jane Lidderdale Estate); the late James Guilford and Ronald Guilford; Keith Haines (Campbell College); Stella Halkyard (the John Rylands Library); the late Dr Cyril Harris; the late Lawrence E. Harvey; Sheila Harvey-Tanzer; the late Josette Hayden; Ronald Hayman; Lawrence Held; the late Martin Held; the late Jocelyn Herbert; Klaus Herm; Aidan Higgins; Jakob Holder (the Albee Foundation); Alannah Hopkin; Susan Howe; the late Eugène Ionesco; Hugo Jehle; the late B. S. Johnson; General Sir Charles Jones; Sheila Jones (née Dobbs); Jan Jönson; Valerie Joynt (née Lawrence); Gottfried Junker; the late John Kobler; Rosemarie Koch; Charles Krance; Barbara Krieger (Dartmouth College); Rolf Kruger; Professor Jay Levy; Antoni Libera; the late Yvonne Lob; Christopher Logue; Sandra and Julian Lousada; the late Reverend Dr Brian McConnell; the late Adelaide Mary McCormick (née Arabin Jones) and Simon and Timothy McCormick; Simone McKee; Rebecca and Miranda MacQuitty; Anna McMullan; Alan Mandell; Jean Martin; Jane Maxwell (Trinity College, Dublin); Bernard Meehan (Trinity College, Dublin); Anthony Minghella; John Montague; Louise Morgan (the National Gallery of Ireland); Neill Morton (Headmaster, Portora Royal School); Caroline Beckett Murphy; Frederick Neumann; Mark Nixon; Edna O'Brien; the late Eileen O'Casey and Shivaun O'Casey; Vibeke Kennair Ottesen; Lois Overbeck; the late Sheila Page (née Roe); Alexis Péron; the late Geoffrey Perrin and Jean Perrin; Richard Pine; Emeritus Professor John Pilling; the late Robert Pinget, Ronald Porter, Executor of the late Peter Woodthorpe; Eric Price (Grove Atlantic); the photographer I. C. Rapoport; Gennet Rich; Mary Rogers; the late Lucien Roubaud; Michael Rudman; Nicholas Ryan (the Thomas MacGreevy Estate); Claude Sarraute and the late Nathalie Sarraute; Jay Satterfield (Dartmouth College); Elliseva Sayers; Robert Scanlan; Michael Schmidt (Editor of *PN Review*) for his advice; the late Alan Schneider; Susan Schreibman; Eva-Katharina Schultz; Dorothy Scott (née Pearse); the late Duncan Scott and Bernadette Scott for permission to use her husband's invaluable notes; Richard and Jeannette Seaver (who are also our publishers in the United States); Morris Sinclair; Emily Skillen (née Lisney); Jerry Speier; Nina Soufy; Tom Stoppard; the late Francis Stuart and Finola Stuart; Moira Symons (née Neill); the late Ursula Thompson and Mima Thompson (now Deborah Charlton); Bud Thorpe; Claire Tomalin; Ann Trimble (née McConnell); the late Mita and Edmund Tuby; Thomas Victor; Dr John A. Wallace; James Walling; Jane Walling Wefelmeyer; Helen Watanabe; Terence West; Francis Wheale; Billie Whitelaw; the late Eileen Williams; the late Professor John O. Wisdom; Diane Worrell; Emeritus Professor Barbara Wright; Jesse Forbes Yates (née Brown); Diana Zambonelli.

Finally, because of its mixed content of interviews, personal reminiscences, especially commissioned pieces and over a hundred photographs this book owes a lot to the skill, dedication, patience, enthusiasm and good humour of the editorial staff at Bloomsbury Publishing in Great Britain: Dr Kathy Rooney, who first commissioned it; Bill Swainson, who took over its preparation and production and became its overseeing spirit; Louise Miller who assisted him capably and enthusiastically and dealt with the photographs; Sarah Hall, the copy editor, who helped to simplify and clarify, as well as scrupulously copy-edit the text and Penny Edwards, who designed and oversaw the book's production. In the United States, we warmly thank our publishers, Richard and Jeannette Seaver, and in Germany, our dedicated editor, Hans-Ulrich Müller-Schwefe, the consistently helpful picture editor, Christine Gröh, Matthias Reiner and our excellent translator, Christel Dormagen.

James and Elizabeth Knowlson

Picture Credits

40 Beckett's friend, Thomas MacGreevy, *c.* 1928. *(Courtesy of Margaret Farrington and Nicholas Ryan)*

42 Emile Delavenay before his wedding, 1928. *(Courtesy of Claire Tomalin)*

44 James Joyce in the 1930s. *(Courtesy of Getty-Images)*

48 Joyce, Giorgio, Lucia and Nora in the 1920s. *(Courtesy of the Morris Library, Southern Illinois University, Carbondale)*

50 Lucia Joyce in the early 1930s. *(Courtesy of The Jane Lidderdale Estate and University College, London)*

51 Paul Léon in the late 1930s. *(Courtesy of the McFarlin Library, University of Tulsa)*

57 Grace West with a group of Trinity College, Dublin students, 1930–1. *(Courtesy of Terence West)*

59 Jack Yeats at his easel, 1950. *(Courtesy of the William MacQuitty Estate)*

60 Francis Stuart. *(Courtesy of Finola Stuart)*

65 Beckett and Thomas MacGreevy, London, 1934–5. *(Courtesy of Margaret Farrington and Nicholas Ryan)*

67 Beckett's wife, Suzanne, at sixty. *(Courtesy of Margaret Farrington and Nicholas Ryan)*

67 Suzanne as a young woman. *(Courtesy of Mita and Edmund Tuby)*

71 Ursula and Geoffrey Thompson, *c.* 1937. *(Courtesy of Mima Thompson)*

73 The Thompsons' wedding, 1935. *(Courtesy of Mima Thompson)*

74 J. M. Coetzee, Nobel Prize winner for literature, 2003. *(Courtesy of the Nobel Foundation)*

76 Beckett's application to the University of Cape Town, July 1937. *(Courtesy of the Samuel Beckett Estate)*

77 Alfred Péron, *c.* 1939. *(Photograph by Samuel Beckett. Courtesy of Alexis Péron)*

78 Jeannine Picabia ('Gloria'), 1939–40. *(Courtesy of her son, Patrick Bailly-Cowell)*

80 Gabrielle Buffet-Picabia in Madrid in 1943. *(Courtesy of Patrick Bailly-Cowell)*

81 Nathalie Sarraute. *(Courtesy of Historisches Archiv, Stuttgart)*

82 Alfred and Mania Péron, 1939. *(Courtesy of Alexis Péron)*

84 Beckett's rented house in Roussillon. *(Photograph by Gottfried Büttner. Courtesy of Marie-Renate Büttner)*

86 Anna O'Meara (pen-name Noel) de Vic Beamish. *(Courtesy of Ursula Greenwood)*

87 Henri Hayden's pen-and-ink sketch of Roussillon. *(Courtesy of The Beckett International Foundation, The University of Reading)*

90 'The Capital of Ruins': the Normandy town of Saint-Lô after the war-time bombing. *(Collection Béziers. Courtesy of Phyllis Gaffney)*

92 Beckett with Simone McKee and friends in Ireland after the war, *c.* 1948. *(Courtesy of Simone McKee)*

93 Beckett in Ireland after the war, *c.* 1948. *(Courtesy of Simone McKee)*

97 The painter Henri Hayden and Samuel Beckett, early 1960s. *(Courtesy of the late Josette Hayden)*

98 May Beckett, 1948–9. *(Courtesy of Dartmouth College Library)*

99 Beckett's 'modest little house' in Ussy sur Marne. *(Courtesy of the Samuel Beckett Estate)*

195 Rick Cluchey in *Krapp's Last Tape*, 1977. *(Courtesy of Rick Cluchey)*

198 Beckett with members of the San Quentin Drama Workshop, 1984. *(Courtesy of Lawrence Held)*

200 Alan Mandell. *(Courtesy of Alan Mandell)*

204 Lawrence Held as Estragon in *Waiting for Godot*, 1984. *(Photograph by Daniel Fogel. Courtesy of Lawrence Held)*

208 Bud Thorpe as Vladimir in *Waiting for Godot*, 1984. *(Photograph by Daniel Fogel. Courtesy of Bud Thorpe)*

212 Beckett in Berlin. *(Photograph by Heinz Köster)*

214 Duncan Scott. *(Courtesy of Bernadette Scott)*

220 Beckett with Gottfried Büttner. *(Courtesy of Gottfried Büttner)*

225 Beckett on the set of *Film*, New York, 1964. *(Photograph by I.C. Rapoport)*

226 Beckett in the 1960s. *(Jay Levy)*

227 Beckett with Alan Schneider, Paris, 1956. *(Courtesy of Syracuse University Library)*

229 Edward Albee. *(Photograph by Jerry Speier. Courtesy of Edward Albee)*

232 Paul Auster. *(Courtesy of Paul Auster and Faber and Faber)*

235 Jessica Tandy. *(Courtesy of Susan Cooper-Cronyn)*

238 Hume Cronyn. *(Photograph by Editta Sherman. Courtesy of Susan Cooper-Cronyn)*

242 Frederick Neumann in his adaptation of *Worstward Ho*, 1986. *(Photograph by Thomas Victor. Courtesy of Frederick Neumann)*

247 Samuel Beckett at the Royal Court Theatre, London, 1973. *(Photograph by John Haynes; gift of John Haynes)*

249 James Knowlson. *(Photograph by Rolf Kruger)*

255 S.E. Gontarski. *(Courtesy of S.E. Gontarski)*

262 Charles Krance. *(Courtesy of Charles Krance)*

268 Michael Rudman. *(Photograph by John Haynes. Courtesy of Michael Rudman)*

272 Jan Jönson. *(Photograph by Beppe Arvidsson. Gift of Beppe Arvidsson)*

277 Spoon Jackson and Twin James in *Waiting for Godot*, San Quentin Prison. *(Photograph by Beppe Arvidsson)*

280 Anthony Minghella. *(Photograph by Brigitte Lacombe. Courtesy of Anthony Minghella)*

288 Jay Levy, Samuel Beckett, Stuart Levy. *(Photograph courtesy of Jay Levy)*

292 Antoni Libera. *(Courtesy of Antoni Libera)*

294 Robert Scanlan. *(Courtesy of Robert Scanlan)*

300 Raymond Federman. *(Courtesy of Raymond Federman)*

305 Beckett in 1985. *(Photograph by Hugo Jehle. Courtesy of the Historisches Archiv, Stuttgart)*

307 Grace West. *(Courtesy of Terence West)*

Preface

Most tribute volumes necessarily focus on the later years of their subject's life, especially when that life has been a long one and when the number of those who are still alive to remember the early years is very small. With this book, published to commemorate the centenary of Samuel Beckett's birth in 1906, we have, however, been able to portray Beckett at many different periods of his life: as a child, a youth, a student, a reluctant teacher and lecturer, a struggling young writer, a member of a British Special Operations Executive cell in Paris during the Second World War, then working with a French Resistance group in the south of France.

In the post-war period, his contemporaries speak of Beckett as the author of the famous novel trilogy (*Molloy, Malone Dies, The Unnamable*) and of the play, *Waiting for Godot*, which had worldwide success in the 1950s (all first written in French); and, finally, friends write of him in physical decline and old age. This wide range of reminiscences is made possible because interviews with members of Beckett's family, his friends and his colleagues were recorded over ten years ago while I was preparing a biography of Beckett entitled *Damned to Fame.** So, although many of the interviewees are now dead, their memories have not been lost with them and can now be included alongside the tributes of the living in the present book, a companion volume to that biography.

A biographer draws on reminiscences of his subject from such personal sources, along with much other written material, especially correspondence, but must necessarily select, filter, as well as reject so many of these memories. And, later, he or she may well come to regret, as I did on a number of occasions, not using a particular quotation or a telling detail. For things tend to come

---

* James Knowlson, *Damned to Fame. The Life of Samuel Beckett* (London, Bloomsbury Publishing and New York, Simon and Schuster, 1996, reissued by Grove Atlantic, 2004.)

to light that throw into new prominence something which at the time appeared unimportant. None the less, I hesitated for several years before concluding that a book which offers the unmediated words of the speakers not only has a distinct fascination of its own but also adds new elements to what is already known about Beckett. Of course, the material still has to be selected, shaped and edited. Yet the personality of the speaker comes through very vividly when his or her words do not have to be paraphrased, summarized or integrated into a complex narrative. For that reason we have deliberately chosen to leave the interviews in their *viva voce* form.*

Quite different views of the man and the writer can be set alongside each other in an oral record in a way that is much more difficult to achieve in a biography. The widely divergent views of Beckett as a lecturer by his former students at Trinity College, Dublin are a case in point. Their opinions were solicited since the publication of my biography and are published here for the first time. Some regarded him as brilliant; others found him bored and boring. In other chapters, those interviewed stress the human traits of a man whom in many cases they knew long before he ever achieved any measure of success.

Alongside these earlier interviews, we also invited a number of Beckett's friends and those who had worked with him over the years to set down their memories of him. Several writers (e.g. Edward Albee, Paul Auster, J. M. Coetzee, Aidan Higgins, Antoni Libera, Raymond Federman) also speak of his work and of the impact that it had on their own writing. We should stress that it would not have been possible to include the memories of all of Beckett's surviving friends. This is necessarily a selection. To take only the example of his publishers, Barney Rosset and John Calder have already spoken about him in their own writing or have given interviews concerning their friendship or collaboration. We also did not want to compete with another book of tributes, *Beckett at 100*, being prepared by John Calder.

Our criterion was rather to seek out those who could speak about him at different points in his life or who could illuminate different

---

* All of the interviews recorded in French are translated by the editors.

elements of his personality. It seemed important for instance to reflect his hypersensitivity to pain and suffering and to point to the significance of this in his writing. We also needed to reflect the depth and intensity of his thinking about life, art and language and the relations that exist between them. The remarkable notes of Patrick Bowles and Lawrence E. Harvey on their own conversations with Beckett satisfy these demands better than most.

In the specially commissioned pieces, contributors were given the freedom to write whatever they wanted but, in order to focus the mind, were asked to limit themselves to about 2,000 words. The only one to whom this rule did not apply was Beckett himself. For the writer gave so few interviews during his lifetime that to possess a whole set of verbatim talks with him, especially ones in which he is speaking about his personal life, is unusual, perhaps even unique. In Part I of this volume, we publish then much fuller, more coherent versions of interviews which were quoted only partially in my biography of Beckett. In the interviews, he speaks interestingly about his family, his early youth, his friendship with James Joyce and the Joyces, his psychotherapy in the 1930s, his work as a liaison officer in the Resistance, his escape from the Gestapo and his life in hiding throughout the rest of the war in Roussillon in the Vaucluse. Sadly, he died before we could progress very far beyond the war in our conversations. Parts of different interviews are merged but never altered. The practice followed with all the interviews is simply to remove the interviewer's questions and to allow the interviewee to speak uninterrupted. Whenever something appears unclear, the editors add the necessary information in square brackets.

For this commemorative volume we have also sought out new or unusual photographs not just of Beckett himself but of family or friends who played a significant part in his life. We thank here the descendants of such friends and colleagues who have hunted through their trunks and boxes for surviving photographic records, occasionally coming up with some surprises, even a few treasures.

Finally, a few years ago, I was contacted by Mrs Grace West (née McKinley), one of Beckett's former students at Trinity College, Dublin in 1930–1, who had kept all her notes on his university lectures on the plays of Jean Racine. With the kind agreement of her son, Terence West, it seemed appropriate to end this book with the thoughts of the 24-year-old lecturer Samuel Beckett on a dramatist who mattered a lot to him at the time and whose own later theatrical development was to be influenced by his meditations on the theatre of that dramatist. Here, as elsewhere in the book, our main object has been to give more substance and significance than is usual in a tribute volume.

James Knowlson, May 2005

Part I

Beckett Remembering

1

The Young Samuel Beckett

Family photograph. *Left to right:* Molly Roe (cousin); Samuel Beckett on his aunt's knee; Frank Beckett (brother); Aunt Rubina Roe; Sheila Roe (cousin); Annie Roe (grandmother), *c.* 1910.

Biography, 1906–27

Samuel Barclay Beckett (1906–89) was born on Good Friday, 13 April 1906 in the prosperous Irish village of Foxrock, County Dublin.

His mother was Maria (known as May) Beckett née Roe (1871–1950), the daughter of a once-wealthy mill-owner in Newbridge, County Kildare. His father, William Frank Beckett (1871–1933) was a quantity surveyor in the Dublin firm of Beckett and Medcalf and the son of a prosperous firm of master builders. His brother, who was almost four years older than Samuel, was Frank Edward.

The family was descended on both sides from solid middle-class, Protestant, Anglo-Irish stock with, on his father's side, a distinct musical and artistic strain: grandmother Beckett and an aunt and an uncle were musical, Aunt Cissie also being a painter. But neither of Beckett's parents was in the least intellectual or artistic.

Sam Beckett was a fearless, adventurous boy who showed as much prowess for sport at school and university as he did for literature and foreign languages. He went to private schools; first to a prep school, Earlsfort House, in Dublin, then to Portora Royal School, Oscar Wilde's old school, in Enniskillen, County Fermanagh, where Beckett's brother, Frank, was already a boarder and where Sam swam, boxed and played cricket and rugby for the school teams.

Beckett entered Trinity College, Dublin in 1923 and read French and Italian in the Modern European Literature course, also studying English literature during his first two years at university. He was deeply influenced by the presence, the lectures and the writings of his professor, Thomas Brown Rudmose-Brown, who inspired in him a love of the poetry of Ronsard, Scève, Petrarch and the theatre of Racine and introduced him to the work of many modern French poets. He also took Italian lessons from a private tutor, Bianca Esposito, with whom he studied Dante's *Divina Commedia*.

Home

*Samuel Beckett** We lived in a very chic kind of suburban setting. My father built the house ['Cooldrinagh']. There were other houses there already, but it never became particularly populated: a very few big houses. It had a back entrance from a lane. The main entrance was, I remember, an iron gate that we opened to let the car [a Delage] through. There was a big comfortable kitchen with a pantry, a scullery and a larder. It had a red floor, a big range, and, outside it, a big yard, with a coal hole where the coal was kept and, a bit beyond it, a henhouse, for bantam hens. A little further on, outside, was the greenhouse where my father grew tomatoes. We knew all our neighbours.

---

* The interviews with Samuel Beckett by JK took place from July to November 1989. Other interviews in this book, unless otherwise stated, were also conducted by JK.

Beckett's family home, 'Cooldrinagh'.

There were two servants. They slept at the top of the house. Frank and I had a room on the same floor as the two maids. I don't know much about them. They mostly stayed in the kitchen. Every night they climbed the steep stair to their little room.* One of them was called Mary Farren. She stayed with my mother after my father's death. My mother later moved into 'New Place'. I think Mary moved and stayed with her. Frank and I had one room which we shared – in the attic. There was a place with the water tank, where the water supply was stored and went through. Frank turned this into a workshop. He used to shut himself up there and make things: you know, wood and so on.

Sheila Page (cousin)† We lived on the first floor and the boys were on the top floor. We had rooms on the same floor as Aunt and Nunc

---

* On a number of occasions during these interviews Beckett adopts turns of phrase which he has already used in his writing. Here he quotes (probably unconsciously in this case) from Winnie's story in *Happy Days*: 'The sun was not well up when Milly rose, descended the steep . . . (*pause*) . . . slipped on her nightgown, descended all alone the steep wooden stairs, backwards on all fours, though she had been forbidden to do so . . .' (Samuel Beckett, *Happy Days*, London, Faber and Faber, 1966 [1st edn, 1963], p. 41; New York, Grove Press, 1961, p. 55.)
† Sheila Page (née Roe) lived with the Beckett family for several years as a child with her sister, Molly, after her mother died and while her father was working in Nyasaland.

Samuel Beckett
as a boy, *c.1910*.

Frank Beckett, Sam's
older brother, *c.1910*.

(I used to call him 'Nunc'). We just fooled about as young people would. We played a lot of tennis and were on bicycles all the time. They had a funny little spinney and we made tents there of branches and leaves that covered them. And we put a rug on it and used to read stories out there. And we used to play bridge – a sort of children's version of bridge, of course. Sam's bridge as an older man was incredible by the way. My sister Molly, my husband, Donald, and Sam and I used to play. We all played bridge. You'd deal out the cards, and normally you'd sort them out. But Sam would shuffle them, not put them in order. Yet he still knew where all the cards were. It was extraordinary.

I think he taught me to play chess, too, as I recall. We used to do those sorts of things. He played chess a lot with Frank. And we used to do jigsaws. We had a playroom, a sort of nursery, at 'Cooldrinagh'. I remember Aunt used to read us stories. Not necessarily at bedtime but, you know, sitting around. Oh yes, the most tearjerking things. One was called 'Froggy's Little Brother', I remember. I always wept solemn tears over that. You know, they were soppy sort of yarns.

Family

Samuel Beckett   They were born in the same year, my father and mother, in 1870 [in fact it was 1871]. My father died in 1933 and my mother died seventeen years later. She was seventeen years a widow. In fact, she hardly left off mourning for the whole time, in the little house, 'New Place', when she left 'Cooldrinagh'.

She was very fond of dogs. The first dog I remember we had at home was a Collie. That was when I was very small. My father couldn't bear cats. He couldn't be in the same room as a cat. So we never had a cat. But he loved dogs and we had a whole series of Kerry Blue terriers. They were terrible fighters. They were used for so-called sports in the west coast of Ireland. 'Drawing the badger', they called it. The badger was put in the closed end of a tunnel or big pipe and they'd send the dog in to draw the badger out. They were both

One of Beckett's dogs.

ferocious beasts. And as often as not the dog was defeated in this horrible concern.

The Kerry Blues were beautiful animals. But you'd go out for a walk with one and he'd see another dog and attack it. There was the bitch and the dam and the grannie. I've remembered their names. Bumble was the first, the bitch, then there was Badger, Wolf and Mac: all Kerry Blues. I remember going on long walks with Badger. I'll tell you an anecdote about my mother and dogs. My father was alive at that time. He was sleeping. She was awake. And there was the sound of a dog barking in the distance, barking, barking, barking. She got up in the middle of the night and went out and tracked down where the dog was by the bark; she followed the bark. It was in the garden of a family called Goode about five hundred yards from the house. She got into the garden somehow and found this unfortunate dog in a trap, trapped. And she released the dog.

*Ann Beckett (cousin)** When Sam's father, Willie, died in 1933, Aunt Molly [Samuel Beckett's mother, May] rented a house in

---

* Ann Beckett (1929–2003). Her father, Dr Gerald Beckett (1884–1950), was Sam's father's younger brother. He was appointed Medical Officer for County Wicklow towards the end of the 1920s. The family lived in the little village of Greystones, on the coast, south of Bray, and it was there that Ann and her twin brother, John, used to see Sam and his mother in the mid-1930s. Beckett played piano duets and golf with their father.

Beckett's mother, May Beckett, with her brother, *c.* 1937.

Greystones so that she could see Willie's grave in the graveyard. As children we adored it because it was a favourite site for all the children of the neighbourhood. They used to beseech me to bring them to my Aunt Molly's house, because she had two Kerry Blue dogs, who were rather scary and sort of slightly edgy. The other thing was that she always kept an enormous jar of bulls-eyes [sweets or candy]. She produced the bulls-eyes and all the kids around used to have some. One day, I remember, I swallowed one the wrong way and – being a nurse and knowing exactly what to do – she just caught me by the feet, upturned me and banged my back. The other kids were fierce impressed by this rapid treatment! I remember Aunt Molly being rather severe. I was slightly in awe of her. She was very tall and rather overbearing-looking and definite in the way she spoke. But at the same time she was rather exciting. There was a warmth from her as well. She was very kind to people. I had a raggle of kids with me, children in the neighbourhood whom I'm sure must have been very annoying to her, a noisy group of children. She never gave us the feeling that she didn't want to see us or anything like that but simply went off and got those bulls-eyes . . .

James Guilford (neighbour)   Mrs Beckett was thin and fairly tall and rather sharp-featured. She had tremendous charm and generosity. I'll tell you one thing that she did. I was a young married man and I built a house nearby and she thought that buttermilk was good for us. So she used to bring us down a pint of buttermilk or a can of buttermilk or whatever every time she got it. From the milkman or wherever she got it. She thought it was good for us. It was sour to taste but I got a taste for it and it was very nice. There was nothing she wouldn't do and she'd keep on doing it, you know. But at that time she was regarded as being something of an oddity. The fact of her wanting to have a donkey of course only added to this reputation. She also had dogs, Kerry Blues. They were big. I had trouble with them because I think Mrs Beckett had two of them at first and they are very pugnacious dogs. I had a cocker spaniel, quiet-natured, and those dogs absolutely tore him to bits. It was an appalling thing to me and I had to try and get the vet to do the best he could. He was never the same again. And what could I say to Mrs Beckett?

Bill and May Beckett with their niece, Sheila Page (*née* Roe) and her children.

Caroline Beckett Murphy (niece) I was in awe of my grand-mother. But she was very kind. I can remember vividly – it couldn't have been easy for her to entertain me – one of the things she used to do in the afternoon – she always had a donkey and she used to get her gardener-cum-handyman to harness up the donkey and off we used to go down Brighton Road to visit various of her old cronies . . . I can also remember going to church with her, to Tullow Parish Church. Church was an important part of her weekly schedule . . . I never remember her wearing any other colour than black. And she always wore a hat.

Sheila Page I used to go for rides with her in the donkey and cart. I was terrified, since I was never quite sure whether the donkey would take off. But I was grown up then and probably married. We used to go for a little drive – it was very countrified, you know, in Foxrock. Down to Findlater's Stores near the station. Then Sam's father got a car. But first he got a motorbike and sidecar, to begin with. He used to put May in the sidecar and I'd sit on the saddle on the back. This was before people got cars. Then he got a Delage and I used to go down with him every morning when he was getting it out to go into the city.

May Beckett, on the right, with (probably) her brother's wife, *c.* 1937.

Aunt May was unpredictable in a way. I remember we were playing hide-and-seek or something on the top floor and they had a wide curtain and I was hiding behind it. Sam pushed the curtain to see if I was there. And I broke the window. Poor old thing. She said, I won't have you children staying here any more. All over in a minute. But it was very kind, having us. And I think the boys probably got bored having us around. Molly [Sheila's sister] was very good with Aunt. She suffered awful fits of her being difficult and so on. But she loved her dearly and Molly was very patient with her. She was a difficult woman. But she must have had a wonderful strain of unselfishness, taking us on.

Samuel Beckett Mother was always in the kitchen, helping and cooking. She was a very good cook and she used to do the shopping. She went to Findlater's shop beside Foxrock Station. It's gone though now. I often did shopping for them myself at Findlater's Stores. She also looked after the flowers and helped in the garden. She looked after the house. The housework. It was a very big house and too much for one servant. [The earlier two servants were later reduced to one.] And in the kitchen, every year, she'd make the marmalade. Huge quantities of marmalade. She'd do that. And prepare it all. And we'd go blackberrying in the fields. My mother had some local friends. Local people. Mrs Coote was one of

Beckett's father, Bill Beckett, *c.* 1928.

them. She is mentioned in one of my stories. I used to go with Frank to work with Mr Coote on his stamps. And Mrs Coote used to come to tea with my mother – the 'wafer-thin bread and butter'.*

Sheila Page   I don't think Sam and his mother ever tuned in the way Bill [his father] and Sam did. She seemed overly anxious about him in some way. I don't know whether it was that he had been a difficult child – I wasn't conscious of it. She could be very stern with him. There was a very tense relationship between them when he was at Trinity [College, Dublin] and so on; that's probably why he took to his heels. If only they could have lived to have seen the success that he's been. But they used to think: 'If only he'd write something we could understand.' And my father said exactly the same . . . Uncle Bill and Sam were very close. They sort of understood each other. Bill was a man's man. They played golf together and went for wonderful walks. They were absolutely tuned in.

Samuel Beckett   My father was a quantity surveyor. And he had this contract with Fred Hicks. And when my father and mother married, they lived for a time in Dalkey, I think it was, while the house was being built. Fred Hicks was the architect and I remember him coming to the tennis parties, sitting on the edge, not playing but watching.

My father was a very kind man. Interested in my progress. I always felt guilty at letting him down. When I was working in

---

* Beckett is (consciously this time) quoting here from his book, *Company*: 'You are alone in the garden. Your mother is in the kitchen making ready for afternoon tea with Mrs Coote. Making the wafer-thin bread and butter. From behind a bush you watch Mrs Coote arrive. A small thin sour woman.' (Samuel Beckett, *Company*, London, John Calder, 1980, p. 28; *Nohow On: Company, Ill Seen Ill Said, Worstward Ho*, New York, Grove Press, 1996, p. 14.)

Trinity College, teaching in TCD, that gave him a great deal of pleasure. He was absolutely non-intellectual. He left school at fifteen. He was taken away. He couldn't stay and he was put to work. He had a big case of books, Dickens, encyclopedias that he never opened. He used to read Edgar Wallace. He was so pleased when I got this job at Trinity and when I got a good degree and then was appointed and had keys opening the gate [of Trinity College] on to the road, on to Nassau Street. We used to open the door and walk through. It was a privilege to have a key. Then when I resigned and gave the whole thing [teaching] up, he was very disappointed.

He was a tremendous walker. He used to walk home from work sometimes. He used to take a train to the suburb of Rathfarnham. And from Rathfarnham he would walk over the mountain road through Dundrum, Sandyford and Stillorgan and home through the race-course premises where he had a friend, Fred Clarke, the Clerk of the Course. He walked all the way home, about an hour and a half it took him. He often did that. We often used to walk a lot together in the mountains. We used to walk to Three Rock Mountain on Sunday morning across the fields. We found a way of avoiding the roads, across the Ballyogan Road, across the highroad, all the time in the fields, then up to the heather and the Three Rock. There actually were three rocks. The further one beyond that is Two Rock. I remember father being very tired and remember leaving him and going on at my own speed as a young man, then waiting for him in the lee of the rock. He had got tired and had to slow down. You can see the sea from there.*

I also remember we used to go once a week to a Turkish baths. I'd go with my father, who was trying to lose weight. And after all the sweating and the cooling off, we'd emerge from the Turkish baths and walk down the street to his club for a drink. I was given a beer, I think, and my father was given a whiskey, which he often used to pretend to drink because he wanted to wait for his own whiskey at

---

* In *Company* a man is 'looking out to sea from the lee of a great rock on the first summit scaled'. (*Company*, p. 17.) 'One day I told him [the narrator's father] about Milton's cosmology, away up in the mountains we were, resting against a huge rock looking out to sea, that impressed him greatly.' (*From an Abandoned Work, The Complete Short Prose 1929–1989*, ed. S. E. Gontarski, New York, Grove Press, 1995, p. 158.) 'JK: Did you ever tell your father about Milton? SB: I did, yes. Milton's cosmology! (*Laughs*).' (Interview with SB by JK.)

home. So he would say goodbye to his friends with a glass in his hand and then give it to the man on the door to drink, as we left! And then drive us home. He left his car in the Automobile Club in Dawson Street. And then he walked to his office from there.

Father gave up fishing. He used to go shooting too – he was a member of a shoot at one time – but he became disgusted with the cruelty of shooting and gave it up. But I remember going fishing with him in a little row boat, fishing for mackerel, with a spinner.

James Guilford   I knew Willie Beckett very well. You see, he was a quantity surveyor – Beckett and Medcalf was the name of the firm – in Dublin and I was in the builders' providers business. So when he was doing quantities for a big contract, if there was any detail that he hadn't got about materials, he'd get on the blower [the phone] and get through to me: 'Jimmy, what's so-and-so and so-and-so?' and I'd have to say: 'It's so-and-so and so-and-so', like that. He didn't even say who he was. I knew his voice.

Billy was a terrific character, a charmer, a real charmer, tremendously energetic, large in figure, heavily built. All he knew about was to get on with things. Even his recreation was walking; he didn't do much else, didn't play games much I think [except for golf and bridge], but he used to walk for miles and miles; and he used to bring Sam particularly with him. And he'd walk over the mountains, my goodness, three or four times as far as we would even think of going. He was never desperately serious unless he was in some interesting topic. Inclined to be jovial, yes, but he was hot-tempered. He'd get angry very easily.

Beckett's brother, Frank.

Samuel Beckett   My brother, Frank, was at Engineering School [in Trinity College, Dublin]. Very good at it, he was. He was an intelligent chap. But

Sam and Frank playing cards, at 'Shottery', Killiney.

he wasn't interested in art or anything like that. He played golf. I played with him. But he was very nervous; an uncertain temper.

After he graduated from Engineering School, my brother got a job on some railway in India. A two-year appointment, it was. When he came back in 1932, not knowing what to do, he had a pause before the next job. My father died in 1933. Frank put in the time. He would help my father during this period in the office. So when my father died, he had to take over the office. He had to pass his examination to become a quantity surveyor. I remember making him laugh by suggesting that he should put an advertisement in the paper saying: 'Frank Beckett, the quality quantity surveyor'. But I think the move was a big mistake. I played the piano at home. I used to play classical music, but Frank played nothing but jazz. I used to play sometimes with Frank and duets with [my uncle] Gerald.

Sheila Page   I think Frank didn't like losing at games. He had quite a temper. But he wasn't the complicated make-up of Sam. I think that life wasn't too easy for him because of the feeling between his mother and Sam. I think that bothered him. Then he went off to India. I think his life when he got married wasn't easy, either. With his mother, I mean. Frank and Sam were very close. In

Frank and May Beckett, *c.* 1948–9.

his latter days, Frank relied on him a lot. And when Sam's father, his mother and his brother died, he was always with them.* That was marvellous of him. I always found Sam so gentle and peaceful.

Samuel Beckett   Frank was always very involved with the church. I think he was a member of the Board of Trustees of the church. As children we used to go to church in the pew. We had a pew near the pulpit, shared by the market gardener, Mr Tyler. He had a big market garden not far from the house. I used to go and buy apples. I used to go there when I was very young. He was 'wall-eyed'. (My father used to have nicknames for people. And he called Tyler 'wall-eyed Watt'.) But Father never came to that church. And later on, I used to be with him on Sundays in the mountains, in the fine weather. When I walked with my father, I wasn't in church obviously. Otherwise I was in church with my mother, who was a very constant attender. She never missed it. Now in the evening my father would condescend to go to a church, but not to the Tullow Parish Church. He'd go to a church near Monkstown, down Blackrock: All Saints' Church, where the parson was a man called Dobbs.† He was a friend of my father's. The All Saints'

---

* Frank Beckett died of cancer on 13 September 1954 at the early age of fifty-two. Beckett stayed at Killiney for several months looking after his brother.
† The Reverend Henry B. Dobbs, BA, Vicar of All Saints' Church, Blackrock.

Church in Blackrock was fairly high. But our own church was fairly low.

The Bible was an important influence on my work, yes. I've always felt it's a wonderful transcript, inaccurate but wonderful. There are some wonderful hymns too. One was written by a man called Lyte. He was at Portora [Portora Royal School, Beckett's old school]. 'Lead kindly Light amid the encircling gloom'. It was either that or 'Abide with Me'. Wonderful. (*He sings.*) 'Abide with me/ Fast falls the eventide/The darkness deepens/Lord with me abide'.*

Music and Tennis

Samuel Beckett   I remember my music lessons with Miss Ida Elsner. She had a sister called Pauline.† In the country that was [i.e. their house, 'Taunus'], on the road to Stillorgan, not very far from home. I remember they had a very big garden. My father measured it out and got some plans prepared for a gymnasium in the garden. Ida Elsner taught me. I've seen it written that she taught me German, as they were German 'émigrés', but that isn't true. I did do some French with her. And music. She used to teach the piano. Then I had some more music lessons at the Leinster School of Music, opposite Harcourt Street Station, at a later stage, from some woman whose name I can't remember: Catherine something, I think. She was very unsympathetic. But I didn't prepare, you know. I was a very bad pupil. Then, later on, I had to walk down to Blackrock to the Skipworths. There were three sisters living there. One of them was a very good musician. And Beatrice [Beckett's music teacher] was the youngest. It wasn't serious. I'd play something for her and she'd make some comment. And we'd have a drink of tea or something. And Father would call for me on his way home from the office and drive me home. Later on I had a piano teacher in Portora. I've remembered her name as well. It was Miss Hunt. I think her first name was Eliza. 'Lizzie' we used to call her, anyway.

---

* Henry Francis Lyte, 1793–1847, wrote 'Abide with Me'. It was Cardinal John Henry Newman, 1801–90, who wrote 'Lead Kindly Light'.
† 'I thought a little of the Elsner sisters. Everything remained to be planned and there I was thinking of the Elsner sisters. They had an Aberdeen called Zulu.' (Samuel Beckett, *Molloy*, London, Calder and Boyars, 1966, p. 113; New York, Grove Press, 1995, p. 144.)

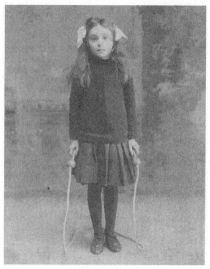

Mary Manning as a child, 1914.

Mary Manning (friend) At the Skipworths' in Blackrock I used to come on in an afternoon before Sam and when I came down, there was Sam lumped up over a book down in the hall waiting to go up for his music lesson. I used to laugh over those lessons with Sam afterwards. He was terrible then. He banged, just banged away remorselessly, not caring a damn. He didn't practise. But the family was very much into music.

Sheila Page They had a piano at home in the drawing room. And we used to queue up for this. Sam loved the Doyle Carte [*sic*] operas, you know. We all used to sing that stuff and Sam used to tinkle it on the piano and sing it madly with a quavering voice. And we'd all be roaring with laughter out in the hall. He was very musical. And Frank used to play jazz. But Sam was all Schubert and so on. I remember them playing duets.

Geoffrey Perrin (neighbour) I really became friendly with Sam and the Beckett family due to our enjoyment of playing tennis. When the weather intervened, we retired to the house, where Sam strummed Sullivan's music on the piano and sang irreverent, ribald Beckett libretti in substitution for Gilbert's words. Both the Becketts and the Delaps [another family of neighbours in Foxrock] had complete sets of gramophone records of the Gilbert and Sullivan operas and we became very familiar with them, as, in between bouts of outdoor activity, playing the operas was our recreation.

Mary Manning Then there were the tennis parties, those historic tennis parties, we used to go to them constantly. Oh, those awful tennis parties. There would be about six boys and six girls. None of us spoke to each other. Sam and Frank never uttered a word to any girl. They were both totally bound up, shy. Nobody – it was awful. We were in our teens. Earlier there were all the children's parties: just a mob of silent creatures. Nothing good – occasionally if they sang together – but they all stayed waiting eagerly for food. That was it. It was just the food. And May knew that, of course. She toiled over the food.

Sheila Page   We usually played tennis on the Beckett's court. But I did play in one tournament. I won the girls' junior at Carrickmines and Sam won the boys'. He reminded me of this not so long ago. The under-twelves or under-fourteens. And he and I, Sam told me, had to play an exhibition game. He was very athletic.

Geoffrey Perrin   My principal memories of Sam were on the tennis court. We played at both our houses and at Carrickmines Tennis Club. We partnered each other in the handicap doubles in both the Co. Dublin and Co. Wicklow championship tournaments for two years. We were about the youngest pairing and must have been reasonably competent as we were never given a fancy handicap, + or − 0.2 was usually our level.

School

Prep school: Earlsfort House

Samuel Beckett   Earlsfort House school was over seven miles from home. We walked to Foxrock Station and then took the train to Harcourt Street. I can still remember every one of the stations from Harcourt Street to Bray on that line: the Dublin Slow and Easy.

John O. Wisdom (fellow pupil; later the author of several books on psychoanalysis)   Earlsfort House was a very small school, only 100 or so pupils, and we had some Roman Catholic boys. That's where I got my first lesson that there were other people around, because we are a Protestant family, though we may not practise, in fact we don't. We all knew who everybody was. You can't be in Ireland and not know. But there was never any offence taken at the other party, and the number of Roman Catholics was a fairly small proportion. I got one of my first lessons [in tolerance]. We were summoned one day by the Headmaster, Le Peton (Lep as he was known)*, and he said: 'We're having a new boy coming to the school on Monday. Now, you have to treat him like anybody else. He may be a little different, but God help you, you'll be flayed alive if you don't.' This was [Edward] Solomons, the first Jew. It was a very good thing for me because I've been mixed up with Jews for so long both in psychoanalysis and at the LSE [London School of Economics] and so I understood then that they were just people . . . and he was the most popular boy in the school.

Samuel Beckett   We had French lessons with Lep. But he wasn't too reliable a character. I think – I don't want to speak ill of the dead – that he was a bit of a rogue. I remember he tried once to borrow money off my father. I think he was a homosexual. He liked friendly physical contact, you know. The serious fellow who ran the school was the man who taught maths, called Exshaw (I think that's how you spell it). My father had a nickname for him; he called him 'Eggshell'. My father had a nickname for everyone!

I played a lot of sport there. On the Leinster sports ground. That's where I first played cricket and tennis. I used to play tennis with Mr Eggshell! I was quite good at tennis – until I was about fourteen, I guess. And I did a lot of running. I was a fairly good runner at middle to long distances. I remember winning a race, coming into the sports ground and seeing my father leaving. He had to go to a meeting just before I went up to the tape.

At Portora, I used to run in cross-country races organized by one of the masters, called Keith Meares. He lived quite near us in Foxrock. Another boy who used to be involved was [A. M.] Buchanan. I think he played rugger for Ireland.† I did some boxing fairly young too.

Portora Royal School, Enniskillen

Samuel Beckett   Portora had a good reputation as a Protestant school, a good Protestant school. That was important. But it was to

---

* William Ernest Lepeton, the Headmaster of Earlsfort House, went on to found Sandford Park School in September 1922. He left the school in 1925.
† He did. A. M. Buchanan, with whom Beckett played, was captain of both Portora Royal School's rugby XV and cricket XI and he later played for Ireland at rugby. He received his first cap against England at Lansdowne Road, Dublin, on 13 February 1926. His club was Dublin University and he represented his country on six occasions during the 1926–7 season. We thank Grainne Gaynor of the Irish Rugby Football Union for her help in obtaining this information.

A. M. Buchanan, Beckett's cricket captain at Portora, is in the centre holding the bat. 1923. Samuel Beckett is seated, the third from the right.

get us away from the troubles. There were some good schools in Dublin: St Columba's High School and Wesley [College]. But it was to get us as far away as possible in Ireland from the troubles. I was in Connaught House. There were Connaught, Munster, Leinster and Ulster. The Connaught President was Micky Murphet. I have very clear memories of Portora.

Charles Jones (fellow pupil; later General Sir Charles Jones) Sam Beckett and I were the closest of friends and moved through the school together. During the holidays he stayed at my home more than once. We moved up the school in the same classes. I had a great affection for him.

Although withdrawn and sometimes moody, he was a most attractive character. His eyes, behind his spectacles, were piercing and he often sat quietly assessing in a thoughtful, and even critical, way what was going on around him and the material that was being presented to him. However, he had a keen sense of the ridiculous and a great sense of humour; from time to time his

Portora Royal Cricket XI. Beckett is seated third from the left.
His friend, Geoffrey Thompson, stands to his left, 1922.

face would light up with a charming smile and change his whole appearance.

From the start, it was obvious that he was very able – most discriminating and critical in thought and blessed with a wonderful memory. His tastes, as one might expect from his subsequent achievements, lay on the literary and linguistic sides and I well remember that he was almost word-perfect over the whole range of Gilbert and Sullivan operas.

Sam Beckett was good at games, playing in the back division for the first XV and as a bat – though he bowled also if I remember aright – for the first [cricket] XI. He was a keen and effective bridge player.*

John A. Wallace (fellow pupil) My main recollections of him at Portora are of his cricketing ability, being a member of a small group of regular morning cold-bathers and of playing some sort of bird-call in a prize-day performance of Haydn's Toy Symphony. He also must have been one of the few boys in V and VI in my time who took music lessons.

---

* The reminiscences of Charles Jones, John A. Wallace and Herbert Gamble are taken from a document sent by Mary Rogers, wife of the Headmaster of Portora Royal School, to James Knowlson, 15 July 1970.

Cyril Harris (fellow pupil)   Sam Beckett was somewhat different from any of the boys that I had been associated with. He was not particularly odd – but he gave the impression of being a solitary, withdrawn person. He was naturally athletic and excelled at games. I shall never forget the way he dealt with me in a school boxing tournament. I met him in a semi-final bout and he quickly knocked me through the side ropes and out of the ring. That was the end of my boxing career.*

Herbert Gamble (fellow pupil; later Governor of the Windward Islands)   I was in the same form as Beckett at Portora. I remember that he was already very good at French and English composition but I don't think he shone particularly in the general examinations, e.g. I don't believe he ever obtained either a Junior or Senior Exhibition.

University: Trinity College, Dublin

Samuel Beckett   My professor at Trinity College was a very human sort of man and an excellent scholar. He introduced me to Racine and passed on his dislike of Corneille. We did *The Kid*, you know – a spoof [of Pierre Corneille's *Le Cid*] – as a play! He was very familiar with contemporary developments in poetry as well: he taught Viélé-Griffin, Le Cardonnel, Jammes. But I didn't meet them, contrary to what Deirdre Bair [a previous biographer] says. The only one of the writers that Rudmose-Brown knew that I met was Valery Larbaud. I suppose he [i.e. Rudmose-Brown] started me working [after graduating] on *l'Unanimisme* and Jules Romains. I was teaching at Campbell College in Belfast at the time. I remember when I was working on that.

Ruddy was a very warm, friendly person. You could talk to him as a student. We used to go out for drives in the country together in his car. We didn't talk about literature all the time, of course! We visited him at his house in Malahide and in a flat he had in Dublin. He used to have parties when he used to

---

* Cyril Harris, letter to James Knowlson, 26 October 1992.

Thomas Rudmose-Brown and a student, Eileen
O'Connor, at Trinity College, Dublin, *c.* 1926.

entertain his students. Very sexy they were! He had the lights down low to make it more relaxed and easier. He was Professor of Romance Languages, you know.

You had to do two languages at TCD at the time, so I chose Italian as my second language. Did I tell you about Sir Robert Tate, who used to teach us Italian language? A bit of a 'dead beat' he was. He wasn't too good at it. But it was my good luck to meet Bianca Esposito. She was a private tutor and she helped me with my literature as well as my Italian language. She used to go through the difficult bits of the *Divina Commedia* with me, I remember. I went to Florence in 1927. My father let me go to improve my Italian before my final exam. I stayed in Florence. Most days I used to go out to Fiesole to see and talk to Bianca Esposito's sister, Vera. She had been married to an Irishman and had lived in Dublin. She had done some acting – she appeared in one or two plays at the Abbey Theatre. You would find her name in some of the programmes from the twenties. She was divorced at the time. Things hadn't worked out with her husband. She'd had a bad time. She went back to look after her mother in Florence (or in Fiesole) while Bianca looked after her father, Michele, in Dublin.* I told you he was director of music at the [Royal Irish] Academy [of Music], didn't I? He played all Beethoven's twelve piano concertos in three separate concerts. He was Commendatore Esposito too. He came from Naples. It is a

---

* Michele Esposito (1855–1929), Professor of Composition at the Royal Irish Academy of Music, founded the chamber series at the Royal Dublin Society in 1886. He also founded and directed the Dublin Orchestral Society (1898–1914) and was active as pianist, concert promoter and adjudicator at musical competitions.

Beckett's notes on Dante – based on Cary's 'The Vision of Dante', 1926.

Neapolitan name, of course. There was a son called Mario. He became very distinguished. He had lived in Dublin, too. But there had been some problem and he couldn't stay. I knew him very well. I even went on holiday one year to the north of Italy with him, for a trip into the mountains, near Lake Como.*

---

* There is an excellent account of the whole Esposito family in Richard Pine and Charles Acton's *To Talent Alone. The Royal Irish Academy of Music 1848–1998*, Dublin, Gill and MacMillan, 1998, pp. 194–9 and passim. Beckett's holiday near Lake Como with Mario is reflected in Beckett's first novel, *Dream of Fair to Middling Women*, as well as in his later play *Endgame*.

Sport and Theatre

Bill Cunningham (friend)   It was at Carrickmines Golf Club that I first met Sam. He was also a student member and our friendship struck up on the golf course. I played a lot with him and on at least one occasion we played in a golf match that was part and parcel of the series of matches that the Golfing Union of Ireland sometimes had. This was called the Barton Cup. It was a foursome and he and I were beaten. I remember we played two people from the Royal Ireland Golf Club and we were beaten at the 21st hole. We were representing Carrickmines. But at the same time I played matches for Trinity and so did he . . . Sam's handicap was always a bit higher than mine: I was a 4 and he was a 7. But he was a good golfer.

In those days he had a motorcycle. I occasionally went out with him to a place called the Royal Dublin Golf Club which was really the centre for the Trinity Golf Club and, when we went out there to play in Trinity competitions, or maybe perhaps in Trinity matches, I used to go out on the back of his motor-bicycle. In those days we had a lot of cobbled streets in Dublin and I remember falling off the back of the motorcycle one frosty morning in a street which we now know as Pearse Street, on the way out to the Royal Dublin. I didn't come to any harm. We didn't have helmets, of course, in those days.

Beckett with his golf partner, Bill Cunningham.

'I like driving fast', Sam said. But I didn't have fear on the back of that motorbike and I would be carrying a bag of clubs as well. It was . . . well, primitive.

Samuel Beckett   I had an AJS motorbike. In fact I had two of them. My father bought me them. It was a four-stroke motorbike, I remember. My brother, Frank, had a Douglas. That was a two-stroke. I used to ride it into Trinity College from Foxrock. I remember bumping into Sir Robert Tate [his Italian teacher and Junior Dean of Students] once on my motorbike with all my gear on.

Bill Cunningham   I used to make my own golf shoes. Money was important in those days. I put brags into my own golf shoes, hammered them in; I had a last. So that was the background. Neither of us dressed very extravagantly. Sam always had the old pair of slacks and a grey suit on. In the photograph, he has the old grey suit, the Galway tweed sports-coat. I had the blazer which was burnt in the Carrickmines fire twenty years ago. And he was the only one, he said, 'Oh my golf clubs were old'. They all claimed a hundred and twenty or thirty pounds [for their losses in the fire], and he claimed thirty bob [shillings] or something.

Carrickmines is a very simple nine-hole course set up round about the beginning of this century. When Sam and I were members there, it was very much a club that had a strong background of conservatism. And if you like to put it as far as that, there was an element of snobbishness about it . . . It was a very pleasant, quiet place, with not a great membership and no great stress laid on the winning of things at golf.

It was a good place for young people to play and there was a very good professional called James Barrett who came from the Greystones area. He used to teach young people like us how to play golf and Sam was very friendly with him. Sam used to play golf with the son. He used to come over here on occasions and used always to go and play, have a round with the son. Sam was what I would have said [was] a very natural golfer.

Samuel Beckett   I suppose I must have had my first clubs when I was about ten. I used to play a lot on my own at Carrickmines Golf Course. A lovely golf course. It's still there. I used to spend hours there hitting the ball by myself. But I had a lot of help from the professional there. I remember his name. It was 'Jem' Barrett. I think his real name was Jim. I remember the groundsman's name too. His name was Condell. He looked after the greens. Isn't it odd the sort of thing you remember?

I used to play cricket for Trinity College. There were only about forty men who played in all, so you didn't have to be too good to get into the team! We played various local Dublin teams. I used to enjoy batting on Trinity Square. It was a very good wicket. I also remember when we played Northants, they were a happy band, drinking and whoring and so on between matches, and I'd go off alone and sit in the church. I wasn't at all what you would call a sociable sort of boy. The main requirement was to be alone.

I also played for Trinity at chess. There were various chess teams all over Dublin. And Trinity had their chess team of six players, I think it was. We used to tour. There was a competition between the various chess groups. There was one in Dún Laoghaire, I think. I forget the names. The Dublin Chess Club was in Grafton Street too. It was called the Café Cairo. That was the headquarters of the Dublin Chess Club. It was not peculiar to Trinity.

Bill Cunningham   We were in the university and the university had a wall around it and, you know, we would talk about our education and what we were learning in the university and various things involved with that sort of world, including the interest in English literature and things like that. We were both interested in literature, so we used to talk fully about all sorts of things, literature and so on and he was brilliant at modern languages. Neither of us had sisters and I would say that we were both completely unaware of the female side of life. This was in 1922–4 and Sam was intensely shy and I was intensely shy.

I admired Sam's brain. I looked upon him as a man of intense ability and intense academic stature. But he was more rounded than that. He had a piano in his rooms and I remember him playing to me. He sat me down and played in his rooms at Trinity. We still used to meet when I went into business and we used to go to the theatre.

There was a play we saw at the Gate Theatre – these were all instances when he came over from France or wherever he was – called *Payment Deferred* by C. S. Forrester, the man who wrote the novel about Captain Horatio Hornblower.* And this was a 'whodunnit'. It wasn't the greatest of plays, but Sam was sitting in the front row of the stalls at the Gate Theatre, and there was some

---

* *Payment Deferred* was a play by Jeffrey Dell, based on C. S. Forrester's novel of that title. It was also made into a film in 1932, with Charles Laughton as William Marble. Interestingly in the light of Beckett's later play, *Happy Days*, the two main characters were known as 'Willie' and 'Winnie'. Winnie Marble was played in the film by Maureen O'Sullivan.

comment made on the stage, and Sam rose to his feet and he said out loud, 'My God, what a profound remark!' And, of course, I shrank down in my seat because everybody was looking at us. Now that's where I saw that Sam was moving away from me: because he was prepared to make such an outburst. It was a very trite remark but I wouldn't have thought to comment.

The second time that disclosed that our minds were going in a different way was – I said to him 'Look, I'm going round Dublin, I'm doing little jobs round town and I went to a little builder's place there the other week and I found a man there whom I would have looked upon as a person who wouldn't have done anything like the reading that you or I would have done and I found that his leisure-time reading was a book called *The Decline and Fall of the Saracens* [*sic*]'. Now it was probably Gibbons [*sic*] because I know that Gibbons wrote *The Decline and Fall of the Romans* [*sic*] but I had never heard of this.* I said, 'What I am finding out now, going out now into the world round me in Dublin, I am finding ordinary people who can give you a lot of interesting information and who are very interesting in themselves, normal people,' I said. Sam looked at me and said: 'I'm not interested in the normal, I'm only interested in the abnormal.'

Geoffrey Perrin I was friendly with Frank and Sam Beckett, especially in 1925 and 1926 during the summer vacation when Sam was in TCD . . . I went to Kenya in January 1927 when Sam was still at home. At that time he was an ordinary, intelligent citizen with a considerable flair in the realm of sport. I had no idea he was to become an intellectual genius. The only sign I can recollect was his enthusiasm for the Abbey Theatre and his liking for abstruse plays. He took me to a performance of 'Oedipus Rex' [*Oedipus the King*] which I thoroughly enjoyed, largely due to the wonderful acting of Frank McCormick.†

---

* In all probability the book in question was Syed Ameer Ali, *A Short History of the Saracens. Being a Concise Account of the Rise and Decline of the Saracenic Power and of the Economic, Social and Intellectual Development of the Arab Nation*, London, Macmillan, 1924.
† This production at the Abbey Theatre was of *Oedipus the King*, W. B. Yeats's translation of Sophocles; first performance 16 December 1926. Frank McCormick (1889–1947), real name: Peter Judge.

Samuel Beckett   They had wonderful actors at the Abbey Theatre: Barry Fitzgerald, Frank McCormick. Beautiful actors. And they all – what's the word? – 'finished up' in the States, Barry Fitzgerald having an international reputation. They were all good. But I admired above all Frank McCormick.* Frank McCormick and Barry Fitzgerald in *Juno and the Paycock* were unforgettable.† Frank refused to go abroad. He was so attached to the Abbey and home that he wouldn't go. Anyhow he died young. But what infuriated me at the time – it was so stupid on the part of [W. B.] Yeats – was to refuse *The Silver Tassie*. They'd done *The Plough and the Stars* and the next play that Seán [O'Casey] came up with was *The Silver Tassie*. And it was turned down by Yeats. It was a monumental mistake. O'Casey left Ireland as a result.

I was a weekly visitor to the Abbey. I always occupied the same seats. Have I told you that story? The balcony was semi-circular with two aisles: a central triangle and two aisles. And if you got a seat at the centre end of the aisles you were as well off as if you were sitting in the centre. You got as good a view. It also only cost you one and six for a side seat as opposed to three shillings in the centre. So (*laughs*) I always had the seat next to the centre! I saw the Synge revivals there. I don't think he finished *Deirdre of the Sorrows*, you know. But *The Well of the Saints* is a beautiful play.

The Gate was hardly really going again [when I was there] and I had no feeling for the two who ran it: Hilton Edwards (who died three or four years ago) and Micheál MacLiammoir; they lived together.‡ MacLiammoir was a very well-known theatre man. He used to travel. He was very good. And he died before Hilton Edwards, who continued to run the Gate until a few years ago when it was taken over [in 1983] by the present chap, Michael Colgan, who has made a great success of the place. I remember

---

* Frank McCormick acted in over 500 plays at the Abbey and was particularly noted for his performances in plays by Seán O'Casey. He toured America five times and played three major film roles, the last being in *Odd Man Out* (1947).
† Born William Joseph Shields, Barry Fitzgerald (1888–1961) recreated his role in O'Casey's *Juno and the Paycock* in 1930 for Alfred Hitchcock in his very first film role. He went on to have a very successful Hollywood career from 1930 to 1959, starring in many films such as *How Green Was My Valley* and *The Quiet Man*.
‡ The Gate Theatre was founded, in the former Grand Supper Room of the Rotunda's New Assembly Rooms, in 1928 by Micheál MacLiammoir (1899–1978) and Hilton Edwards (1903–82).

seeing a play [*Youth's the Season*] there by Mary Manning, Mary Manning Howe. Denis Johnston's plays were also put on at the Gate. Then there was The Gaiety. And The Queen's was in Dame Street. I remember well The Theatre Royal, The Queen's, The Olympia, The Abbey, The Gate, and The Peacock. Lennox Robinson was a director at the Abbey. The Abbey was destroyed by fire, of course, years ago.

2

Reluctant Teacher and Lecturer

Beckett as a student.

Biography, 1927–33

In 1927, Samuel Beckett graduated from Trinity College, Dublin with a First Class degree and a Gold Medal and began to work towards an MA thesis on Pierre-Jean Jouve and the French literary movement, *Unanimisme*. He taught briefly (and somewhat reluctantly) at Campbell College in Belfast in 1928, while waiting to take up an appointment as *lecteur* in English at the prestigious Ecole Normale Supérieure in Paris.

He also began a two-year love affair with his first cousin, Peggy Sinclair, who lived with her family in Kassel in Germany. His visits to Kassel established what was to be the beginning of a long and enduring contact with German art and literature.

In Paris, he was introduced to the writer James Joyce, by his fellow Irishman, Thomas MacGreevy, Beckett's predecessor as *lecteur* at the Ecole, who became his close friend and confidant. Beckett was strongly influenced by the force of Joyce's personality, the range of his culture and his total dedication to his work and he found it hard to escape from Joyce's influence in his own writing and to discover his own distinctive voice. While living in Paris, he wrote poetry, including his first published work, *Whoroscope* (1930), an essay on Joyce's *Work in Progress* (which was to become *Finnegans Wake*) and a critical study of *Proust* (1931).

He returned to Dublin in the autumn of 1930 to take up the post of assistant to Professor Rudmose-Brown in Trinity College, teaching French to undergraduates, taking over Rudmose-Brown's lectures on Racine and lecturing on the Romantic poets, Balzac, Stendhal, Flaubert, Proust, Gide and Bergson. While he was lecturing in Dublin he met the Irish painter, Jack B. Yeats, whom he greatly admired and with whom he remained friendly until Yeats's death in 1957.

But Beckett was almost pathologically shy and detested the self-exposure that was involved in lecturing. So he resigned his appointment after only four terms. After a short stay with the bohemian family of his aunt and uncle, Cissie and William Sinclair, in Kassel at the beginning of 1932, he returned to Paris, where he wrote the major part of a novel, *Dream of Fair to Middling Women*, which he had begun in Dublin a year earlier. The book was rejected by several publishers and only appeared posthumously in 1992.

Only weeks after his cousin, Peggy Sinclair, died from tuberculosis, Beckett's father died at the end of June 1933, leaving him feeling guilty and depressed; guilty at having, as he saw it, let his father down by resigning his academic post, depressed on account of the death of his father and of serious concerns about his own health.

Campbell College, Belfast

Beckett (*centre, in his academic gown*), Campbell College, Belfast, 1928.

Samuel Beckett   After I graduated, I had six months. I'd already been nominated at the Ecole Normale, but the appointment didn't have to be taken up until the fall. There was a blank period that I filled as best I could with this job at Campbell College. I didn't like it, though I made some good friends. I don't remember their names any more. But I played cricket with the boys.

Brian McConnell (pupil)   [On the staff at Campbell College] there were the old stagers, professional teachers who had made a life career of it; and there were the young men who came and went. Among the latter was included for a very short time a myopic young man who strode gloomily about the classroom making a half-hearted attempt to teach French. The name was Beckett – Samuel Beckett. My term report from him was not favourable, but it was the only report I ever got on which the head had added some words of comment. He wrote 'I do not agree with this report'. Unfortunately I no longer possess this, as it would be of some interest and value.

Sam Beckett has, I believe, applied to the boys at Campbell the probably not original saying 'They were the cream of Ulster; rich and thick'. But the ethos of Campbell in those days was probably quite alien to Beckett, for it was very British indeed. The sterling qualities which made for the successful administration of the British Empire were certainly instilled into us, and the fact that the 'Empire Day' was observed with pomp and ceremony was more significant than most of us realized.*

The Sinclairs and Kassel

Samuel Beckett   My aunt Cissie was the only daughter [in grand-father Beckett's family]. She married a Jew called William Sinclair. They had a shop in Dublin. Cissie was musical. But she had a very difficult time with her husband. He had some political troubles in Dublin and had to leave. That's why he went to Germany. I don't know why he went to Kassel. Yes, I do know why. There was a friend of his there: the poet [and painter] Cecil Salkeld. He was there. That's why he chose Kassel. I met him [Salkeld] when I was there. But then, of course, because he [Sinclair] was Jewish, he had to come back because of the Nazis. Well, with his brother, Harry – we used to call Cissie's husband 'Boss' Sinclair – he had an art shop in Nassau Street in Dublin. They made some very remarkable discoveries. I remember they discovered a Rembrandt somewhere in the country. They worked together, until 'Boss' got into some political trouble and had to get out. And I know that Cissie's association with Boss was looked on with some disapproval by the family. Snobbish you know – again because he was Jewish and a naughty chap, the family wouldn't have anything to do with him. She had a big family, Cissie, no money, and a wild husband. 'Boss' used to give English lessons in Kassel. He had 'Englische Sprache' written on the door. He didn't have many pupils! But he had some good German pictures. He knew about German art.

Aunt Cissie was a wonderful person. She came after my father in the family. ['Boss' and Cissie] had a lot of children. There was Sally who married a Cusack (Ralph), Peggy and Deirdre,

---

* Reverend Dr Brian McConnell, letter to James Knowlson, 15 February 1992.

Peggy Sinclair, 1928.

and Morris. I used to call him 'Sonny'. He was a good violinist. There was a sort of unofficial engagement with his sister Peggy. Then, for some reason, I don't know why, I broke it off. And she married some German. [She was engaged, not married to Heiner Starcke.] But she died very young of tuberculosis. She was very artistic: a good musician. Peggy was a student of the piano. She was at some music school near Vienna. She was a very lively girl, full of life. She's the Smeraldina [Rima] in my work, yes. There was a very easy-going, friendly atmosphere in the family. I enjoyed going to Kassel to stay with them.

I used to go to the gallery there, oh sure. We used to go to the Wilhelmshöhe, on the hill; we used to go there in parties and expeditions; and I went with Peggy, of course. Oh, Peggy didn't need any chasing! There were four daughters: Deirdre, Peggy, Nancy and Sally. Then Morris was, I think, the youngest.

*Morris Sinclair (cousin)** Sam played the piano a lot in Kassel, *quatre mains* [duets] with Peggy and with my mother, as well as on his own. The music played: classical overtures, *Egmond, Coriolan, Magic Flute*, etc.; Schumann string quartets; all the symphonies by Beethoven (except the 9th, I think); late Mozart symphonies; Haydn; Schubert unfinished; Tchaikovsky's 5th and 6th symphonies. There was in those days no gramophone or radio in the house . . . Sam loved the Beethoven 7th.

In his visits to the Sinclairs in Kassel, he brought in something musically new, at least to me. He introduced me to Granados, Poulenc, MacDowell. He may well have played some Debussy, but I cannot now recall what, though the well-known *Fille aux cheveux de lin* is a likely candidate . . . As I remember, he gave passionate renderings of Mozart's A-minor sonata and the last movement of Beethoven's early C-minor sonata. John Sebastian [Bach] he could not abide. For Sam he was a mere technician, filling page after page

* Morris Sinclair (1918–), the son of William and Frances ('Cissie') Sinclair. Letters to James Knowlson, 1991–2, text agreed by Morris Sinclair in 2005. Morris played the violin. He gave Beckett German lessons in the mid-1930s; in exchange Beckett gave him French lessons. They became close friends, although it was very much a master/ pupil relationship, with Beckett, the master, offering Morris advice on his career prospects.

Peggy and Morris Sinclair in Kassel, 1929–30.

of rule-correct counterpoint. There is a line in one of Mac-Greevy's poems à propos Bach's *Magnificat*: 'The self-satisfied [Lutheran] music circles on . . .'.* Sam, I imagine, was in harmony with that line.

Sam and I also made a start of playing violin and piano sonatas, notably Mozart. It is imaginable that the lack of dark spots in some of Mozart's music might have prompted Sam to an adverse remark about this or that piece. But as a general judgement I think it must be repudiated. The A-minor sonata which I remember Sam playing in Landgrafenstrasse is certainly a dark piece and so is the G-minor string quintet (K516), which touched him deeply. Going for the dark pieces does not mean shoving the rest aside. I forget the exact context but I hear Sam saying (in the rue des Favorites [where Beckett lived for many years from 1937]): 'Lucky enough to find somebody who likes Mozart'; i.e. a musician who likes playing Mozart.

It could perhaps not be said that he had a highly developed technique as a pianist, but I remember well with what conviction and *élan* he would play the last movement of Beethoven's *Pathétique*. The intensity of his absorption was almost ferocious. Not in Landgrafenstrasse, I don't think, but later on he used to hum while he played, not at all in tune with the music, and admitted that it was a bad habit. But it showed how completely absorbed he was in the music in a subjective way and how little concerned he was with a rendition for others.

He was a frequent concert-goer in London and also in Paris. He

---

* Thomas MacGreevy's poem was entitled 'Anglo-Irish'. The line quoted above is explained by the earlier lines 'And the gramophone starting/Bach's *Magnificat*.' *Collected Poems of Thomas MacGreevy*, an annotated edition by Susan Schreibman, Dublin, Anna Livia Press and Washington DC, Catholic University of America Press, 1991, p. 25.

walked out of [a] concert in Kassel, a recital given by the violinist Vasa Prihoda,* which he attended with a group of the Sinclairs, including myself. The barren display of technique was not to his liking. It should not be concluded that virtuosity in his view was undesirable. Among pianists he greatly admired were Cortot, Solomon, Brailowsky.

My debt to Sam is great indeed not only because of what he wrote and published (everybody's debt) but because he was my friend – nearly the brother-in-law – mentor and teacher: language, literature, painting, philosophy. All the family loved him.

The Ecole Normale Supérieure, Paris

Samuel Beckett   I graduated in '27 and started doing a thesis on *Unanimisme*. I met [Pierre Jean] Jouve in Paris when I came here. I was a great admirer of his early works. He occupied a big place in my scrappy work on *Unanimisme*, which I was supposed to do after leaving Trinity. And Rudmose-Brown got me this appointment as *lecteur d'anglais* at the Ecole Normale but not to take over the job until the autumn of 1928. Now, when I got to the Normale, Tom MacGreevy was already there – to the great annoyance of Rudmose-Brown. He hadn't been appointed by Rudmose-Brown. It was some influence that got him the appointment. So he was there when I arrived. And for a year, the two of us were in the Ecole Normale. He had rooms inside. You can still see them there. But the railings that I used to climb when I came home at night are changed. I couldn't climb them now – not even as I was then.

I struck up a friendship with Tom MacGreevy. I liked him. Our rooms were next door, up the stairs, on the first floor, I seem to remember. It was through him that I met James Joyce.

My work was supposed to be teaching English. But there was no one taking it. It was just a joke. I taught Georges Pelorson, but I think it was in the second year that I taught him. [This is not true: Pelorson was taught by Beckett in his first year in Paris, 1928–9 and Beckett also forgets that he helped some of the postgraduates,

---

* Vasa Prihoda (1900–60) was the most internationally successful Czech violinist of his generation and also perhaps the most controversial. He was thought of by some as a 'string gymnast' with his playing of Paganini and Bach.

Beckett's friend, Thomas MacGreevy at the Ecole Normale Supérieure, *c.* 1928.

Alfred Péron and Emile Delavenay, with their prose translations for the *Agrégation* examinations.] He'd remember better about that than me. He's at Aix. You know he got into trouble in the war. He was Pelorson and changed his name afterwards to Belmont. We didn't have any contact of course in those days. I was on the Péron side. [Beckett was a member of the Resistance cell 'Gloria SMH' with his good friend Péron. See Beckett's comments later on the war years, pp. 79ff.]

I used to play the tin whistle by the way at the Ecole Normale, a rusty old tin whistle. I had a tin whistle and I used to tweetle on it, and in Dublin too.

Georges Belmont (Pelorson) I was nineteen years old and I was the only Anglicist in the 1928 year. We started by reading some Shakespeare together – but that was never Sam's forte. I am not even sure we ever reached the end of *A Midsummer Night's Dream.** He was as embarrassed as I was by this and asked me what I wanted to do. We met first in his room. I no longer remember how often each week – but regularly. And then Sam said it might be more interesting if we were to meet outside in a café or a bar. And that is what we did. We soon started just to talk rather than to read Shakespeare. We didn't have actual lessons; we just chatted. It was purely social. Always in English. He was very scrupulous about that. He would ask me what I was reading . . . and we spoke about literature, mostly modern French literature and theatre and cinema. It was a conversation, nothing academic about it at all. Later on, when I was in Dublin as the *lecteur*, he used to speak to me in French.

As soon as I got some money then, I went out and bought myself an expensive gramophone and tried to persuade Beckett that he would come to love Wagner. So I forced him to listen to it. Not being at all impressed when he was listening to Wagner's *Le Crépuscule des Dieux* – in which there would be all these cymbals clashing – he would get his own back by going up to the gramophone and saying: 'That's a beautiful flute you can hear there. Ça, c'est merveilleux' ["Now that, that's wonderful"]'.

---

* Georges Belmont (Pelorson) later recalled that it was *The Tempest* that he and Beckett read together. 'Remembering Sam', *Beckett in Dublin*, ed. S. E. Wilmer, Dublin, The Lilliput Press, 1992, pp. 111–12.

Emile Delavenay before his wedding,
Stratfield Saye, 1928.

Emile Delavenay The summer of 1928 was the time when I presented my Mémoire de Diplôme on Barrie to my examiners. I had just got married and this was the time when McGreevy [MacGreevy] arranged for the meeting with Joyce. Beckett arrived in the following autumn term. I was then again in Cambridge, coming to Paris for the periods when the Cambridge term was over or not started, and the Sorbonne operated. McGreevy was still living at the rue d'Ulm and I saw quite a lot of him although his teaching duties were over. Péron and I were preparing for the *Agrégation* competition and worked hard with Beckett when we could lay our hands on him . . . most of our study times with Beckett were at the [Café] Mahieu or the less resplendent café next door, the Départ, opposite the Gare de Sceaux . . . He was a late riser. So was McGreevy and we used to go after eleven in the morning and he had his breakfast then . . . Our Sorbonne professors were there for the hard, methodical work on the history of literature, and the comradeship of people like Tom McGreevy and Beckett introduced into our studies something vividly different. It is difficult to put it into words, but I am sure that, on balance, we learnt more from those extremely informal and almost casual encounters with McGreevy and Beckett at the Mahieu than from the formal teaching . . .*

[Beckett] was not sociable. He was brusque and he always gave me the impression of great purity of character. And when I saw him

---

* The first paragraph of Emile Delavenay's memories of Beckett and his predecessor at the Ecole Normale, Tom MacGreevy, is a fusion of a letter to Richard Ellmann, 17 March 1982 (copy sent to us by Emile Delavenay) and a personal interview by the editors with Delavenay at his home in Vence in 1991. The rest is taken from that same 1991 interview. The extract from the letter to Ellmann is printed by kind permission of Delavenay's daughter, Claire Tomalin, and Lori Curtis of the University of Tulsa.

when we were, after all, in our late seventies and early eighties, I found he hadn't changed. He was the same, the eyes, the blue eyes, the friendly look. He looked you straight in the face. We all liked him.

It was after I retired from UNESCO. We talked a good deal about the old days and we talked about old friends. Perhaps the last time but one that I met him at the PLM St Jacques I was writing my memoirs at the time* and I said, 'Look, we've come to an age where there isn't much future, there is only the past to talk about.' And he sort of looked up and said, 'Oh not at all, don't you believe it.'

Lucien Roubaud (with whom Beckett played rugby for the Ecole Normale team)   I have a very different picture of Samuel Beckett as a rugby player from that of Jean Rolland.† Like him, I ran behind Beckett, expecting him to pass back to me, and saw him go flying, as his feet could not keep up with him. Like him, I heard Beckett twice mutter to himself 'Never again'. But my impression was very different from that of Jean Rolland. The graphic picture presented by the incident was for me quite secondary. As I was a Toulonnais and had played rugby far more than the other members of the team, I understood that Beckett was going to execute a manoeuvre which was performed by a famous scrum-half in the Toulon Rugby Club and which I later saw executed by Gareth Edwards. Beckett failed to exploit what would have been, in itself, remarkable, creating a hole in the opposing defence. He tried the classic scrum-half's dummy, feigning a move in one direction which forced the opposing backs to rush to defend, so leaving a gap into which Beckett, with a sudden change of direction, thrust himself. It was worthy of a real rugby player, even of a great rugby player. And after the game as Beckett left the changing rooms, saying to himself 'Never again', I felt really sad at heart for his tone was both resolute and bitter, almost desperate.

Finally I'll give you an example of Beckett's style which seems to me rather piquant. The team had all gone to the station at Moulins and were in a rather sleazy bar, waiting for the train. I was sitting at

---

* Published as Emile Delavenay, *Témoignages. D'un village Savoyard au village mondial.* 1905–1991, Aix-en-Province, Diffusion Edisud, 1992.
† Jean Rolland was a member of the Ecole Normale rugby XV with whom we were not able to get in touch. The 'Never again' story referred to here was also recounted to James Knowlson in letters from two other members of the team, Ulysse Nicollet and Camille Marcoux. See *Damned to Fame*, pp. 93–4.

a table with Beckett when a brassy-looking waitress came up to us and asked for a cigarette. Beckett held out a packet and told her to keep it. The woman hitched her skirt up as far as possible and tucked the packet into her stockings. Beckett, looking very solemn, said: 'So, Madame, do you put everything in your stockings?' Then, after a silence, he added enquiringly: 'Even your legs?'

Beckett on the Joyces

On James Joyce

Samuel Beckett I was introduced to Joyce by Tom MacGreevy. He was very friendly – immediately, to the best of my recollection. I remember coming back very exhausted to the Ecole Normale and, as usual, the door was closed and I climbed over the railings. I remember that: coming back from my first meeting with Joyce. I remember walking back. And from then on we saw each other quite often. I can still remember his telephone number! He was living near the Ecole Militaire. I used to come down sometimes in the morning from the Ecole Normale to the concierge and he used to say 'Monsieur Joyce a téléphoné et il vous demande de vous mettre en rapport avec lui'. [Mr Joyce telephoned and wants you to get in touch with him.] And I remem-

James Joyce in the 1930s.

ber the concierge, he was a southerner. He used to say 'Sé-gur quatre-vingt-quinze vingt' [pronounced 'vent']. And it was always to do with going for a walk or going for dinner. I remember a memorable walk on the 'Ile des Cygnes' [The Isle of Swans, the island on the Seine] with Joyce. And then he'd start his 'tippling'. And we'd have an appointment with Nora at Fouquet's. And there was another one we used to go to at that time, not Fouquet's. Léon's or some such place. No, that was later, another time. It was there I remember meeting [Ezra] Pound with Joyce in that restaurant.

I was very flattered when Joyce dropped the 'Mister'. Everybody was 'Mister'. There were no Christian names, no first names. The nearest you would get to a friendly name was to drop the 'Mister'. I was never 'Sam'. I was always 'Beckett' at the best. We'd drink in any old pub or café. I don't remember which. He was very friendly. He dictated some pages of *Finnegans Wake* to me at one stage. That was later on when he was living in that flat. And during the dictation, someone knocked at the door and I said something. I had to interrupt the dictation. But it had nothing to do with the text. And when I read it back with the phrase like 'Come in' in it, he said 'Let it stand'.

We shared our . . . [common background]. He was at the National University, of course, and I was at Trinity – but we both took degrees in French and Italian. So that was common ground. It was at his suggestion that I wrote 'Dante . . . Bruno . Vico . . Joyce' because of my Italian. And I spent a lot of time reading Bruno and Vico in the magnificent library, the Bibliothèque of the Ecole Normale. We must have had some talk about the 'Eternal Return', that sort of thing. He liked the essay. But his only comment was that there wasn't enough about Bruno; he found Bruno rather neglected. Bruno and Vico were new figures for me. I hadn't read them. I'd worked on Dante, of course [at Trinity College, Dublin]. And we did talk about Dante. But I knew very little of them. I knew more or less what they were about. I remember I read a biography of one of them. I can't remember which.

I remember going to see Joyce in the hospital. He was lying on the bed, putting drops in his operated eye. I don't remember having read to him though. I used to go there in the evening sometimes, when he had dinner at home. It was at the later stage when he was living in the little impasse off the long street. There wasn't a lot of conversation between us. I was a young man, very devoted to him, and he liked me. And he used to call on me if he needed something. For instance, someone to walk with him before dinner.

He was a great exploiter. Not perhaps an exploiter of his friends. In the Adrienne Monnier book, it's told how we did the translation of 'Anna Livia Plurabelle', [Alfred] Péron and I. And Joyce liked it.

But he organised a committee of five, which used to meet in [Paul] Léon's house to revise it, including Adrienne Monnier (who was quite unqualified) so that he could talk about his *septante*, those five and Péron and myself. Why he wanted to talk about his *septante* devoted to him I don't know. I remember at Adrienne Monnier's a reading of our fragment of 'Anna Livia Plurabelle', Péron's and mine, as corrected, so-called, by the Joyce clan. But there was a reading of this with Joyce in Adrienne's bookshop, a public reading. I remember being there and Joyce was there; [Philippe] Soupault read it, I think.

And I brought him home drunk one night, but I won't go into that! [He drank a lot] but in the evenings only. I remember a party. He was a great man for anniversaries. Every year he would celebrate his father's anniversary, 'Father forsaken, forgive thy son'. On that occasion he would give me a note, in francs. I don't know how many francs it would be. A note. To give to some poor down-and-out in memory of his father. Towards the end of the year, in December, the date of his father's birth was celebrated or commemorated every year and I was given on several occasions, when I was available, this note to give to some down-and-out in memory of his father. [Recites his own version of Joyce's moving poem 'Ecce Puer' on the death of Joyce's father and the birth of his grandson, Stephen]: 'New life is breathed upon the glass etc.'

It's a poem of Joyce. It's not in *Pomes Pennyeach*. I don't know where it will be. It's part of a longer poem but I remember the verse, 'A child is born. An old man gone'. When his father died, he was very upset.

I played the piano once at the Joyces'. I forget what I played. But he, when he had enough taken, at these 'at home' parties, receptions at home, with various friends, he would sit down at the piano and, accompanying himself, sing, with his marvellous remains of a tenor voice [*sings*]:

> Bid adieu, adieu, adieu
> Bid adieu to girlish days.

I remember myself accompanying Giorgio. When he was living with Helen. I remember accompanying him – in what? Ah yes. [Then he sings part of Schubert's Lieder, *An die Musik*.] Oh, by the way, I've found the name of the street where Joyce lived when I first met him in Paris. Yes, it's a little street off the rue de Grenelle; this goes from the Latin Quarter to the Avenue Bosquet near the Ecole Militaire. It goes through the . . . And just before it comes to the end of the rue de Grenelle near the Avenue Bosquet, before it 'débouches' on the Avenue Bosquet, there's a little street on the right-hand side. It was an impasse in those days. It still exists but it's a square. The Square Robiac. I remember it as an impasse. You go in to the right off the rue de Grenelle. It was very short. And on the right-hand side was the house where Joyce had his flat.

I admired Joyce's *Portrait of the Artist as a Young Man*. There was something about it. The end – when he is so self-sufficient at the end. He got pompous about his vocation and his function in life. That was the improved version; he reworked it.

On His Debt to Joyce

Beckett to James Knowlson   It was Maurice Nadeau who said it was an influence *ab contrario*. I realized that Joyce had gone as far as one could in the direction of knowing more, in control of one's material. He was always *adding* to it; you only have to look at his proofs to see that. I realised that my own way was in impoverishment, in lack of knowledge and in taking away, sub-tracting rather than adding. When I first met Joyce, I didn't intend to be a writer. That only came later when I found out that I was no good at all at teaching. When I found I simply couldn't teach. But I do remember speaking about Joyce's heroic achievement. I had a great admiration for him. That's what it was: epic, heroic, what he achieved. I realized that I couldn't go down that same road.

Beckett to Martin Esslin   [On being asked by Esslin, 'Are you influenced by Joyce?' Beckett replied] 'Not really, except that his seriousness and dedication to his art influenced me. But', he added, 'we are diametrically opposite because Joyce was a synthesizer, he wanted to put everything, the whole of human culture, into one or two books, and I am an analyser. I take away all the accidentals because I want to come down to the bedrock of the essentials, the

Joyce, Giorgio, Lucia and Nora in the 1920s.

archetypal'.* And that is exactly what the clown/tramp [in *Waiting for Godot*] is. The clown is not an allegorical figure but is a man who hasn't got any possessions and can't be defined by the fact that he runs a Mercedes car. In other words, if you take away all the unimportant accidentals, you come to a human figure that is completely real but at the same time not encumbered by any sort of accidentals. Whether somebody has got a nice suit or not a nice suit has nothing to do with his essential soul. And therefore if you put him into a tramp's clothes, people don't think about the suit.

Beckett to Duncan Scott: Comparing his way of working with that of James Joyce, whose method he called accretion, he said 'Joyce was a greedy writer'.†

On Nora Joyce (née Barnacle) and the son, Giorgio

Samuel Beckett to James Knowlson Nora was in many ways distant, you know. She wasn't interested in the work at all. There's a book on her. [Brenda Maddox's *Nora. The Biography of Nora Joyce* which we know Beckett read.] But I liked Nora. She was an extraordinary woman.

Giorgio was a baritone; he had a good voice. I liked him very much. He married that woman, Helen Fleischmann. She had lots of money; very wealthy. I saw a lot of Giorgio. I used to go out with him and I used to go to the house near the Ecole Militaire. I remember he had an audition somewhere but was turned down. In England, I think.

On Lucia Joyce

Lucia was there [when I went to see her father], already very disturbed mentally. Sometimes she was perfectly normal. I had to tell her finally that I went to the house not to see her, but to see Joyce. Joyce was my interest. And, according to some accounts, Joyce was very upset. What the bloody hell is the book I've been

---

* Beckett's reply is taken from JK's interview with Martin Esslin.

† Duncan Scott's memory of a conversation with Beckett about Joyce is published for the first time with the agreement of his widow, Bernadette Scott. For further information about Duncan Scott, see Ch. 7, 'Memories of Beckett in London and Berlin', pp. 214ff.

Lucia Joyce in the early 1930s.

reading? I think it was in the book on Adrienne Monnier.* And, according to that, my relationship with Joyce was poisoned at that stage. I used to go out to see her in that place where Artaud was [at Ivry] and Joyce used to go to see her too. And we used to walk, when she was perfectly normal. And then she had these crazy spells. I never saw her in them though. They all understood that she was incurable. But Joyce could never agree with them. He was all for trying different treatments, with Jung and so on.

She was very good-looking. She had a slight squint but she was still very attractive. And I remember seeing her dance – at the Bal Bullier. She danced in a dancing competition at the old Bal Bullier. We all met afterwards at the Closerie des Lilas, including Joyce and the whole family. She was very gifted as a dancer.

[Joyce in Vichy in 1940] I think there was some sort of problem with his passport or visa, I think it was. He was very anxious about

---

* Beckett may well have had in mind here Richard McDougall's *The Very Rich Hours of Adrienne Monnier. An Intimate Portrait of the Literary and Artistic Life in Paris between the Wars*, London, Millington, 1976, but there is no reference to the quarrel between Joyce and Beckett in this book. He may have confused it with Noel Riley Fitch's *Sylvia Beach and the Lost Generation. A History of Literary Paris in the Twenties and Thirties*, New York/London, W. W. Norton, 1983, which lay on his desk during several of my own (JK's) visits to see him and in which the upset of Joyce over Lucia and Beckett is indeed discussed, pp. 303, 307.

Lucia as well. She had been moved from the hospital at Ivry, to somewhere down south, near Toulouse I think it was. You know Joyce was the only one who believed she could be cured. Everyone else had written her off. Giorgio thought she was mad and nothing at all could be done for her. Joyce tried so often to get her help – he was the one who got her to see Jung at the Tavistock Clinic. It's possible I think that Jung had her in mind at the lecture I went to in London when he spoke about the girl 'who had never really been born'. She would suddenly get violent. When I used to visit her in Ivry, we would go for a walk in the gardens. Everything would be calm and peaceful and all of a sudden she would become extra-ordinarily violent and aggressive.

On Paul Léon

I remember Paul Léon [Joyce's amanuensis] very well. I used to call on them [Paul and Lucie Léon]. You know when Joyce left Paris in 1940, Léon did too. And I was told that he was advised very strongly by the Jolases, who had a school near Vichy, not to return to Paris. But he was so concerned with his son's *baccalauréat* or something that, against all advice, he returned to Paris and was arrested.

Paul Léon used to go to Fouquet's. He didn't join the Joyce table, because he would sit on his own at a nearby table and have his meal and say goodbye and go. But he did all the dirty work for Joyce. He was his secretary. Léon was an enormous help to Joyce. It was he who collected the books Joyce left behind; he collected all the materials, the papers and so on and eventually gave them to the National Library in Dublin with an injunction not to open them for 100 years or something like that. They could tell you all about that in Dublin. I liked Paul. He was a nice man.

Paul Léon in the late 1930s.

Trinity College, Dublin*

'I don't want to be a professor (it's almost a pleasure to contemplate the mess of this job).'†

Robert Burkitt   I fear that my memories of Sam Beckett are very inadequate. It is not that I don't remember his lectures – I remember them extremely well and can still see his tall, lean frame, leaning rather nonchalantly against the wall as he gave his lectures – in very informal attire, but with a gown, which was of course obligatory in those days. I rather think he only lectured to us for one year and I am ashamed to say that I have no recollection as to the writers on whom he lectured or on the sort of information that he imparted. All I can remember was that he didn't take the whole thing very seriously, and we didn't either. They were in the form of personal opinions and friendly chats rather than formal lectures.

Meta Buttnick (née Bloom)   I recall Samuel Beckett's lectures very well. He lectured on Racine. I especially remember his talks on Phèdre, how her appearance engenders a sense of darkness. I have quoted many times how he said you can never quantify how a human being will react. You can put a bunch of tongs in the fire and they will all turn red. Ten human beings faced with a situation will react in different and unexpected ways. As he said, 'we do not know what a human being is made of.' My memories of him as a lecturer are that he was brilliant and interesting. A listener could develop a whole treatise from one of his sessions. I remember Ruddy [their Professor, Thomas Brown Rudmose-Brown] standing with us after an examination, saying that Beckett had written 'a laconic letter' saying that he was not returning next term [the spring term, 1932]

---

* All these memories of Beckett as a lecturer in French at Trinity College, Dublin were written down in 1997–8 when, almost two years after the publication of the biography, *Damned to Fame. The Life of Samuel Beckett*, we sent a circular letter with many questions to students who had been taught by Beckett in 1930 and 1931. These reminiscences, unless otherwise noted, are taken from their replies to our questions. We are grateful to Professor Barbara Wright, then the Dean of the Faculty of Arts in TCD, for putting us in touch with the Alumni Office and to the staff of that office for kindly supplying us with a list of the addresses requested.
† Samuel Beckett, letter to Tom MacGreevy, 11 March 1931, TCD.

'telling nothing else, where he was going or what he was going to do'.

Evelyn Nora Goodbody (née Strong)   The authors Beckett lectured on were André Gide, Maurice Barrès, François Mauriac, and of course his great love, Proust. He talked of D. H. Lawrence, Lafcadio Hearne, Nietzsche, Schopenhauer – strangely I don't think he ever spoke of Joyce. I only knew him as a lecturer but have always heard and talked about him to my friends, the Sinclair family [Cissie Sinclair was Beckett's aunt]. His dislike of lecturing to us was almost tangible but when he warmed to his subject he was really inspiring. Here I'll add my personal feeling at the risk of your finding me rather tiresome. To me the thoughts he expressed were so new, so unusual and so different to any I had heard before that I felt this is a new sort of mind, I'm really in the presence of someone outstanding. Now I'm sure you will think – easy to say that now when his fame is worldwide.

Sheila Jones (née Dobbs)   I think Sam Beckett was there only for one term, perhaps two. He gave one the impression of being a tall thin streak of misery – standing in front of the fireplace, leaning against the mantelpiece, a large lock of hair falling down on his forehead. He hardly ever looked up at us. The term he was missing, I asked 'Where's our Sam?' Someone replied: 'Gone to Paris to commit suicide.'

Mary A. McCormick (née Arabin Jones)   Sam Beckett was *not* a good lecturer – in fact even the most earnest and serious students found him boring . . . My first memory of him is of a tall, gaunt, bespectacled, pock-marked man gazing out of the window into the New Square. I can only remember his lectures on Proust and I wish I had been more attentive then as for a long time I have been very interested. I remember him drawing diagrams on a blackboard and saying 'The Proustian equation is not a simple one' etc.* Once I plucked up courage and asked him the meaning of the word 'persiflage' and he translated it in such a convoluted fashion that I

---

* The opening sentence of Beckett's study, *Proust*, London, Chatto and Windus, 1930, p. 3, is 'The Proustian equation is never simple'.

was completely confused. I can't have been the only student who was so baffled, as soon afterwards in the Valentine edition of the *T.C.D.* magazine there was one addressed to him with the quotation 'I wish you would explain your explanations'. I haven't any notes of his lectures, am afraid that all thought him rather odd, and I know how he despised us all and that wouldn't make him an inspiring lecturer. On one occasion he told one of his really very intelligent students that if she weren't interested and continued to read novels throughout his lectures she might as well leave the room. Things were different in those days!

Elliseva Sayers   Sam always fascinated me, rather than the stuff he taught. I wondered about him. He was so unlike the other teachers or lecturers as they were called. As I was about nineteen then, and understood little or nothing of the subjects he talked about – more like rambled on about, to us, anyway – except that it was way above our heads – he was like in the clouds, did not look at us or address any of us but appeared to be talking to himself. Our (or rather my) thoughts were more the romantic kind – he was tall, handsome, mysterious – so I imagined having personal conversations with him in which he explained himself or whatever susceptible nineteen-year-olds think. Anyway, when we lunched in Paris at the Closerie des Lilas in the 1950s, I asked him about it. He said he was terrified of us and didn't himself know what he was talking about – as if he were in a trance of some kind – it looked that way . . . Beckett lectured on Proust, which I tried to read and understand, but though I am told I was a good student, I could not summon up much interest in him.

Dorothy Scott (née Pearse)   My very hazy recollection of him is of a very quiet, possibly almost shy young man, perhaps even not altogether completely happy in his role of 'teacher'. As we got on with our work, he would stand facing out of the window that was beside his desk, as if perhaps deep in thought – as no doubt he was. Naturally I had no idea, then, of the genius that was inside him, and even though I was so unsuccessful [she failed her French exams], I feel proud, now, to think that I had actually been in his class. As far as books on the course are concerned, I can only recall one – Balzac

– but what it was called, or what it contained, I can no long remember.

I felt rather sorry to think that my term with him was his last as a Trinity lecturer. It would be a sad thought, wondering if we could really have been so bad, that he wanted to leave. Trinity was such a happy and delightful place really – a little world of its own – that it is hard to imagine anyone not being happy there.

Emily Skillen (née Lisney)   Yes, I attended Samuel Beckett's lectures but do not recall specific authors on which he lectured, but remember being fascinated by his ideas, especially his idea of 'motion in a stasis' which I suggest is the main theme of his plays in line with ancient mystery plays and Greek drama – to hold an admonitory mirror up to people in every walk of life. So many lives are merely a minimum of motion in a moribund stasis.

Jesse Forbes Yates (née Brown)   I attended Samuel Beckett's lectures and the only author I can remember is Sterne's *A Sentimental Journey* with which he seemed obsessed and made us translate into French. He was such a dull lecturer and such a dull man, as he thought himself too good for the job and held his students in contempt. The only thing which roused us from our somnolent lethargy was when he set himself on fire by letting the sleeve of his gown drop into the open fire when he was leaning his fevered brow on the marble fireplace.

Moira Symons (née Neill)   Sam Beckett wasn't with us for very long, as far as I remember. I do not remember a thing about what he lectured on. But one thing came across very clearly: that he hated the job. I can see his face now in the classroom. We had a saying that 'he despised us with the utmost despision'.

Rachel Burrows (née Dobbin)   Professor Rudmose-Brown had such admiration for his junior lecturer that he gave him his lectures on Racine, which he usually took himself. Beckett shared his liking for Racine and his dislike for the heroics of Corneille. I remember so well his search for the subconscious in Racine, his pinpointing the solitary nature of every human being. In his essay on Proust, which began, 'the

Proustian equation is never simple,' he said, 'We are alone. We cannot know and we cannot be known,' a theory which could be applied to his own work. But in those days, you see, we didn't think of Beckett as a writer . . . I don't believe any of our year knew him well, except perhaps Leslie Daiken [Yodaiken], who wrote to me shortly before he died saying, 'Sam is in London. We are having great fun.' Seems an odd word to use in connection with Sam Beckett. He seldom smiled. His Valentine in *T.C.D.* [college magazine], February 1931, reads as follows: 'An exhausted aesthete who all life's strange poisonous wines has sipped and found them rather tedious.' He was a very impersonal lecturer. He said what he had to say and then left the lecture room. But he was very courteous and always willing to elucidate a point, if anyone had the courage to ask him a question.

I believe he considered himself a bad lecturer and that makes me sad because he was so good. Many of his students would, unfortunately, agree with him, and they made little effort to try and understand him . . . This may have been why we so seldom saw the genial side of his personality. He probably felt that we were as bored with him as he was with us. In my case, it was far from the truth. Looking back, I'm glad, as young as I was, I was just nineteen, I was aware that here was a brilliant mind. Here was exciting material that could not be found in a book . . .

He had an odd delivery. He would make long pauses between phrases, or very often pause in the wrong place, after a word, which might make you lose the thread of his thought . . . In lecturing, some people like Beckett are creating as they go along. Suddenly he would come up with something better than what he'd been going to say . . . People would say he couldn't teach, but he even got down to the nitty-gritty of showing us how to write an essay on the lesson, with proper headings. He was really trying to help us pass the exam. And this is what people will not give the man credit for.*

Grace West (née McKinley)   My years at Trinity College were from 1928 to 1932 so I was one of a class in 1931 taught by Samuel Beckett and I remember him with admiration. We were a small class,

---

* These reminiscences of Rachel Burrows are reprinted with permission from 'Interview with Rachel Burrows, Dublin, Bloomsday, 1982' by S. E. Gontarski, Martha Fehsenfeld and Dougald McMillan, *Journal of Beckett Studies*, nos 11 and 12, 1989, pp. 6–15.

Grace West (seated on the left) with a group of Trinity College, Dublin students, 1930–1.

I think, perhaps ten to fifteen (the memory dims!) and 1931 was within a year of Moderatorship, so we regarded his lectures very seriously and recognized a very original mind. As far as I can recall, he lectured entirely without notes, which impressed us greatly, so it is sad to think that he considered himself a failure as a teacher at that time. I think I particularly enjoyed his lectures on Racine but he also dealt with twentieth-century French Poetry and the Novel.

He seemed a sad young man – almost depressed – and it was rumoured that this was due to an unhappy love affair. I believe none of us knew him personally as a man or were aware of his home background. We knew he had just returned from the Ecole Normale and would have been aged twenty-five and had written his short book on Proust, a copy of which I possessed much later when I had moved to England.

There was something unique about Beckett. He lectured to us in a mixture of English and French. I loved his lectures on Racine. [See Appendix for extracts from Mrs West's unpublished notes.] He was always talking about Dostoievsky, 'Crime and Punishment'. I once said to Leslie Daiken that there are one or two phrases of Beckett that I remember so well. One of his favourite phrases was 'Phèdre is bathed in white light'. I think that is a wonderful phrase. It was a dark play. And all of the light is on the front of the stage. Beckett seemed very conscious of lighting. He had a very acute sense of dramatic effects. Leslie Daiken could remember most clearly Beckett's thoughts on Rimbaud and Verlaine: 'Rimbaud harpooned his similes, but Verlaine netted his.'

I also remember that he lectured to us on Balzac and I have notes on his lectures on Balzac. I also seem to remember that he lectured on Stendhal but I don't seem to have those notes . . . With Beckett's lectures, it always seemed to be winter and his gloom matched the weather!*

Beckett on Jack B. Yeats

Samuel Beckett　I knew Jack Yeats well. I had two pictures by him. I gave one to Jack MacGowran and Edward [Beckett, his nephew] has the other. [This picture is now in the Jack B. Yeats collection of the National Gallery of Ireland.] Of course, I lost touch with him for six years during the war years. I used to go to his 'at homes' in Fitzwilliam Square. You used to go up there, and he was very hospitable. His wife never appeared. And he'd greet you in his studio. Tom MacGreevy would often come. He was very close to him, Tom MacGreevy. He was with him when he died in the Portobello Nursing Home, the Private Nursing Home. And he would go behind a sort of screen and bring out a painting and put it on the easel for me or anyone to look at. And then he would produce some sherry I think it was. I remember the gesture he used when he served the sherry. Then he would squeeze a lemon with a gesture of his hand. We used to go for walks, through the Park. We didn't talk much. I didn't admire his writing too much. He had one play at the Abbey. What was it called? *In Sand*, that's it.

But his paintings were wonderful. He said he was completely impervious to influence. I think he thought he was the only painter. He said all the painting must have some 'ginger of life' in it. He was detached . . . He was very Republican. And he didn't at all agree with his brother's [W. B. Yeats] attitude in 1916, when the rebellion broke down. He was exclusively Republic. He broke up indefinitely

---

* Grace West's remarks are taken from a letter to James Knowlson, 4 July 1997 and from an interview with her recorded in 1997. I thank Mrs West's son, Terence, for the photograph and for the use of her lecture notes later in this book (see Appendix).

Jack Yeats at his easel, 1950.

with his brother, with whom he had never been close. He dismissed all that senatorial activity. He used to go off with [John Millington] Synge, you know. They got permission to go to the North for a tour. He was always polishing up his Irish.

I would make an appointment to go for a drive or for a walk. We'd drive out to a park and leave the car. Then we'd walk. To Leixlip or somewhere. Then have a meal together and then walk back. Then I'd drive him back along the quays.

I was in Ireland just before the war, seeing my mother, about 1939 [probably 1936]. It was at that period that I bought the painting *Sligo Morning* for 20 pounds [30 pounds] I think. And I paid him in instalments. Then six years later after the war, on my return to see my mother, I again contacted him and bought the second painting, *Regatta Evening*, for 40 pounds! I had it with me in Saint-Lô [after the war when he went as a storekeeper and interpreter with the Irish Red Cross Hospital], hanging on the wall.

Francis Stuart* on Beckett

Francis Stuart.

Francis Stuart   I knew Beckett when he was on the staff of Trinity College [in 1930–1]. I had come down from Antrim. I hadn't

---

* Francis Stuart (1902–2000). Irish writer; author of over thirty novels and a famous autobiographical work entitled *Black List, Section H*, Carbondale, IL, Southern Illinois University Press, 1971. He held the position of Saoi, the highest honour which the arts body of Ireland, Aosdana, can bestow on an artist. Interview with JK.

published anything; nor had Beckett. We were both from Protestant backgrounds, although I had become a Catholic when I married, which I did when I was very young. We were both awkward, as I remember, Sam Beckett and I. We used to go to this pub, Davy Byrne's. There was a back room there which we used to go to. When I say 'we', there was a varying collection of would-be writers I think, mostly, and what in those days were called 'bohemians', I suppose, and people who weren't really writers, sort of hangers-on to the arts. Some were quite wealthy people, actually. There was Cecil Salkeld and 'Con' Leventhal, who, later on, was a close friend of Beckett's. I was very uncouth. I don't know if Beckett was uncouth but he felt 'out of it' and that brought us together.

I remember he used to have a ploy, which I didn't have. He would ask one of the girls for a pair of nail scissors and then he would be doing his nails, which gave distance to him. I would sit, miles from anyone, more awkward than he. He never missed anything but he was doing something, you know, and that struck me as . . . [rather odd]. And there was another funny thing I remember. We had a game: whoever could stick a stamp highest on the wall got a free round of drinks or something like that. Beckett was tall, but he wasn't the tallest. We had a heavyweight boxer in Ireland called Jack Doyle who used to come there.* I knew him quite well. He was from Cork. He was one of the Irish . . . not quite a stage Irishman but with a sort of panache about him. I think he got friendly with the then Prince of Wales, who became Edward VIII. He moved in those circles. But he didn't train. In his first fight he knocked out quite a good English heavyweight, but then he didn't train. Anyway, he was there with us and it was a foregone conclusion that he would put the thing [highest] and when he came, he put his stamp, of course, beyond our reach. The rule was that you couldn't take your feet off the ground, naturally, so when it came to Beckett's turn, Beckett put a stamp just higher than Jack Doyle's and yet we never saw how he did it; he was so lithe, reaching up. He was very athletic.

---

* Jack Doyle (1913–78), known as the 'Gorgeous Gael', was a boxer, singer, wrestler, and playboy. He achieved fame, not to say notoriety, in the 1930s and during and after the Second World War.

I also saw Beckett in Paris. I went to Paris with the typescript of my first novel, which I had also left with Cape [his publisher] to read.* I met Tom MacGreevy there, whom I knew already – well I knew Beckett, too, already and we used to meet in the Café Dôme at teatime and I remember how we walked back, towards evening, to the Closerie des Lilas, which is very fashionable and expensive now, but it wasn't then. It was a bistro. It's surprising how it came [into fashion]. Now it's only a wealthy tourist haunt. So we'd go along the Boulevard Montparnasse and I always remember the way we'd stop, Beckett would stop, for some messages and he'd buy two ounces of cheese in a little *charcuterie*, presumably for his supper. And then we'd go on to the Closerie des Lilas and have a last drink and Beckett would say 'Goodnight' and disappear up towards his [lodgings] – I never knew exactly where he lived. I used to see MacGreevy more.

Then, much later, during the war, I was living in Berlin and Sam Beckett was in occupied Paris. We couldn't write home, at least I couldn't write home. I imagine Beckett couldn't have written home, I don't know, but we could write to each other. And he wrote to me a long letter which very unfortunately disappeared under strange circumstances. Among other things, he said, 'I've nearly finished a novel, that is to say, I've written the first chapter.' I understand that as a novelist myself, if I've written a chapter which I'm not going to tear up, which I consider is two-thirds of the way there. I don't know what novel it could have been [the novel was *Watt*]. I treasured this letter and when we left Paris, that is myself and my late wife – although we were not married then – in the early '50s I should think, I left a lot of stuff with my French publisher, who had offices in the rue Jacob and who had a lot of space to store books and manuscripts and so on, and I left this letter.† We moved

---

* Francis Stuart, *Women and God*, London, Jonathan Cape, 1931.
† This letter from Beckett is referred to in a diary entry made by Stuart on 9 August 1942. 'Selections from a Berlin Diary, 1942', *The Journal of Irish Literature*, vol. IV, no. 1, Jan. 1976. Some doubt has since been cast on the authenticity of this entry. Beckett himself neither remembered writing it nor thought it likely that he could have written from Paris to an address in Germany at that time (letter to Francis Wheale, 10 August 1981). However, if the political circumstances allowed such a communication, it would certainly have been possible, as Beckett's chief Resistance friends were not arrested until 14, 15 and 16 August and Beckett and Suzanne did not flee from the Gestapo until 16 August 1942.

to London. When I went back to Paris and went to see him, he had no recollection of this at all. I said, 'Well, will you have a search made of your cellars or archives?' and I don't know whether he did or didn't but nothing came up. Quite a long time later, when I told the story to Geoffrey Elborn, a close friend of mine, who was writing my biography, he said, 'I'll go to Paris' but he had no more success.* In the course of this letter, Sam Beckett said, 'When I was walking up to Long Hill' (that's a long hill going down to where I lived in Ireland) 'I saw you coming down in your car', but he didn't even stop me, you know. It must have been shortly before the war. Then there was the war and our paths diverged.

Then we came to live in Paris in 1949 and we lived there for a few years. I knew Beckett was in Paris but I didn't actually contact him. I hesitated to, you see I'd been under suspicion, I'd spent a long time in Allied custody or whatever you call it, whereas he'd been decorated by De Gaulle, so I said, 'No, I can't very well'.† Although I did mention that to him later and he said, 'You should have.' And so I should have, you know, because whatever Beckett personally might have thought you must judge a writer by his [work].

The last time I met Sam Beckett was in that very cold winter in Paris in '87. He gave me an appointment in this hotel. I was a bit early so I went to a café near it. Then I went into the vestibule. I hadn't seen him for exactly fifty years, which must have been '37. And there he was, standing by the reception desk in, as it was very cold, a sort of overcoat and beret, ready, it looked to me, for flight – which was chilling. And the first few minutes were chilling. We went into the lounge and he ordered some wine. For the first five minutes I was sorry I had come. It wasn't particularly easy, not easy at all but gradually it warmed up and there was real warmth, I felt, and for me it was a moving experience, and we talked. He said, of course, he was through with Ireland. I knew what his attitude was already, but he asked about Dublin and about mutual [acquain-tances]. Of course, when I came back to Ireland and met one or two gossip columnists, to whom I said that I did meet him, there were certain things which I did not repeat, naturally. One thing that he

---

* Geoffrey Elborn, *Francis Stuart: A Life*, Dublin, Raven Arts Press, 1990.
† Francis Stuart was imprisoned and interrogated after the war for his broadcasts to Ireland while he was living in Berlin.

said was, 'You know, Francis, my days are filled with trivia'. And that is sad. And I said to him how much I admired, as I did, and do, the Trilogy [*Molloy, Malone Dies, The Unnamable*]. Geoffrey Elborn had met him, a year or two before, and he had given Geoffrey a first edition of this Trilogy inscribed for me and I said how grateful I was for that. And then he said, 'You know, Francis, a different person wrote that'. And it all seemed to me sad.

3

The Bad Years

Beckett and Thomas MacGreevy, London, 1934–5

Biography, 1933–9

A few months after the death of his father in the summer of 1933, Beckett left Dublin for London to undergo a course of psychotherapy to help him to cope with his increasingly frequent attacks of panic and depression. These were, as Beckett himself described them, 'bad days' both for his psychological and emotional stability and for his efforts to make a living as a writer.

The stories that he had written about an Irish intellectual, Belacqua Shuah, were published in 1934 as *More Pricks than Kicks*, but they had little commercial or critical success. His poems were then published in 1935 by a friend's small private press, under the title *Echo's Bones and other Precipitates*, but, again, they made little impact. His attempts to carve out a career in London as a reviewer and critic also failed. He worked on a novel, *Murphy*, which, when completed in June 1936 after his return to Dublin, was turned down by numerous publishers until it was finally published by Routledge in 1938. But again it sold fairly badly. While he was living in London, he read widely, including several books on psychology and psychoanalysis and went to a number of classical concerts. He also visited the Bethlem Royal Hospital (a mental hospital) where one of his old friends, Geoffrey Thompson, worked as a doctor. His visits to the hospital had a major part to play in the new novel, *Murphy*.

Returning to Dublin, his relations with his mother deteriorated badly and there were countless arguments and quarrels. Things came to a head in 1936 when Beckett (considered by his mother as unemployed, although he was trying hard to write) drank heavily, had an affair with a childhood friend of the family – a married woman at that – then smashed up his car, injuring another woman whom he adored. In an attempt to escape from these troubles and dogged by ill health, he toured Nazi Germany from October 1936 to April 1937, where he indulged his passionate interest in painting and met a number of Jewish painters who were the victims of Nazi persecution. He also witnessed at first hand the furore that modern art was creating inside the Nazi party – many paintings were being physically removed from the walls of galleries during his stay.

On returning home, under pressure to find gainful employment and not wishing to remain in Ireland, he applied for a lectureship in Italian at Cape Town University in South Africa. Failing to be appointed, he upset his mother still further by agreeing to act as a key witness in a celebrated libel case that his uncle, Harry Sinclair, was bringing against Oliver St John Gogarty. Then, after a blazing row with his mother, he left Ireland definitively to settle in Paris late in 1937, renewing his friendship with the Joyces and becoming friendly there with a number of painters and writers. Soon after that, in January 1938, he was stabbed by a pimp, the knife narrowly missing his heart.

He had a number of affairs in Paris, including one with the American art collector, Peggy Guggenheim, and another with a Frenchwoman, Suzanne Descheveaux-Dumesnil, an accomplished

Beckett's wife, Suzanne, at sixty.   Suzanne as a young woman.

pianist, whom he had met ten years earlier and who renewed their acquaintance by visiting him in hospital after the stabbing. Although they lived together soon after their reunion, they did not marry until 1961.

Beckett described these years in Paris before the outbreak of the Second World War as a 'period of lostness, drifting around, seeing a few friends – a period of apathy and lethargy'. None the less, he was evolving in different directions as a writer, writing poems in French and translating *Murphy* into French, with the help of a friend, Alfred Péron.

Psychotherapy and *Murphy*

Samuel Beckett   After my father's death, I had trouble psycholog-ically. The bad years were between when I had to crawl home in 1932 and after my father's death in 1933 [when I was] in London. I'll tell you how it was. I was walking up Dawson Street and I felt I couldn't go on. It was a strange experience I can't really describe. I found I couldn't go on moving. So I had to rush in to the famous pub in Dawson Street, Davy Byrne's. I don't know where I was going, maybe up to Harcourt Street [station]. So I went into the nearest pub and got a drink – just to stay still. And I felt I needed help. So I went to Geoffrey Thompson's surgery. Geoffrey at that time was still working in Dublin, working in the Lower Baggot

Street Hospital as a heart specialist. And he wasn't there; [he was] still at Baggot Street. He hadn't finished his consultations. So I waited outside. When he got there, I was standing by the door. He gave me a look over, found nothing physically wrong. Then he recommended psychoanalysis for me. Psychoanalysis was not allowed in Dublin at that time. It was not legal. So in order to have psychoanalysis, you had to come to London. He himself wanted to get some training as a psychiatrist. So very bravely he took himself off to London – he was an established doctor in Dublin at the time. Before you could become a psychiatrist, you had to undergo psychoanalysis yourself. So he tried to get it arranged so that I could go to the man he was going to see [J. A. Hadfield]. I don't know why but I finished up with [Wilfred Ruprecht] Bion to whom I used to go, I think, twice a week. It was going to cost about £200. So, of course, there was no question of my financing the course myself. So my mother paid for my course of treatment; she decided that she would finance me. The allowance from my father's will wasn't enough to pay the fees. So my mother gave me the money. That was when I started psychoanalysis with Bion. I used to lie down on the couch and try to go back in my past.

After about six months [a gross underestimate of the time that he spent with Bion, which was almost two years] I decided that I'd had enough. We decided to call it a day and we parted very amicably. Well, I thought it wasn't doing me any good. I was using my mother's money and she couldn't afford it. But I think it probably did help. I think it helped me perhaps to control the panic. I didn't have that feeling of panic or dizziness or something. I think it all helped me to understand a bit better what I was doing and what I was feeling. I certainly came up with some extraordinary memories of being in the womb, intra-uterine memories. I remember feeling trapped, being imprisoned and unable to escape, of crying to be let out, but no one could hear, no one was listening. I remember being in pain but being unable to do anything about it. I used to go back to my digs and write notes on what had happened, on what I'd come up with. I've never found them since but maybe they still exist somewhere. I stayed on in London, seeing Geoffrey Thompson of course. He was working at the Bethlem Royal Hospital [a famous mental hospital]. He had finished his analysis and was working at this first job as a psychoanalyst. Or perhaps it was simultaneous and he hadn't quite finished. But he had got this job in order to make enough money to pay for his analysis. And then I went to the Bethlem and saw him. I remember going to visit him at the hospital. I remember the man that I wrote about in *Murphy*. I remember him very clearly. Mr Endon was loosely based on him.

*John Kobler** One night in June 1971 [in Paris], as we were strolling after dinner at the Closerie des Lilas, Sam got to talking about how he had worked years ago. When writing *Murphy*, he had needed a psychiatric clinic upon which to model his own Magdalen Mental Mercyseat. Being a friend of the psychiatric resident at the Bethlem Royal Hospital, near London, that was the institution he chose, visiting frequently between 1935 and 1938.† 'I often saw a patient who claimed he had hereditary syphilis and begged the doctors to kill him,' Sam recalled. 'I finally said to him, "You have knives and forks at meals. Why don't you . . .?"' The madman was furious, as Sam suspected he would be. 'No real encounter was wanted', Sam continued. 'Stop the game.' In the novel, Murphy, an avid chess player like his author, is a ward supervisor in a madhouse. Mr Endon, his opponent, is a mad man. They make meaningless manoeuvres, the pieces soon returning to their starting position. 'Stop the game', Sam concluded. 'No encounter wanted. I think that's what the chess game in *Murphy* meant.'

Duncan Scott‡ He told me once about a man undergoing voluntary hypnosis, and who was gradually being taken back to the moment of his birth: first three years old, then two, then one, then . . . the birth itself. At this point the man cried out, 'I've got a terrible

---

* The quotation from John Kobler (1910–2000), biographer of Al Capone and John Barrymore, among others, and journalist, is borrowed from 'The Real Samuel Beckett: A Memoir by John Kobler', *Connoisseur*, July 1990, p. 59. Kobler recounted the same story to me [JK] in an interview, but it is better expressed here.
† Beckett visited the Bethlem Royal Hospital much less frequently and over a shorter period of time than this suggests. Thompson left as Registrar in fact after a nine-month-long appointment which was extended for three months more and in any case Beckett returned to Ireland in December 1935.
‡ Duncan Scott's memories of a conversation with Beckett about his days in London and about *Murphy* are published for the first time with the agreement of his widow, Bernadette Scott. For information about Duncan Scott, see 'Memories of Beckett in London and Berlin', pp. 214ff.

pain in my neck.' Sam: 'Well, the whole thing seemed highly
theatrical and suspect, but I liked that. Birth is a pain in the neck.'

This tale led him to another, about the time when he was living in
World's End, writing *Murphy*, and receiving psychiatric treatment,
which his mother paid for. He went because he was suffering from
terror in the night. His heart would thump wildly and he would be
totally unable to sleep. Others were lodging in the same house, but
he couldn't even cry out for help. The psychiatrist eventually
explained that something must have seriously alarmed him in
the womb, when he would have been similarly helpless and unable
to cry out. It wasn't clear whether or not Sam believed the
explanation, but he said that it cured him so effectively that he
was quite happy alone in his cottage in the Marne Valley where
there was no one to appeal to for help (Suzanne refused to visit the
cottage because she disliked it), even though, at his age, he was
more likely to need it at any time.

We were crossing Hyde Park, he naming the various locations as
we came to them. He spoke of *Murphy* as if he [Murphy] had been
of flesh and blood. 'It's Murphy's old haunt.' He said. 'He used to
walk about here a lot. They used to fly kites, but I was here the other
day and they don't do it any more.' There was disappointment in
his voice. A few minutes later, we crossed the Broad Walk. A
solitary kite soared in the sky. Sam beamed with pleasure.

I did not ask him why, since he had hated so much living there,
he kept returning to World's End. It had occurred to me that he
may have been exorcizing old ghosts. ('That time. Do you remember that time? When was that?')* He told me that he had gone
there on his previous visit to London as well, looking for the house
he used to live in, but it had been pulled down. He had been very
poor in those days, which constituted one of the most unhappy
periods of his life.

Ursula Thompson†   My husband [Dr Geoffrey Thompson] was a
close contemporary of Sam Beckett. He went to a Quaker school in

---

* An allusion to Beckett's play *That Time*, although not an actual quotation from it.
† Mrs Ursula Thompson (1911–2001), widow of Dr Geoffrey Thompson (1905–76), the
psychoanalyst who helped Beckett to embark on a course of therapy with Wilfred R. Bion
at the Tavistock Clinic in London in 1934–5. Interview with JK. We are most grateful to
their daughter, Mima Thompson, for her help.

Ursula and Geoffrey Thompson, *c. 1937.*

the south of Ireland and Sam was already at Portora Royal when Geoffrey transferred there at about the age of fifteen. They soon became very good friends. Cricket was a shared interest and they played together, both at Portora and at Trinity College, Dublin. He and Sam also went to the Abbey Theatre a great deal together. Geoffrey was very interested in George Bernard Shaw and the Irish writers of the time.

I first met Geoffrey in September 1934, when he came over to England to do psychiatric medicine at the Maudsley Hospital. He had been a consultant physician at the Baggot Street Hospital in Dublin, specializing mainly in the heart, I think.

Sam was already in London in 1934 and I met him then through Geoffrey, who was working as a Registrar at the Bethlem and the Maudsley. To become a psychoanalyst you have to have a long training and nobody in Ireland could give him that. Catholicism was strictly against psychiatric medicine in those days and it could not be practised at all in Ireland. Geoffrey had to start immediately with an analysis. It was called a training analysis, with a man called Hadfield, a senior man, very well qualified, at the Tavistock Clinic at the beginning of 1935. In those days psychoanalysts were often not very well qualified in medicine but Geoffrey was and, as such, he was a valuable asset to the field.

He mentioned Sam very early to me. Sam was really ill in 1934 and Geoffrey was very worried about him. And in those days there was little help for any kind of psychosomatic illness (panic attacks and so on). He was a physician but learning in psychiatric matters. And Geoffrey advised Sam about psychoanalysis. Sam and he spent a lot of time together in 1935, when Geoffrey was at the Bethlem Royal. He took Sam, dressed in a white coat, around the Bethlem to see the patients.* Sam was curious, interested in the patients. He regarded himself as a bit of a 'loony' and wanted to see the other 'loonies'!

When Geoffrey and I got married, he left the Bethlehem and began to think of setting up on his own in psychoanalysis. Then Hadfield offered to take him on at £600 a year, while he started his own practice, to help him with his extra patients. He suggested that we ought to leave the scruffy flat in Pimlico and take a place in Harley Street, which we did. So Geoffrey had private patients in Harley Street but he also worked at the Tavistock Clinic, where he knew W. R. Bion, Beckett's analyst.

We lived in a little attic on the top floor in Harley Street and Sam used to come and visit us there. They played chess together. The door bell would go, the butler [from downstairs] would open the door and we would peer over the banisters to see who it was and see the top of Sam's beaver hat, a large rather artistic type of hat, sombrero style, which young men interested in poetry often affected at the time. We still have the armchair he used to sit in, where he made a cigarette burn between the arm and the seat! I felt that he did not think I was the best choice for Geoffrey and viewed me as 'a silly ass of a schoolgirl'. [Ursula was teaching gymnastics and dance in Croydon High School when Geoffrey Thompson met her.] But he was awfully nice to me, none the less.

I married Geoffrey on 2 November 1935. Sam was our best man, although I don't remember him making a speech. The wedding was in a village called West Lulworth in Dorset, where my parents lived. We went down to Lulworth on the Friday night with Geoffrey driving a hired car and Sam sitting shivering in the back, because he had no overcoat – either because he hadn't got one or because he hadn't brought it with him. It was a Protestant church wedding, a small wedding; we walked to and from it. There is a wedding photograph with Sam in it. My aunt Sarah, the headmistress of a

---

* Beckett toured the wards at the mental hospital in mid-September 1935. This is established by a letter to his friend, Tom MacGreevy, undated but 23 September 1935 (TCD). The tour represents an important moment in the writing of his novel *Murphy* (1938).

The Thompsons' wedding 1935. Beckett is standing on the left in the second row.

school in Leicester, said at the wedding: 'You're marrying the wrong one'. She had fallen for Sam. Everyone did fall for Sam.

When Sam was stabbed in 1938, Geoffrey heard it on the wireless, and rushed over to Paris at once. Then, after the war, whenever he came over to London, Sam came to see us. I remember him not seeing very well [on account of the cataracts on both of his eyes]. He is our son Dan's godfather. ['The principle of selection escapes me but I'll be glad to do it', commented Beckett, as none of the family was religious.]* He was always very sweet towards the children. He used to bring them toys, the first they had after the war. There was a good wooden construction kit for Dan and a teddy with real fur.

---

* Beckett's comment on being chosen as godfather was reported by the Thompsons' daughter, Mima.

J. M. Coetzee*: Samuel Beckett in Cape Town – An Imaginary History†

J. M. Coetzee.

J.M. Coetzee In 1937 the University of Cape Town advertised a vacancy for a lecturer in Italian. Applicants should hold at least an honours degree in Italian; the successful candidate would be expected to teach, for the most part, beginning Italian language. Perks would include six months of sabbatical leave every three years, and assistance with travel expenses (by ocean liner).

The advertisement was brought to the attention of T. B. Rudmose-Brown, Professor of Romance Languages at the University of Dublin, who promptly contacted one of the better students to have graduated from his department and suggested that he apply.

The student in question, S. B. Beckett, MA, followed Rudmose-

---

* J. M. Coetzee (1940–). Nobel Prize Winner for Literature 2003. Author of *Dusklands*, *In the Heart of the Country*, *Waiting for the Barbarians*, *Foe*, *Age of Iron*, *The Master of Petersburg*, *Elizabeth Costello*, and *Slow Man*. Both the *Life and Times of Michael K* and *Disgrace* won the Booker Prize. His non-fiction includes: *Boyhood: Scenes from Provincial Life* and *Youth*. He wrote his PhD thesis on Samuel Beckett's novel, *Watt*.

† Copyright © J. M. Coetzee, 2004. An earlier version of this piece appeared in *Passage* (Sydney), no. 2, 2003. It was revised by J.M. Coetzee for this volume in 2005.

Brown's suggestion, though without enthusiasm. He sent in an application but failed to get the job. The job went to a specialist in the Sardinian dialect.*

Even if S. B. Beckett had been offered the lectureship, he would in all likelihood not have accepted, for his ambitions stretched in another direction. He wanted to be a writer, not a language teacher. On the other hand, he had no prospects at home, where at the age of thirty-one he was living off hand-outs from his brother. Penury might have forced his hand; he might indeed have found himself, in 1938, at the southern tip of Africa.

In that case, the outbreak of war would have trapped this citizen of neutral Ireland seven thousand miles from home. What might then have followed?

Conceivably, after years of easy colonial life, he might have found a return to war-ravaged Europe unappealing. Conceivably he might even by then have met and married a South African belle, and settled down and had children.

Just possibly, then, S. B. Beckett, appointed as lecturer in Italian, and advanced in the course of time to a professorship in Italian or even in Romance Languages, might still have been in residence at the University of Cape Town when, in 1957, I enrolled at that institution as an undergraduate.

Knowing no Italian and only a few words of French, I would not have been able to study in Professor Beckett's department, but I would certainly have heard of him as the author of *Waiting for Godot*, and perhaps even attended a performance of the play written in an English scandalously inflected with the argot of the Cape Flats. Professor Beckett might even have consented now and again to conduct the Wednesday-afternoon creative writing class to which students from all faculties were invited to bring their handi-work.

Since I would have been no less resistant to adopting Professor Beckett or anyone else as a spiritual father than Professor Beckett would have been to adopting me as a spiritual son, I would in all

---

* The specialist on Sardinia was M. F. M. Meiklejohn, who later became Professor of Italian in the University of Glasgow. He was also a distinguished ornithologist.

likelihood have left South Africa once I had graduated – as indeed happened – and have made my way, via England, to the United States. But I would certainly not have spent my time at the University of Texas labouring over a doctoral dissertation on Professor Beckett's prose style.

Whether I would have shaken off the influence of that prose style on my own – whether I would have wanted to shake it off – is another question entirely.

S. B. Beckett's laconic letter of application has survived in the University of Cape Town archives, as have the testimonial Rudmose-Brown wrote for him in 1932 and the letter he wrote in 1937 in support of his candidacy. In his own letter Beckett names three referees: a doctor, a lawyer and a clergyman. No academic referee. He lists three publications: his eccentric book on Proust, his collection of stories (which he cites as *Short Stories* rather than by its proper title, *More Pricks than Kicks*), and a volume of poems.

Rudmose-Brown's two letters could not be more enthusiastic.

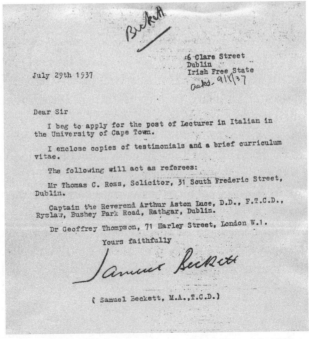

Beckett's application to the University of Cape Town, July 1937.

He calls Beckett the best student of his year in both French and Italian. 'He speaks and writes like a Frenchman of the highest education,' he writes. 'As well as possessing a sound academic knowledge of the Italian, French and German languages, he has remarkable creative faculty.' In a P.S., he notes that Beckett also has 'an adequate knowledge of Provençal, ancient and modern'.

One of Rudmose-Brown's colleagues in Dublin, R. W. Tate, adds his support. 'Very few foreigners have a practical knowledge of [Italian] as sound as [Beckett's], or as great a mastery of its grammar and constructions.'

Biography, 1940–6

Following the fall of France in June 1940, it was Beckett's French friend, Alfred Péron, who persuaded him to work for a Resistance cell of the British Special Operations Executive (SOE) called 'Gloria SMH'. 'Gloria' was the Resistance name of Gabriele-Cécile (known as Jeannine), the daughter of the painter Francis Picabia and his writer, lecturer and art critic wife Gabrielle Buffet-Picabia.

(Jeannine Picabia related in her 14th March 1943 debriefing at SOE head-quarters in London how she had come to meet Péron. 'I wanted to organize some-thing in Nantes and Lorient and through Sam Beckett, an Irishman whom I knew before the war, I met Alfred Péron who had groups of *paramilitaires*, and a woman called Suzanne Roussel, whose working name was Hélène . . . Péron had a wireless somewhere in the North

Beckett's own photograph of Alfred Péron, his friend, tennis partner and fellow Resistance agent, c. 1939.

Jeannine Picabia ('Gloria'), the head of Beckett's Resistance cell, 'Gloria SMH', 1939–40.

of France, around Lille I believe. When we had urgent messages to send we sometimes sent them through him.')

Beckett recounts below his clandestine activities as an agent and his enforced flight from the Gestapo with his partner, Suzanne, when the cell was infiltrated and betrayed and when many of his co-workers were arrested and then deported to Ravensbrück and Mauthausen concentration camps. He and Suzanne lived out the rest of the war in the little Vaucluse village of Roussillon, where Beckett wrote (in English) a large part of a daring, radically innovative novel, *Watt*. Returning to Paris late in 1944, he was decorated after the war with the medals of the Croix de Guerre and the Médaille de la Reconnaissance Française, telling no one, not even his closest friends, about these decorations.

Having returned to Ireland at the end of the war to see his mother, Beckett found it difficult to return to France. So he volunteered to work as an interpreter, storekeeper and ambulance driver for the Irish Red Cross Hospital in Saint-Lô in Normandy, which had been destroyed by allied bombings and shellings after the D-Day landings. He returned to Paris to endure some of the most poverty-stricken years of his life.

Beckett and the French Resistance

Samuel Beckett [After the declaration of war in September 1939] I went back [to France from Ireland] straight away – the next day. If I hadn't, I would have never got back. Even then I had difficulty in leaving England at Dover. They didn't want to let me through. No way. I didn't know what to do. I managed to wangle my way. I went back to talk to them, saying Ireland was not England, Ireland was not at war and so on. I managed to get through.

Alfred Péron* was the one who got me involved in the 'Gloria' Resistance group. It was at the time when they were rounding up all the Jews, including all their children, and gathering them in the Parc des Princes ready to send them off to extermination camps. Information came in from all over France about the German military movements, about movements of troops, their position, everything that concerned the occupational forces. They would bring this information to me on various bits, scraps of paper. There were about forty agents in that group. It was a huge group. It was the boy-scouts! They brought it all to me. I would type it all out clean. Put it in order and type it out, on one sheet of paper, as far as was possible. Then I would bring it to a Greek [named Hadji (André) Lazaro]† who was part of the group. He lived in what is now the rue de Coty I think. And he would take photographs. And my sheets would be reduced to the size of a matchbox. All the information. Probably unreadable but it could be magnified. And then he would give them to Madame Picabia, the widow of Picabia, the painter. And she was a very respectable old lady. Nothing could be less like a Resistance agent. And she could get

---

* Beckett had known Péron since his student days in Dublin, when Péron had been the French *lecteur* at Trinity College. They had also worked together in 1930 on the translation of James Joyce's 'Anna Livia Plurabelle' and on the French translation of Beckett's own novel *Murphy*. Alfred and Mania, his Russian-born wife, stayed firm friends with Beckett throughout the 1930s. Then he and Alfred were to work closely together as fellow members of the Resistance cell in Paris until Péron's arrest in August 1942.

† André Lazaro, the photographer of 'Gloria SMH', also known to the group as 'Jimmy le Grec' or 'Jimmy the Greek', survived imprisonment in Mauthausen concentration camp and died in Paris in November 1996.

Gabrielle Buffet-Picabia (*left*) in Madrid in 1943 after her escape from the Gestapo. The friend with her is unknown.

over to the other zone, the so-called unoccupied zone, without any difficulty. And so it was sent back to England.

When the whole thing blew up, as soon as we knew – the same day – I went to tell the Greek, but he didn't take it seriously enough and he was arrested. There was an informer in the group.* Everybody used to know everybody else. There used to be meetings in the evening. Everybody knew everybody. I'll tell you what happened. In August of 1942, Suzanne and I were at home. Mania and Alfred Péron were on holiday at the time, when Alfred was picked up by the Gestapo. And Mania sent us a more or less uncoded telegram, which we understood to mean that Alfred had been arrested by the Gestapo. I remember we got it at eleven and we'd gone within the hour. First we went to Marcel Duchamp's and Mary Reynolds'. They had a house in the rue Hallé, where we hid out for a night. It's near here. I'll show you sometime. That was our first refuge. Then some of Suzanne's communist friends found us another safe place where we lay low for a time while we were provided with forged papers.

[One of the places where Beckett and Suzanne hid out was in Janvry with the French writer, Nathalie Sarraute. She relates here what happened.]

---

* The informer was a Catholic priest named the Abbé Robert Alesch. See *Damned to Fame*, pp. 311–18.

Nathalie Sarraute* During the Occupation, my daughter, Claude, who spoke English well – she started to learn it at the age of two and was bilingual – used to take lessons in English literature with Samuel Beckett. We knew that he and Suzanne were very badly off, so we tried to help him out by paying him for lessons. She read Shakespeare with him. [Claude Sarraute informs us that their lessons were held inside a tent that Beckett had erected in the apartment in the rue des Favorites because it was so cold and there was a great fuel shortage that winter.]† I didn't know him myself personally then. I only

Nathalie Sarraute, who sheltered Beckett and Suzanne when they were on the run from the Gestapo.

knew him through our mutual friend, Alfred Péron, for whom Beckett used to translate messages received from London. Péron was quite an important figure in the Resistance. These messages were retyped and translated by Beckett. Claude came home one day from Beckett's flat and said how extraordinary it was that Péron had come to see Beckett while she was there and that they'd spoken about serious matters to do with the Resistance that she shouldn't be hearing. Beckett's own wife reproached them even for their lack of discretion. Péron was also careless enough to have a notebook in which he had written down the names of eighty or so [*sic*] members of his Resistance cell with him when he was arrested.‡ Fortunately,

---

* Nathalie Sarraute (1900–99), born in Ivanova in Russia as Nathalie Ilyanova Tcherniak. French novelist and critic. During the Nazi occupation, after she sheltered Beckett and Suzanne, she was denounced as being from a Jewish family and was forced to go into hiding under the name of Nicole Sauvage, posing as the governess of her own three daughters. Later in this recorded interview, in a passage not quoted here, she related in detail what happened to her and her family. Before the war, she had already published *Tropismes*, Paris, Denoël, 1939. Interview with JK
† Claude Sarraute, telephone conversation with JK, 22 September 2004.
‡ Clearly the truth of this statement cannot be checked.

Alfred and Mania Péron, 1939.

my husband belonged to another cell in Paris. Anyway most of the members of Péron's cell were soon arrested. But Beckett was warned in time and managed to escape before the Gestapo went round to his flat to arrest him.

Péron's wife, Mania, was a childhood friend of mine. She was eight years younger than me but my mother-in-law and her mother were good friends. She was Russian and had two children, the twins Alexis and Michel. So Mania asked me if I would shelter Beckett at our house, since she knew that Claude had been having lessons with him. As you can imagine, there was no question of our saying 'no' at the time. So he turned up with Suzanne.

In our house at the time there were my three daughters, my mother, myself and a young Jewish girl who was living with us with false papers. Her name was Liber but she had papers in the name of Gauthier-Villar, because she was a distant relative of the Gauthier-Villars. We were all living cooped up together in a little gardener's house at Janvry in the Vallée de la Chevreuse (which is still there, by the way, on the village square). It belonged to a gardener called Monsieur Mariage who owned this little cottage. It was very primitive: there was running water only in the kitchen and the toilets were at the bottom of the garden. It was heaven's punishment inflicted on human beings. So when the Becketts arrived, Claude and Anne moved into a dark little room behind the kitchen which was normally used as the dining-room. We put a mattress in so they could sleep there. Naturally they were very unhappy with the arrangement. The Becketts slept in their bedroom, which was fairly basic, not particularly attractive, but perfectly acceptable. It was the best and the sunniest room in the house. The children had the dark room which overlooked the street. Beckett and Suzanne stayed with us for ten days. Then we sent them on to some Russian friends in Paris and these friends found a way of getting them across the line into the Free Zone. Beckett had a very, very strong accent in French. Indeed, he did not speak French particularly well or write French well at that time. And I remember my husband saying to Beckett: 'The first thing you must do is shave off your moustache, because you look just like an English civil servant, or even an English officer!' Suzanne helped me in the kitchen and with the shopping.

As the children were living in what was the dining-room, we used to eat our meals in the kitchen. So, in order to go to the toilet at the end of the garden, the Becketts had to pass through the kitchen. They did this every day about half past one or two o'clock while we were eating. And my mother said, 'I've never seen anyone so badly brought up in my life. How long are they going to stay here?' And when Beckett came through, chamber-pot in hand, she used to say to me – in Russian – 'There is the madman who always comes through when we are eating!' The Becketts used to go out for walks at that time. It was considered safe enough. And when my husband came out for long weekends, Beckett would go out for long walks with him. My husband got on as well with Beckett as I got on badly. Beckett couldn't seem to bear that I should have the least literary pretention. Even though at the time he admired enormously Simone de Beauvoir, my own aspirations seemed to annoy him. He had lent us the French translation of *Murphy* and when the Gestapo came to pick up my husband as a hostage, we had *Murphy* on the table. They wanted to take it away with them. He said, 'Why ever do you want that? That is of no interest to you'. But they took it away none the less.

The word 'grateful' didn't seem to be in Beckett's vocabulary. An old friend of mine, an American woman who knew him well, once said: 'Oh, he never forgives you for any service you do him. He doesn't like to be in anybody's debt.' You call that pride, do you? I would call it unworthy. As Proust says, 'un homme très ordinaire peut habiter un génie' ['a very ordinary man can inhabit a genius']. We are not talking of the genius that you can see in his work, but the man that inhabits the genius. And after the war, he came here once when my father was very, very ill. He stayed for only a quarter of an hour, then he left. According to Mania, it seems he was unhappy because my father was not very agreeable to him. Now my father could hardly walk at the time and used to get very impatient and cross as a result.

I empathized very much with Mania. She helped Beckett a lot with his French after the war. She was an *agrégée d'anglais*, you know, although she spoke English with an incredible Russian accent, whereas she spoke excellent French. Beckett used to send her *pneumatiques* [i.e. telegrams delivered speedily in the Paris area] to ask her how to say something.*

Escape to the South

'Nous avons fait les vendanges, tiens, chez un nommé Bonnelly, à Roussillon' ['We were picking grapes for a man called Bonnelly, in Roussillon.'] Vladimir in *En attendant Godot* (*Waiting for Godot*).

Beckett's rented house in Roussillon.

Samuel Beckett We tried to get over the line [between the Occupied and the Unoccupied Zones] at Chalons. We just didn't

---

* He certainly wrote several letters to Mania Péron in which he asked her questions concerning French usage or vocabulary, although he did not always accept her judgements. These letters still exist today.

know where to go. I think we finished up in Toulouse. Then Suzanne remembered friends [Marcel and Yvonne Lob, née Deleutre, and Yvonne's brother, Roger] she had in a little village in the mountains that was Roussillon [in the Vaucluse]. We went there and lay low. I remember staying in a little hotel [known locally as the Hôtel Escoffier, after the name of the owner] before some friends got us a bedroom and a bathroom in an unoccupied house. That was where we met Josette and [the Polish-born painter] Henri Hayden. I used to play chess with Henri. He came to play with me.

Bonnelly was the one with the vineyard. We used to pick grapes for him. I also remember the Audes. Aude had a large family with two daughters. One of them used to cycle up the hill. Their farm was down the road. We used to go and work on the farm. They'd give us food. And once a week we used to go and eat as much as we could, I remember!

I didn't really get involved in the local Resistance until the last few weeks when the Americans were coming. I remember going out at night and lying in ambush with my gun. No Germans came, so I never had to use it.

I only wrote in the evenings. We used to work during the day. I started writing *Watt* in the evenings.

[There was] Miss Beamish.* She used to live with an Italian woman called Suzanne Allévy. She [Suzanne] was small, dark-haired. Miss B was the masculine one of the couple. She used to dress more like a man. Do you know where the house is? There are still people there who will remember me. It's a very different place now. We had a room with a kitchen on the ground floor, I remember. Just outside Roussillon, on the road to Apt, on the corner. Miss Beamish was facing us. She had the whole house, and her girlfriend, and her dogs, her Airedales. Did you know she used to breed Airedale terriers in a kennel in Cannes? She was very

---

* Anna O'Meara de Vic Beamish, author of over twenty novels, wrote under the name of Noel de Vic Beamish or simply De Vic Beamish. She wrote two books on dogs and did quite a lot of research for her swashbuckling historical novels, especially on the Middle Ages, and was very knowledgeable about wine and the history of wine. She had acted earlier on the London stage and had translated two plays from the Italian, one the well-known *The Mask and the Face* by Luigi Chiarelli. After travelling widely in Europe, she lived for a long time in Cannes with her companion, Suzanne Allévy. She was a very picturesque figure in Roussillon, helping the local Resistance group by hiding arms in the garden of the house opposite Beckett.

Anna O'Meara (pen-name Noel) de Vic Beamish,
Beckett's neighbour, with her Airedale terriers.

likeable. She used to walk out with her dogs; she'd go down to do
some shopping in the village. We weren't far from the centre.

At the end of the war, it was terrible! The forces just opened up
the extermination camps as they came through. They had nothing
to eat, those of them who were left alive. So there was cannibalism.
Alfred [Péron] wouldn't do it. Amazingly he got as far as Switzer-
land and then he died of malnutrition and exhaustion. After the war
we saw quite bit of Mania, Alfred's widow. She used to check on the
French [of my work], I remember.

Fernand Aude*   Samuel used to come to work with us on the farm
almost every day. At that time I was seventeen years old and he was
forty-odd [in fact Beckett was not quite as old as this: he was thirty-
six to thirty-eight during his stay in Roussillon]. He worked
regularly on my father's farm. And he worked for nothing. We
wanted to pay him – but he wouldn't hear of it. I used to say: 'Stop,
Sam, you're exhausting yourself'. But he would answer, 'No, no.
I'm fine. If I help you, you'll finish a lot faster' . . . He used to eat
with us sometimes in the evening. We would eat very late. He would
bring in the milk and collect the eggs before supper. Suzanne used to

---

* Fernand Aude was the son of the farmer Albert Aude on whose farm Beckett worked.
Interview with JK.

Henri Hayden's pen-and-ink sketch of Roussillon.

come with him as well and eat with us. It was about five kilometres from Roussillon to Clavaillan. But they used to come on foot, and then they would walk home about eleven or twelve o'clock at night, since we didn't have room to put them up for the night. Suzanne was very nice; she helped my sister a little in the kitchen, getting the meals and so on. But she didn't like work too much. Whereas Sam, oh, he would do absolutely anything: climb trees, pick cherries, gather melons, pick grapes. He helped us with harvesting the wheat and with the ploughing; we used to plough between the vines . . .

Someone else who Sam knew locally, someone he worked for cutting up wood and so on, a farmer, Monsieur X . . . profited from the black market. He tried to feather his own nest. Samuel did not like that. He was such an honest man, Sam, as straight as a die.

*Yvonne Lob** My brother, Roger Deleutre, was a friend of Suzanne's and it was through him that the Becketts came to Roussillon. As soon as the Nazis arrived in Paris, Roger came to join us here, where we had been settled for some months, living off the land. My husband [Marcel] had lost his university post because he was a Jew. And when Sam had trouble with the Nazis in Paris because he was in the Resistance, my brother wrote to him to let him know that he could come here and we would find some way to put them up.

The problem was that Sam was a foreigner and this made things difficult. However, my husband [Marcel] went to see the Secretary General of the Préfecture in Avignon, whom he knew, saying that he was a friend of my brother and he managed to get permission for him to stay, as long as he did not move from Roussillon. He was, after all, from Ireland, a neutral country, and they knew where he was. But it did mean that he could never leave Roussillon for the whole of the time he was here.

Sam and my husband never really got on together or, more precisely, my husband did not get on with Sam. He was the exact opposite. For me, Sam was a saint with all that the term implies, whereas my husband was a pure rationalist. There were times when

---

* Yvonne Lob (OBE). Before the war, as a well-qualified *agrégée* in English, she was a teacher of English in Nice, where her husband held a university post. This is a brief extract from a much longer interview with JK.

I found it quite difficult to keep the peace within the house because there were a lot of us and, as well as the family, we also sheltered refugees from time to time. My husband was never easy-going but losing his post at the university simply because he was of Jewish origin – he was not even a practising Jew at that – embittered him greatly. I understood how he was suffering. But he really was very intransigent.

I remember one day Sam was given a piece of beef by the Audes, on whose farm he worked. Meat was, of course, extremely rare in those days of rationing. Sam brought it to me and so I said, 'If you are giving me meat, then you must come over for dinner this evening.' So I cooked it. There were a lot of us round the table when, over something too trivial even to remember, Marcel took offence, lost his temper and left the table. On that occasion, I went after him and persuaded him to come back again but that was the kind of thing which happened, preventing our relationship with Sam and Suzanne from being all that it could have been. Despite both of them being intellectuals, Sam and he never really hit it off.

Sam and Suzanne came round quite often and I remember one time saying to Sam, 'You know, if you fancy reading anything in English I have a lot of English novels.' 'That's an idea', he replied. There must have been times when he didn't feel inspired to write and preferred to read and I introduced him to works he didn't know. I told him to take whatever he wanted and he did. 'Ah', he said, 'That's not bad'. It was Hugh Walpole. I introduced him to Hugh Walpole whom he had never read before.*

I knew Suzanne first but I got on well with Sam because we had certain things in common. We didn't speak English together because those around us didn't speak English. His French was very good but sometimes, when we discussed books, we spoke in English. We got on very well. I found him very human and easy to become friends with.

After the war Sam and Suzanne returned to Paris as soon as they could. I never saw them again except for one time when I went to

---

* A fuller account of Beckett's reading in Roussillon and the echoes of this in his novel, *Watt*, partly written in the village, is given in *Damned to Fame*, pp. 326–7. There is also a lot to suggest that Beckett's knowledge of rural life which appears in *Malone Dies* derived from his stay in Roussillon.

spend Christmas with Roger and Denise [his wife]. We went to a concert on the Champs-Elysées and in the interval my brother told me that Sam and Suzanne were there with a niece from Ireland [Caroline Beckett] who had come to spend a few days with them. It gave me real pleasure to shake his hand. That was the only time I saw them after they left Roussillon.

I must say one thing. Apart from *En attendant Godot*, which is accessible, I have never been able to read anything of his. Never. I am probably just too Cartesian. I am open to a lot of English literature, because it was my profession, and when the first volume of *Molloy* came out I thought I really must buy that. I tried to read it but I simply couldn't stomach it and gave it away.

The Irish Red Cross Hospital, Saint-Lô*

'The Capital of Ruins': the Normandy town of Saint-Lô after the war-time bombing.

Samuel Beckett   Saint Lô, 'The Capital of Ruins'. [After the war, when he had returned to Ireland] I went over with Colonel McKinney and Dr Alan Thompson [brother of his old schoolfriend, Geoffrey] to set things up. We went over in the boat with the first lot of stores. At first they were stacked up on paper. I don't know

---

* Phyllis Gaffney, the daughter of Dr Jim Gaffney, the pathologist with the team, has written excellently about the Irish Hospital in *Healing amid the Ruins, The Irish Hospital at Saint-Lô (1945–46)*, Dublin, A. and A. Farmar, 1999.

where they were being kept but they weren't ready for shipping. I can remember them all piled up on the quayside; a large amount of stores. Then we were joined by the rest of the group, Dr Arthur Darley, and the surgeon, Freddie McKee, some others, and then Tommy Dunne joined us. He was my assistant storekeeper in Saint-Lô. I remember Tommy Dunne well, a nice fellow; I got on well with him. Eoin O'Brien told me recently that Tommy had died. His widow, whom Eoin had traced, wrote to me and told that they'd had ten happy years together before he died. Then there was Jim [Gaffney], the pathologist. He died in an Aer Lingus crash, you know. It was my job to store the supplies and do the driving. I used to do a lot of driving, drive the ambulances and the truck. It was a big concern. We had about six ambulances plus the trucks. I used to drive up to Dieppe to get supplies and bring back nurses. McKinney was the organizer. He used to drink quite heavily, when he wasn't in the brothel!

Simone McKee* My future husband, Freddie, said to my parents, 'I really must bring a friend called Samuel Beckett out to meet you', and one day he turned up with him. Both he and my parents were musicians – my father was a very good pianist – and we had a piano that had come more or less unscathed through the bombardments so when Sam felt like playing he used to come out to my parents' home to play. They also used to sing French songs together.

The job he was doing was really not his kind of thing at all. He had to do quite a lot of administration and he was not a methodical, practical person. As far as his driving ambulances goes, he was a terrible driver. He could hardly see; he was so short-sighted. It was dreadful – really terrifying. He never had an accident but his driving was appalling. When he visited us in Ireland after the war he would sometimes pick me up and take me with my baby, Jean-Luc, out to the seaside but I used to be afraid of being in the car with him, especially with the baby.

I found him reserved but not cold. There was a woman called Mrs Barrett, a Frenchwoman who was married to an Irishman and who came to the opening of the hospital in Saint-Lô as a member of the Red Cross. She didn't speak much English and after I got

---

* Simone Lefèvre married the Irish surgeon, Frederick McKee, and lived for many years in Dublin. Interview with JK.

Beckett with Simone McKee and friends in Ireland after the war, *c.* 1948. Left to right: back row, Samuel Beckett, Madeleine Barrett, Mr Barrett; front row, Yvonne Lefèvre (Simone McKee's sister), Mrs Barrett, Simone McKee.

married and went to live in Ireland she often invited me to her home about six miles to the north-west of Dublin. On one such occasion she invited me along with my sister and Sam Beckett. She was always taking photographs and Sam detested that. After the first few when she suggested, 'Shall we take another one?' Sam said, 'I could always turn my back, just for a change' . . . and that was in 1948!

He often came to see us in Dublin when he came to visit his mother. I remember how he loved lobsters. My husband loved them too and used to get them from some people he knew who sold them at the market in Dublin. My heart would sink when I saw him come in with them because of having to cook them and break them up. I can still see my husband and Sam on the garden steps, cracking lobsters.

When his mother died [in 1950], Sam came to our house and asked Freddie to go with him to choose the coffin. Freddie was a bit taken aback, it was such an unusual request. Sam had all the measurements and so on with him. It was all rather morbid, I felt. It was only after *Godot* and what followed that I thought back to those outings to the sea with Jean-Luc when there was no thought of his being so intelligent, so learned and so exceptional, when to us he was just the most natural of men.

Beckett in Ireland after the war (almost turning his back), *c.* 1948.

Part II

Remembering Beckett

4

Post-war Success: The French Novels and *En Attendant Godot*

The painter Henri Hayden and Samuel Beckett at dinner
in the Haydens' house at Reuil in the early 1960s

Biography, 1945–55

Returning to Paris from his work with the Irish Red Cross Hospital in Saint-Lô after the war, Beckett and Suzanne endured some of their most difficult years. To earn money in those inflationary times, he did many translations and taught English; she did dress-making and gave music lessons to children.

From February 1946, Beckett wrote in a frenzy of activity – and now he wrote in French. After a short story, *La Fin* (*The End*), there followed a shortish novel, *Mercier et Camier*, and three more stories,

L'Expulsé (*The Expelled*), *Premier amour* (*First Love*), and *Le Cal-mant* (*The Calmative*). A year later, he wrote a play which has still to be produced, *Eleuthéria*. Then he began a major novel trilogy in French: *Molloy*, *Malone meurt* (*Malone Dies*) and *L'Innommable* (*The Un-namable*), all of which took him over two and a half years to write.

Eventually, after many rejections, Suzanne, to whom Beckett in his own words 'owed everything', found a young publisher named Jérôme Lindon, who had taken over the former underground publishing house of the Resistance figure Vercors, Les Editions de Minuit. Lindon was prepared to publish all of Beckett's novels and promptly offered him a contract. So began a close relationship between the two men which was based on mutual respect and trust. Lindon did far more for Beckett than most publishers ever would for their authors. But Beckett repaid that faithfulness and con-scientious concern with personal friendship and total loyalty, as well as with practical help and financial support in difficult times.*

Although the novels received a high level of critical acclaim, success of a more public nature eventually came to Beckett in his mid-forties in the shape of a play which many have seen as transforming twentieth-century theatre. This was of course *En attendant Godot* (*Waiting for Godot*), written between October 1948 and January 1949. It was published, as were all the later plays

May Beckett, 1948–9.

in French, by Jérôme Lindon. Two of the actors involved in the first productions, Jean Mar-tin, who played Lucky in the French world première, and Pe-ter Woodthorpe, who played Estragon in the English-lan-guage première, speak here about their experiences of working on the play and about their meetings with Beckett.

Having become distanced from his native language throughout

---

* Many instances of the friendship, close co-operation and mutual debt of Beckett and Lindon are described in *Damned to Fame. The Life of Samuel Beckett.*

the war, Beckett at first opted to collaborate with others in translating his French stories and the first of his published French novels, *Molloy*. We publish the fascinating first-hand accounts of Richard Seaver, who translated 'The Expelled' and 'The End', and Patrick Bowles, who worked intensively with Beckett on the English translation of *Molloy* and had numerous fascinating and profound conversations with him.

Two personal events marked Beckett very intensely at this period of his life. In 1950, his mother, May, became critically ill with advanced Parkinson's disease and dementia. She died in August 1950, Beckett staying in Dublin to care for her during the final few months of her life. With the money from the sale of her property after her death, he had a modest little house built in the country village of Ussy in the Seine et Marne region. He used to love to go there to write. At the beginning, Suzanne accompanied him, but later she took against the house as being too quiet and remote from all the things that she enjoyed in Paris: friends, music, theatre, bustle.

Almost as traumatic was the death of his brother, Frank, in September 1954. Again Beckett devoted several months to caring for him, and this experience seems to have had a major impact on several of his later plays, most notably *Endgame* and the 1956 radio play *All That Fall*.

Beckett's 'modest little house' in Ussy sur Marne
with (*from left to right*) Donald Page, Suzanne, Beckett.

Richard Seaver on Translating Beckett

Richard Seaver, seen here in the 1950s, editor in chief of Arcade Publishing in New York, was an old friend of Samuel Beckett's from the 1950s. In 1952 he first brought Beckett, then virtually unknown, to the attention of the English-language public in a laudatory essay in *Merlin*. Seaver has been a distinguished publisher in New York for over forty years, during which time he has translated over fifty books from the French, including works by Marguerite Duras, Françoise Sagan, André Breton, Eugène Ionesco and Beckett himself. Contribution especially written for this volume.

Paris, 1950s

Some people make their own luck, others have it thrust upon them, by timing, by geography, or the gods. In my case, it was a combination of timing and geography, for in the fall of 1951 I moved from my eighth-floor aerie (read: maid's room) in an abominable *pension de famille* on the rue Jacob to a much larger lodging at 8, rue du Sabot, hard behind St-Germain des Prés.

To reach St-Germain, with its throng of welcoming cafés, I had

almost inevitably to traverse the rue Bernard Palissy, a tiny cob-
blestoned street that housed a baker, a greengrocer, a launderer, a
joiner, and, of all things, a fledgling publisher, Les Editions de
Minuit. Until recently, the premises occupied by Minuit had been
the local bordello, shut down three years before by a band of anti-
sex crusaders, in a vain attempt to cleanse the Gallic soul, and with
it hopefully the body as well. But a key point in that exchange of
professions was that the premises at 7, rue Bernard Palissy were
equipped with two display windows, one on either side of the door,
formerly filled with the images of enticing young female bodies,
now with freshly minted books. As I passed Number Seven almost
daily on my way to my hangouts at the Deux Magots and Royale
cafés, I could not help but check the titles, especially two set cheek
by jowl, *Molloy* and *Malone meurt*, bearing a name that rang a
more than faint bell: Samuel Beckett. I was deeply into Joyce at the
time, for me the blessed saint of modern literature, and the Beckett
name had appeared frequently in the Joycean context. All I knew of
him was that he too was Irish, he had come to Paris from Trinity
College, Dublin as a *lecteur* at the Ecole Normale Supérieure – a
signal honour – that he and a French friend, Alfred Péron, had
translated the 'Anna Livia Plurabelle' episode of *Finnegans Wake*
into French, and that he had contributed the opening essay to the
collection of twelve odes to the Master, appropriately entitled *Our
Exagmination Round His Factification for Incamination of Work
in Progress*. I also seemed to recall that he had published a novel or
two in England, to little or no success. But what, my mind kept
asking, was he, an Irish writer, doing in the window of Minuit, a
French publisher? Ah, I decided: it must be a translation. So I
hurried off first to the English bookshop on the rue de Seine, where
the proprietor Gaït Frogé said she had never heard of either *Molloy*
or *Malone* in English, then on to George Whitman's Librairie
Mistral, where the response was the same. So, I semi-concluded,
the books must have been written in French. Bizarre . . .

Then, if I may quote myself, a passage written thirty-plus years
ago:

'Finally, curiosity won out over avarice: one morning, on my trek
to St-Germain des Prés, I went into Number 7 and bought both
books. Later that day I opened *Molloy* and began to read: '*Je suis*

dans la chambre de ma mère. C'est moi qui y vis maintenant. Je ne sais comment j'y suis arrivé . . . Before nightfall, I had finished *Molloy*. I will not say I understood all I had read, but if there is such a thing as a shock of discovery, I experienced it that day. The simplicity, the beauty, yes, and the terror of the words shook me as little had before or has since. And the man's vision of the world, his painfully honest portrayal thereof, his anti-illusionist stance. And the humour; God, the humour. . . . I waited a day or two, then reread *Molloy*, tempted to plunge into *Malone* but resisting the temptation as one resists the seductive sweet. The second reading was more exciting than the first. I went on to *Malone*. Full worthy of the first. Two stunning works. Miracles.'*

Shortly thereafter I became involved in a new literary magazine published in Paris, *Merlin*, whose first issue appeared in the spring of 1952, edited by a talented, charismatic Scotsman, Alex Trocchi.† When we met I overwhelmed him with my exuberant, long-winded description of Beckett's work. 'I've never read anyone like him,' I insisted. 'Totally new, totally different. Maybe more important than Joyce.' Finally, probably to stem the flow, Trocchi said: 'Well, if this man is so wonderful, why don't you write a piece about him?' Which I did, in the second issue. Entitled 'Samuel Beckett: An Introduction', it began:

'Samuel Beckett, an Irish writer long established in France, has recently published two novels which, if they defy all commentary, merit the attention of anyone interested in this century's literature . . .'

If one excepts the phrase 'if they defy all commentary', that opening sentence is one I still stand by.‡

When the issue appeared in the fall, I took a copy over to Minuit

---

* Richard Seaver, 'Introduction' *I Can't Go On, I'll Go On: A Samuel Beckett Reader*, New York, Grove Press, 1976, pp. ix–xlv.

† Alexander Trocchi (1925–84). In Paris, in 1952, he founded *Merlin* with Richard Seaver, wrote several novels including *Young Adam* (1954), *Cain's Book* (1961), a collection of stories, *The Outsiders* (1961), and a collection of poems, *Man at Leisure* (1972). He also wrote several erotic novels for Maurice Girodias's Olympia Press.

‡ For the simple reason that, over the next five decades, those two novels, and indeed all of Beckett's work, have been probed, dissected, analyzed, subjected to more academic scrutiny than perhaps any other contemporary writer, including Joyce. Often when we met in later years, as Beckett insisted we do whenever my wife and I were in Paris, he bemoaned the 'ridiculous exegesis', adding, 'It's a wonder, all the things they're finding I never knew were there myself!'(RS)

with a note to the publisher, Jérôme Lindon, asking if he would kindly forward it to Beckett. When Lindon's secretary told him the purpose of my visit, he apparently told her to send me right up, for what I did not then know was that his opinion of his Irish discovery more than matched mine. A tall, ascetic-looking man with an already receding hairline – he was still in his twenties – and a gaze as intense as I had ever seen, he was impeccably clothed in a dark suit and matching tie. In my Army-surplus khaki fatigues, I felt more than a little uncomfortable and out-of-place, but he soon put me at ease. He assured me he would forward it to Beckett, then let drop that, while he was now writing exclusively in French, Beckett had during the war written a still-unpublished novel in English, entitled *Watt*. I must have half-risen from my chair. Could we see it, with a view towards publishing an excerpt in the magazine? He did not know the status of the work, he believed it was circulating in England, but would enquire. I left elated at the news.

Weeks went by with no response from Beckett. Either he had disliked my piece, I decided, or was uninterested in showing us *Watt*. By that time, late fall, my rue du Sabot lodgings had become the world headquarters for *Merlin*, where all involved would meet two or three times a week to discuss the magazine, the state of the world, and the seductive merits of Paris. We had all but given up hope about Beckett when, one late afternoon in early November, during a not untypical Paris downpour, a knock came at the door. I opened it to confront a tall, gaunt figure in a dripping raincoat, from beneath whose folds he produced a rain-soaked package. 'Here,' he said, 'I understand you asked for this,' turned, and disappeared into the night. Opening the package, it was indeed the long-awaited *Watt*, delivered in person by the mysterious Mr Beckett. Most of the *Merlin* crew was there that day, and I have recounted elsewhere how we stayed up most of the night, reading pages in turn until our voices gave out, or until our tears or laughter stilled our lips.

We published a long excerpt of *Watt* in our next issue – Beckett had dictated which passage we could use: Mr Knott's inventory of the possibilities of his attire ('As for his feet, sometimes he wore on each a sock, or on the one a sock and on the other a stocking, or a boot, or a shoe, or a slipper, or a sock and a boot, or a sock and a shoe, or a sock and a slipper, or nothing at all . . .') and the various permutations of the furniture in his room ('Thus it was not rare to find, on the Sunday, the tallboy on its feet by the fire, and the dressing-table on its head by the bed, and the night-stool on its face by the door, and the wash-stand on its back by the window; and on the Monday, the tallboy on its head by the bed . . .' etc.). I suspected then, and later confirmed, that in so specifying that passage, Beckett was testing the literary fibre of the magazine, for taken out of context it could have been judged pedantic or wearily over-experimental, which indeed, according to some of our readers' letters, it was. But we didn't care: we had a mission, and Beckett was our leading man. In fact, in virtually every issue thereafter some-thing by Beckett graced our pages. What was more, having lost minor but painful sums on the magazine itself, the next year we decided to expand and see if we could compound our losses by publishing books. And, of course, the first book we chose was *Watt*.

In my research for my article on Beckett, I discovered that he had earlier published two longish short stories written in French, one called 'Suite' in Sartre's *Les Temps modernes* and the other 'L'Expulsé' in *Fontaine*.* Both were superb, and I asked Beckett if we could publish one or the other. 'The only problem,' he said, 'they need to be translated, and I've neither the time nor inclina-tion to do so.' Then he brightened. 'Why don't you try your hand at one?' I hesitated. 'When you've finished I can go over it with you,' he assured. In the folly of my youth, I said yes. Folly because here I was sitting with a man whose mastery of English was extraordinary, perhaps unique – I had stated so in print – and I was to recreate, in his native language, his own words. Still, I set to work, sure I could finish the task in a couple of weeks, urged on by Trocchi, who wanted the story for the next issue. Two months later I was still hard at it, revising, thinking: how would Beckett say that? Finally I could do no more and dropped the pages in the mail.

A few days later he dropped me a postcard, saying what a fine job I had done and suggesting we meet at the Dôme to 'give it a glance'. We met promptly at 4:00 p.m., an hour when clients were scarce, in

---

* Beckett later changed the title of the first of these stories to 'La Fin', 'The End'.

the back, where we were alone.* Beckett had my pages and the French edition opened side by side, ready to begin. Our beer orders before us, we looked at my opening lines:

'They dressed me and gave me some money. I knew what the money was to be used for, it was for my travelling expenses. When it was gone, they said, I would have to get some more, if I wanted to go on travelling.'

Beckett studied first the English, then the French, then back and forth another time, his wire-framed glasses pushed back into the thick shock of graying hair, squinting, then shaking his head. My heart, to coin a phrase, sank. Clearly my rendition was inadequate. But I was wrong; it was the *original* that displeased him. 'You can't translate that,' he said, referring to a passage further along, 'it makes no sense.' More squinting and cross-checking produced a more optimistic report. 'That's good,' he murmured. 'Those first few sentences read very nicely indeed. But what would you think if we used the word 'clothed' instead of 'dressed'? They *clothed* me and gave me money.' Do you like the ring of that better?'

Yes, clearly, 'clothed' was the better word.

'In the next sentence,' he said, 'you're literally correct. In French I spelled it out, said "travelling expenses" alright. But maybe we can make it a bit tighter here, just say something like "it was to get me going", or "it was to get me started". Do you like either of them at all?' On we went, phrase by phrase, Beckett praising my translation as a prelude to shaping it to what he really wanted, reworking here a word, there an entire sentence, chipping away, tightening, shortening, always finding not only *le mot juste* but the *phrase juste* as well, exchanging the ordinary for the poetic, until the prose sang. Never, I am sure, to his satisfaction, but certainly to my ear. Under Beckett's tireless wand, that opening passage became:

'They clothed me and gave me money. I knew what that money was for, it was to get me started. When it was gone I would have to get more, if I wanted to go on.'

During those several (for me) edifying sessions, Beckett was

---

* Beckett was the most punctual person I have ever met. He would arrive for an appointment on the dot, and if one was late you could feel the judgement, kind but firm. I erred once, but thereafter always arrived five or ten minutes early, to be on the safe side. (RS)

often visibly suffering, for revisiting a text he had left behind some years before, and from which he had progressed to other levels and other considerations, was clearly painful. Finally, during one of our afternoon sessions, in response to a particularly long moment of despair on his part, I blurted: 'But Mr Beckett, don't you realize what an important writer you are? Why, you're a thousand times more important than . . . than Albert Camus, for example!' Grasping for superlatives, I had lighted on the contemporary French writer who at the time was world famous. At that youthfully enthusiastic but obviously outlandish declaration, Beckett gazed compassionately across at me, his hawk-like features mirroring a response halfway between disbelief and despair. 'You don't know what you're saying, Dick,' he said, shaking his head sadly. 'No one's interested in this . . . this rubbish,' and he gestured contemptuously toward the untidy pile of manuscript pages on the table. 'Camus,' he laughed. 'Why, Camus is known even on the moon!'

Beckett's sincere self-deprecation saddened me, for if there was one conviction I had held unfailingly since my initial encounter with Beckett's work, it was that, sooner or later, the world would catch up with and give due recognition to this great man. Yet it was not as though his negative assessment of his work was based solely on his own predilection for pessimism. After all, the man had been writing incessantly since he was twenty-two, and here he was pushing fifty with no more than a handful of friends and fanatics like ourselves caring about his work.

When we had finally finished 'The End' to his satisfaction, Beckett asked me – to my surprise but none the less pleasure, for a vote of confidence from him restored in large measure the humbling experience of our joint endeavour – if I would translate another story, 'L'Expulsé', 'The Expelled'. I hesitated. 'Are you sure you wouldn't prefer to do it yourself?' I ventured. 'Not at all,' he said. 'I couldn't. . . . I simply couldn't. No, it's a great help, Dick, believe me.' So I said I would, and did.

What neither of us knew during those long – and for me privileged – autumn afternoons was that Beckett's life was about to change, and change dramatically, for his second play, long kept from the boards by whims of fate and theatrical mishaps, was about to open early the following year, propelling him suddenly to the fame he deserved and changing his life, public and private, for ever. Aptly titled for a man who had waited so long, it was called first *Waiting*, then altered, finally, to *Waiting for Godot.*

Patrick Bowles on Beckett in the Early 1950s

Patrick Bowles (1927–95), seen here (*seated reading*) with Jane Lougee and Christopher Logue, Paris, *c* 1953. He lived in Paris in the early 1950s and published fiction and poetry mostly in *Points*, *The Paris Review* and *Merlin*. He translated a number of European writers, including Heinrich Böll and Friedrich Dürrenmatt, as well as Samuel Beckett. He worked intensively with Beckett for fifteen months on the translation into English of Beckett's novel, *Molloy*.

[We reprint here some of the most interesting extracts from the long essay which was originally published in *PN Review*, 96, vol. 20, no. 4, pp. 24–38 and has been largely ignored in Beckett criticism. This fascinating memoir, which describes some of Bowles' many meetings with Beckett and the subject of their conversations, reveals, along with the notes of Lawrence E. Harvey printed in the next chapter, how intently Beckett thought about his work and his role as a writer. Bowles' own later additions to his notes made on his meetings with Beckett are marked with decorated brackets { }. Editorial explanations continue to appear between square brackets [ ].]

TUESDAY. SEPT. 15, 1953

He talks of his books as if they were written by someone else. He said that it was the voice to which he listened, the voice one should listen to. 'There are many things I don't understand in my books. *"Rien n'est plus réel que le rien."* [Nothing is more real than nothing.] They are a positive statement of a negative thing'.

He said he tried to get to the core of it, without all this superfluity, etc. He said he was *horrified* at the fact that one could not open one's mouth without some falsity coming out. There was a continual protest at the things one's voice, one's mouth, said. Finally his books become no more than the mouth speaking, then the voices, coming from one cannot tell where.

But the 'summary' of it is in this brief Democritan statement [i.e. 'Nothing is more real than nothing'] which cannot be explained; it is an intuition one has and is, when one has it, as incontrovertible, I think he meant, as it is non-explicable. [. . .]

Suddenly realize that I began translating *Molloy* in July '53 and now it is January 26 1954, and the damned thing is only half finished.

{One reason for the translation taking so much time was that it was not a translation as that term is usually understood. It was not a mere matter of swapping counters, of substituting one word for another. It was as far apart from machine translation as one could imagine. Time and again Beckett said that what we were trying to do was to write the book again in another language – that is to say, write a new book. When we were stuck for a word or a phrase he would ask, 'what have you got there?', and I would read out my draft. Then he would ask, 'what does it say?' Meaning the original, as if he had not written it himself. Until we produced a phrase that he found acceptable.} [. . .]

'My writing is pre-logical writing. I don't ask people to understand it logically, only to accept it.'

We often talked of what he could possibly do or say afterwards. {Because he seemed to have taken both his thought and his style so far, they were at a dead end. However, he did go on.}

'Perhaps if I'd done it in English instead of French I'd have been able to take it more slowly, without missing so many of the details, leaving so many gaps. And yet in French, without all the old associations English has for me, I was able to get at it more clearly, the outlines were clearer.'

{I have often been asked why Beckett did not translate *Molloy* into English himself, and I also once asked him if he would not have preferred to do it alone – our method of work was extremely taxing, to put it mildly – and he replied that not having spoken or worked in English for seventeen years he felt out of touch with the language and wanted to work with an English writer for a while so as to feel his way back into the language. Beckett's way of speaking French was very French (unlike Joseph Conrad's English, for example).}
[. . .]

On the importance of spirit

NOVEMBER 10, 1955

Talking of the 'contemporary malaise', 'It has been the malaise of all time,' Beckett said. 'People are not in touch with their spirit. What counts is the *spirit*,' he said with great emphasis. 'I cannot see it historically,' he said, differing in a way from myself.

I had said that philosophy had to be seen as the development of ideas, from one man to the next. We changed subjects, of course, and were talking at cross-purposes for a moment, but that does not matter. What is important is the point raised.

'Ninety-nine per cent of people are out of touch with their spirit,' he said. 'History, for me, it's a black-out.' And he added, 'All the rest is frills.'

Then: 'It's the *extreme* that's important. Only at the *extreme* can you get to grips with the real problem.'

He mentioned a scenario written on request (of someone called, I think, Derek Mendel) for 'a dumb white clown'. [This was the mime, *Acte sans paroles I (Act without Words I)*, written for Deryk Mendel.]

'It's quite a good idea: when words fail you, you can fall back on silence!'

The dancer mimes it.

On language, meaning and meaninglessness

SUNDAY, NOVEMBER 13, 1955

Meeting with Beckett. He told me that he once went to hear a lecture by Jung, with a psycho-analyst friend [his own therapist, Wilfred R. Bion]. Jung was describing a young girl he had been treating, when, improvising, he suddenly stopped, thought, then said, 'Her trouble was, she had never been *born*.' She felt herself outside life, Beckett explained.

I had been describing that mysterious point where one seems *between* the moments of willing to do something, and doing it. Picking up an object, for example. Are the two moments in reality synonymous? Is there in fact *no* between?

Yet there often *is* a 'between'. 'I will get out of bed.' One doesn't. 'I will get out of bed.' And then one does, as if by magic. By magic being what we don't understand. I told him, one says to someone in a catatonic stupor apparently, 'Make an effort of will.' Ridiculous. 'Make an effort of will.' Still nothing. One talks, exhorts. Even shakes them. There is no response. When they begin talking lucidly as if their earlier rigidity had never happened, one can never know what made them break the circle, within which they circled. One moment they were in it, then not. Beckett said, 'It is as if there were a little animal inside one's head, for which one tried to find a voice; to which one tries to give a voice. That is the *real* thing. The rest is a game.'

For Beckett had begun, when we sat down, by saying to me 'I have been thinking about that phrase of Blanchot you quoted to me, last week.' (I had said, Blanchot is given to reasoning like this, and cited, '*Toute philosophie de la non-signification reste sur une contradiction, dès qu'elle s'exprime.*' ['Every philosophy of non-meaning rests on a contradiction as soon as it expresses itself.'] I had maintained that this was a fallacy; that it confused two levels which should be kept separate, and that, if each were allotted the level proper to it, there was no contradiction involved. On one level, there was the world, futile, 'meaningless', a gratuitous confusion. On another level, the level of language, this 'meaningless' world of fact could be very clearly described, using the means of language at our disposal so long as we did not lose sight of what our language meant. In fact, two levels, one the world, the other the language of description.)

Beckett disagreed. There are not two levels, he said. There is only one level. In this sense: for the traditional artist (and here he added that in his opinion painting in the Renaissance tradition was for these reasons a fake) there has been one thing, the world, and the second, language. However, the world, meaningless, cannot be rendered truly in a meaningful language for the very reason that the artist himself is a part of the world, is he not? And for him to render a meaningful account of the world – the conclusion is obvious. There is the contradiction. *If* he is in the world, as he is, is he not, and if the world is meaningless, or whatever more embracing word you choose (as it is, is it not), then to render the world truly a man must represent himself as a part of this process, this movement of the unmeaningful, in whatever direction it seems to be moving, if any. The point is, he cannot represent himself as outside it, for that is to say at the same time, the world is mean-ingless (use this word) and at the same time it is not, since I give an account of it.

I asked him, at this point, if it is meaningless, then it must be so in terms of something else that is meaningful. In terms of what is it meaningless? It cannot be an absolute and universal meaningless-ness, for in that case our judgement that it was meaningless would itself have no meaning; it would be like applying another universal name under which everything was subsumed. And if *everything* were meaningless, then 'meaningless' became a word which, having unrestricted application, was itself (as I understand language) meaningless.

Within the universe, we perceive divisions, which we name. Within a universe called meaningless, I continue to perceive divi-sions of the relatively meaningful. What is the meaning of the word, meaningful, under such conditions? Final ends, being unknowable, are undiscussable, their existence is a matter of fancy, we are all free to fancy anything. *Passons.* No first causes, *pas d'horlogerie* [no watchmaking]. The significant is reduced to a matter of what can be described, within the limits of our understanding, according to the structure of our language. What then do I feel myself to be? A matter of chance, among other things. There we are, back again, with this difference, that the meaningless is reduced to matters of chance which I describe to the best of my uncertain ability. This is no joke.

But yes, Beckett says, I know, that is all very well for scientists, and for those who make a game of writing, but *if* you want to render the world *truly*, call it chance if you like, you cannot represent yourself as being outside it, you are *not*, you and I are part of chance and must represent ourselves as blindly immersed in it, for no reason, with no object, by no intention.

Beckett mentioned that self-immersion going by the name of schizophrenia. When that little far-away inner self and voice that *alone* is the real, for him, when it is abandoned, forgotten, when the catatonic leaves his stupor and redirects his attention to the outer world of frills and customs and the conventions of verbal clarity, then he has left what is for him the most profound fact of his existence.

I understand that very well. I said to him it was a kind of eternal malady.

The one that counts, one of us said, or I thought.

Why? Because it is there that all the values of the world break down, as they *should* and *must*, if one is to see it honestly. The rest is convention. Necessary no doubt but not necessary in reality, only for society. There is no logical necessity about it and furthermore a consciousness of what is unchanging in the human condition can dispense with it. What, particularly, *is* unchanging? Consciousness, by which I mean the consciousness of consciousness. Not merely the consciousness *of* some object, but the awareness of being *awake*, if you like. Leave that for the moment. Rests: where all values are reduced to this arbitrary choice depending only on each man's particular aims in life for which he can never give more than wistful, 'persuasive' reasons, then any thinking man must only see an immense confusion. This confusion, this chaos, is one of his own conduct. It does not seem to me to be connected in any necessary way with the vast movements of the galaxies which, being beyond our control at least for the moment, can only terrify us, or console us, whether or not we think we understand them, and do not concern us so intimately as what we ourselves are personally, inwardly aware of as our own particular dilemma. Between what do we choose, in daily life? No, for that depends on a more primary dilemma. Where is the world? You're in it. In what world? And what do we mean by world? The world of the personal, inward spirit, perhaps. What do we mean by spirit? Precisely, that consciousness within ourselves of the movement of thought whose subject can be said to be that energy . . . No, No, No! [. . .]

NOVEMBER 18, 1955
Meeting with Beckett. He said: 'This kind of writing can even *kill* a man. There are men who have been killed by it.'

{Some forty years later I can still remember clearly this particular series of meetings and talks, mostly in the evenings at the Café Sélect, Montparnasse, with Beckett attired in his usual grey clothes – grey sports jacket and trousers, grey roll-neck jersey – quiet, lean and thoughtful but by no means humourless.}

We had concluded that our last talk had ended not in disagreement but misunderstanding. The departure was the phrase of Blanchot – all philosophy of non-meaning rests on a contradiction as soon as it is expressed. I had objected that the contradiction was only apparent. I had understood Beckett to believe that it was real. We had been using these words in different ways. The 'spiritual dilemma', in his own words, seems essentially simple. This writing is the only way of living, for those who understand it. What writing? The writing that becomes a *part* of living. That point at which words break down because, in life, there are wordless situations, that words shatter, or where 'words fail you', then, once you admit and understand how it is possible for words to fail you, then you must admit that words are not omnipotent, that there are times when they can be employed with success, and times when their very employment is inappropriate, out of the question; if you like, a 'contradiction'. But not a contradiction in *logic*: merely a *contradiction of the situation*. And therefore here the word contradiction means not contradiction, but *denial, disavowal*.

I said, there are times when speech is not significant in the sense that the words *mean* something, merely significant as any other human noise or act is significant. The words then become not symbolic. They are themselves an act, a part of life, as the breaking of a bough from a tree is an act. Beckett agreed.

Speech must always be contrasted with silence.

It must always be thought of in relation to silence.

Scientific language has no relation to silence, in this sense, for the reason that scientific language is essentially concerned with *meaning* something. The noise the language of a scientist makes when spoken is an irrelevance, it might just as well not be, it could be any other collection of symbols whose only standard and *raison d'être* is the collection of 'facts' to which they refer. Our language, the language of life, on the other hand, very often has as its only function the particular and sometimes very subtle relation it bears to silence.

When the chaos of the world is apprehended as chaos, we may none the less give expression to it in more or less lucid language. There are many situations which are not susceptible of lucid explanation or description. These can only be suggested, felt after, in obscure and apparently confused language.

(Beckett was interested in Joyce's experiments with this so-called language of the night.)

Jean Martin on the World Première
of *En attendant Godot*

Jean Martin (1922–), seen here as Lucky (*left*) with Roger Blin as Pozzo (*right*) in *En attendant Godot*, Théâtre de Babylone, January 1953. French stage and film actor and a close friend of Beckett and Suzanne, Martin played the roles of Lucky and Clov respectively in the world premières of *En attendant Godot* (*Waiting for Godot*) and *Fin de partie (Endgame)* and was directed by Beckett in *La dernière bande (Krapp's Last Tape).* Extracts from two interviews with JK.

[The story of the staging of the world première of *En attendant Godot* (Théâtre de Babylone, January 1953) has been recounted in some detail by Jean Martin himself in 'Creating Godot', *Beckett in Dublin*, ed. S. E. Wilmer, Dublin, The Lilliput Press, 1992, pp. 25–32. We include therefore only those parts of the interviews with

Jean Martin which add to these accounts or which relate closely to Beckett the man.]

We only rehearsed *En attendant Godot* for a few weeks you know. In fact, I rehearsed for only about three weeks in all. Sam said practically nothing while we were putting it on. You see he was extremely shy and very, very discreet. He has never been talkative and he didn't explain very much. In fact, if you asked him to explain something, he used to say that he didn't know what explanations he had to give. He relied entirely on Roger Blin [his French director, who also played Pozzo]. Of course, he hadn't got the Nobel Prize then and he knew very little about the theatre. But he came to rehearsals every day, but every day. And Suzanne came very often too. But they didn't offer any advice. He knew what he didn't want but he wasn't at all clear about what he did want. And in any case he was just surprised to see his play on the stage.

Our lives became quite intertwined at that time, then and after *Fin de partie*, since Sam and Suzanne were living in the rue des Favorites and I was living in the Porte de Versailles. We would often walk back in the evenings after rehearsals of *Godot* together from Sèvres-Babylone to the rue de Vaugirard where I was living. I had an apartment in which there was no shower, so Suzanne would say to me 'Come round and have a bath' in their place in the rue des Favorites. You know at that period Sam and Suzanne were living very economically indeed, rather precariously in fact, because before *Godot* there had been the war, and then the Liberation and they had considerable financial problems.

I had a doctor friend called Marthe Gautier and I said to her: 'Listen, Marthe, what could I find that would provide some kind of physiological explanation for a voice [of Lucky] like the one that is written in the text? And Marthe Gautier, who was working at the Salpêtrière Hospital, said: 'Well, it might be a good idea if you went to see people who have Parkinson's disease.' So I asked her about the disease and she told me how Parkinson's manifests itself. She explained how it begins with a trembling, which gets more and more noticeable, until later the patient can no longer speak without the voice shaking. So I said, 'That sounds exactly what I need.' So I began to rehearse like that. But I also told myself that I had to find a way of making him tremble. I made him stand on one foot, this Lucky, and, as the other foot doesn't rest on the ground, this makes him tremble and that leads to a trembling of the arms, then of the whole body, and to a tremor in his voice, finally to a sort of delirium. And I began to rehearse like that. And Blin said, 'I don't know, I honestly don't know whether I like it or not; it's important it doesn't become too clinical.' And Sam said nothing at all. And Raimbourg and Latour [who were playing Estragon and Vladimir] said, 'Oh là là, Oh là là, whatever are you doing?' So I finally said to Roger: 'Listen I am not absolutely obsessed with playing it like this, you know. But let me try it as far as I can, and if it doesn't work I can always go back. But I need to try it at least once from start to finish'. And Roger let me do it, but wasn't at all convinced. Nor was I.

Then four or five days before we were due to open, the costume lady at the theatre was there with her husband, whose job was emptying dustbins. She was a charming but simple, down-to-earth lady. We still didn't have a suitcase for Lucky to carry and Roger said, 'We need an old, battered suitcase.' And she said, 'My husband works on the bins and I am sure he could find you the props you need.' And one evening her husband turned up with a big case that he'd found in the bins. It's the one on all the photos of the first production. When Roger saw it, he said, 'That's marvellous. That's exactly what we need.' And, by way of thanking her and her husband, he said to them, 'Look, if you haven't seen a rehearsal, stay in the theatre and watch', warning them that it wasn't perhaps the kind of play they would enjoy. And so the bin-man and his wife went into the theatre and when I started my monologue – they had been a bit put off by the first part of the play – and as I worked up to my frenzy, because I started calmly, just trembling a little, then at the end finishing in a state of real delirium, at that point the costume lady started to cry out and to vomit, saying, 'I just can't stand this.' And Roger Blin said, 'Well, if it has an effect like that, you must keep it!' And we did.

[*Fin de partie* (*Endgame*). First production (in French) at the Royal Court Theatre in London, April 1957, then at the Studio des Champs-Elysées in Paris. Jean Martin played Clov.]

Sam had become much more confident as far as directing was concerned after *Godot* and he let things pass on that production that he wouldn't let through on *Fin de partie*, things that were not really the way he saw them. He had become much more intransigent at rehearsals. So there were, not exactly difficulties, but certain tensions with Sam in as much as he wanted us to adopt a way of speaking in a very slow monotone. But when we tried . . . well, the problems began when Sam got a bit desperate when we couldn't do what he wanted us to do in the way we said our lines. 'It needs a rhythm that you're not getting at the moment', he said. So – in English – he started to deliver Clov's opening monologue: 'Fini, c'est fini, ça va finir, ça va peut-être finir' ['Finished, it's finished, nearly finished, it must be nearly finished'] and Sam said: 'Finnnniiishshed', just like that. And Roger and I looked at each other and I said, 'But, Sam, I understand perfectly well what you have in mind. But what you want can be done with English words, but you can't do the same thing with French ones. You can't say something like "shshsh" in French. It's not possible.' It is not that we had an actual dispute with Sam. But at first we didn't manage to get the right rhythms for the play, because the problem didn't lie with its interpretation but with physically executing what Sam wanted. The problem lay in the rhythms, the way of delivering the text, if you follow me.

As with *Godot*, so with *Fin de partie*, Sam cut quite a lot out of his texts, between what was printed and what was performed on stage. Some cuts were already made in the first production; then he made even more substantial ones for some later revivals. He always worked towards a great economy of means, finding some things unnecessary. It's important to stress this because a play is no longer played in the same way when it has a faster rhythm. And what worried Blin and I with *Fin de partie* was that Sam explained that he wanted not just a kind of lassitude in the characters but also that the vocal rhythms he wanted us to adopt finally slowed the play down: 'weighed it down' isn't exactly the word; but it certainly changed the way in which everything went.

Sam changed a lot over the years, I think, in his way of presenting his plays. Because when *Godot* and *Fin de partie* were first put on, I don't think he was too happy when, deliberately or not, there were certain moments in the play that caused the audience to smile or even to laugh. Sam on the other hand found humour in deeply sad, even dreadful situations which didn't make the public laugh at all. But over the years – and especially after he directed *Godot* himself in Berlin – I think he began to realize that the play should be played using faster, livelier rhythms. So I think the difficulties we experienced at the beginning with *Fin de partie* were not because we were not doing what he wanted us to do but because Sam himself was not fully aware of the ways of doing it. It was not a question of adding anything to what was already there, but of focusing on the way it was done.

Peter Woodthorpe on the British première of *Waiting for Godot*

Peter Woodthorpe (1931–2004). British actor who played Estragon in the British première of *Waiting for Godot*, directed by Peter Hall at the Arts Theatre, London, in August 1955. He went on to have a highly successful career in theatre, film and television. Beckett very much admired his acting. Interview with JK.

I was a biochemistry student at Cambridge University, where I played King Lear as a freshman. This was reviewed by Harold Hobson and it changed my life. Then I played the Yorkshire lad in the musical *Zuleika* – the one who says 'I'm too young to die' – and I was in the 'Footlights' revue at the Scala Theatre when Anne Jenkins, Donald Albery's factotum, phoned me to say, 'Peter Hall would like you to play a part in a new play at the Arts Theatre.' Eight pounds a week; only luncheon vouchers at rehearsals! It was later [when it transferred to the West End] that I got £40. I was sent the script and had a fit. I couldn't understand a word. But I had signed a contract, so I went to rehearsals and said 'Sir' to them all. After that I left Cambridge and never finished my degree.

The important thing Peter Hall said when he started was: 'I don't understand this play and we are not going to waste time trying to understand it.' And the other thing he said was 'And we are not going to play it in Irish or it will be dismissed as another of those Irish plays.' And a lot of Beckett still has been.

The nerves built up on the first night. I have never seen people so ill. Peter Bull [who played Pozzo] was vomiting in basins and running to the loo. It was really panic. Then Peter came on and within two pages he jumped, in his nerves, eight pages. He played five of them, then suddenly realized his mistake and went right back to the beginning. And no one ever spotted that we had done those pages before! He also got the rope caught in his sleeve. It was my first professional experience and the audience shouting at us didn't worry me as much as it did the others. I didn't understand the play but I know that I felt how to do it. Its poetry spoke to me and its humour. And once I got it, I never lost it. I played it by instinct and feeling.

On the first night there was only one curtain call and there were boos and cat-calls. One was: 'This is why we lost the colonies!' I remember the night that was shouted. Business was bad and hostile. And they told you they hated it. But then the whole atmosphere changed – dramatically changed – after the Sunday reviews by Hobson and Tynan. There were two shows on a Sunday and they were sold out. Cheers and bravos and laughter. Altogether different. What it was was the power of those two papers [*The Observer* and *The Sunday Times*] with the theatre-going public. Nobody bothered with the 'dailies'. They booked on what they read.

[The initial controversy about Beckett's play did not subside later on either.] At the Criterion Theatre, this party had arrived in full evening dress on the front row. And one of the ladies shouted out at Peter Bull: 'I *do* wish the fat man would go.' And Peter ran off stage. 'You're going the wrong way', said Vladimir. 'I need a running start', said Pozzo and Peter came back on again. And there was a clattering in the wings as Timothy Bateson [playing Lucky] falls over. Bull stopped in centre stage and, quivering with rage, he leant over the footlights and he looked at the woman full in the face and said, 'And adieu to you too, Madam!' And, as one, the six of them in this party got up and left the theatre. Hugh Burden [who by then was playing Vladimir] put his hand up and said, 'She must have been Godot.' This got the house back brilliantly. There was another wonderful moment at the Criterion when Hugh's teeth fell out and they flew past me so the whole audience could see. And he looked at them and then looked at me. And, without thinking, I said 'Pick 'em up'. And he said, 'Do you think so?' And I said, 'You might as well.' So he went across, picked them up and said, 'That's better.'*

We heard that Sam Beckett was over in London to see the show [when it had transferred to the Criterion Theatre]. After the show he came round to the dressing-room. And there was for me this very frightening man; his appearance was extraordinary. It gave me a frisson: the recession of the eyes, and the lightness of them, a piercing blue. And I thought of him as a giant bird, a giant crow. It was my immediate reaction. Then suddenly his face changed totally. There was a beautiful smile and he just said, 'Bloody marvellous!' And he held me. But he disliked the production. He told me he disliked it, so there you are. He hated the set with the walk-on. Three walks-on. I didn't like it because it made it all look a bit chi-chi, weird, in the wrong way weird. Peter Hall hadn't trusted the play and had commissioned a set. Beckett didn't like the scene with the boy messenger because it became poesy. And even Paul [Daneman, who acted Vladimir at the Arts Theatre] played it wrong. I hated it. It should have been kept the same way.† Peter Hall thinks it was his success to this day. Well, it wasn't really. It was the play's success. Beckett also said to me about 'Godot' that he deeply regretted calling

---

* We have included a few of the anecdotes recounted by Woodthorpe about the first British production for the sheer exuberance and delight of his account. They complement Peter Bull's reminiscences in his book *I Know the Face, but . . .*, London, Peter Davies, 1959.
† 'He [Beckett] particularly erupted when the Boy at the end of the second act pointed to the heavens when he was asked by Vladimir where Mr. Godot lived'. Alan Schneider, *Entrances. An American Director's Journey*. New York, Viking Penguin, 1986, p. 225. In fact there is a problem with Schneider's reading of the text here, although the gesture itself may have occurred, since Vladimir never puts this question to the boy – in either act. But, in the notes that Beckett sent to Peter Hall, he stressed that Vladimir should adopt a 'dead numb tone' at the end of the play, underlining that phrase. Notes reproduced in *No Author Better Served. The Correspondence of Samuel Beckett and Alan Schneider*, ed. Maurice Harmon, Cambridge, MA, Harvard University Press, 1998, p. 5. It was Hugh Burden, not the original Vladimir, Paul Daneman, whom Beckett saw when he went with Schneider to the Criterion Theatre in London.

it 'Godot', because everybody interpreted it as God. Now that he saw it in English. And all the things that people made of it. He said it had nothing to do with God. He was almost passionate about it.

The real success of the play was that it broke all frontiers, not only in writing; it broke the expectation of success from stardom. It was the star actors' theatre at the time. You didn't put a show on without a star. You didn't think of it. And for this little play to run, that half the world didn't understand – and booed at first – with no one in it, for months and months and months was a tremendous shock to the theatre establishment of the day. The only person I remember who welcomed it with open arms and understanding beyond anyone else was Vivien Leigh. She had a brain like a razor. And she came round and sat in my dressing-room and laughed. And she just told us what she thought the play was about. And it was magic: it had no pretence and it was about relationships and philosophies and essential needs and how people behaved, she said. She was wonderful. It was astonishing. She became a star in my eyes that night.

I met Beckett two or three times while he was in London and one night he took me to his cousin John's house. There was a cellist there that night. It was a musical evening somewhere in Hampstead. It was all a bit overwhelming. And in the cab coming back, I did say to him 'What is it [*Waiting for Godot*] all about? Everybody is coming round saying different things.' And we laughed a lot. He said, 'But it's all symbiosis, Peter.' That is what he said. But I didn't really have the ability to create a friendship with him. I was too young.

Ruby Cohn on the Godot Circle

Ruby Cohn (1922–) Professor Emerita at the University of California, Davis (seen here in the early 1960s); a friend of Beckett for almost thirty years. She has written many books on European and American theatre and several books on Beckett, including *Samuel Beckett: The Comic Gamut, Back to Beckett, Just Play*, and, most recently, *A Beckett Canon*. She has edited *Disjecta*, a collection of his critical writings, as well as two casebooks on *Waiting for Godot*. Contribution given earlier as a lecture but revised by Ruby Cohn especially for this volume.

Like many others, I first encountered Samuel Beckett through *Waiting for Godot*, or, more accurately, through *En attendant Godot*. In 1952, I was a student of comparative literature at the Sorbonne, and an addict of theatre everywhere I wandered. My small, unheated top-storey room on the rue Huysmans was a few streets away from the Théâtre de Babylone, which was located not on the rue de Babylone, but, with the logic for which the French are famous, on the Boulevard Raspail. Passing by the Théâtre de Babylone one cold morning of the new year 1953, I noticed a poster about the première of a new play by 'un compagnon de James Joyce, l'Irlandais Samuel Beckett' ['a friend of James Joyce, the Irishman Samuel Beckett']. Little dreaming that the play would focus the rest of my life, I went to see *En attendant Godot*.

Over half a century has passed since then, and I have read and even written so much about that performance that I can no longer rely on the purity of my memory. In January 1953, it never occurred to me to seek out the author of *En attendant Godot*, about whom none of my fellow students had heard. At that time I read few reviews. I did hear – I can't recall where – a rumour about an earlier radio broadcast of excerpts from *En attendant Godot*. Its producer, twenty-year-old Michel Polac, had asked Beckett for a few words of introduction to his strange new play, which the playwright surprisingly supplied. Several scholars have described the first French *stage* performance of *En attendant Godot*, but no scholar has described its first *radio* broadcast. Perhaps no one heard it. I certainly didn't, for I didn't even own a radio at that time. Much later, thanks to Angela Moorjani, I read Beckett's introduction to that French radio broadcast, from which I quote a few excerpts, in a different translation from the one published in *The New Yorker* of 1 July 1996:

> I don't know who Godot is. I don't even know (above all don't know) if he exists. And I don't know if they believe in him or not – those two who are waiting for him. The other two who pass by towards the end of each of the two acts, that must be to break the monotony. All that I knew I showed. It's not much, but it's enough for me, by a wide margin. I'll even say that I would have been satisfied with less. As for wanting to find in all that a broader, loftier meaning to carry away after the performance, along with the program and the Eskimo pie, I cannot see the point of it. But it must be possible . . . Estragon, Vladimir, Pozzo, Lucky, their time and their space, I was able to know them a little, but far from the need to understand. Maybe they owe you explanations. Let them supply it. Without me. They and I are through with each other.

However, that was wishful thinking on Beckett's part. Since *Godot* remains Beckett's best-known work, he was never able to be quite 'through with' it.

I was enthralled by *En attendant Godot*, and I saw that first French production twice more – once in Germany. I read what little else I could find by Beckett – as I remember, only the novels *Murphy* and *Molloy*, both in French. Back in the United States, I embarked on doctoral study, and, independently, I continued to read Beckett's works, which were slowly being published by Grove Press, in Beckett's translations into English. When I had to choose a dissertation subject, Beckett's work seemed to me ineluctable.

During the course of my research on Beckett, I listed what seemed to me errors in the Grove Press editions, but after reading Beckett's novel *Watt*, I became unsure that these *were* printing errors, rather than authorial subversions. I therefore wrote to Grove Press with a list of eight errors in the novel, *Watt*, fourteen errors in *Molloy*, and a mere four errors in *Malone Dies*. I was informed that Grove Press would ask Mr Beckett, who soon replied that my list was virtually a compilation of errors. Only after I made Beckett's acquaintance did I learn how punctilious he was about reading proofs, and perhaps I made Beckett's acquaintance *because* I was punctilious about reading texts.

Once my dissertation was complete, but not yet published, I summoned the courage to write to Beckett directly, c/o Les Editions de Minuit, his French publisher, but I wrote in English. I informed Beckett that I would be in Paris during the summer of 1962 and, although I knew that he never granted interviews, it would be a privilege to meet him, and I promised not to ask him to interpret his work. Beckett replied – in what I later learned to recognize as his company handwriting that was quite legible. He would call for me at my hotel at 8 p.m. on 23rd June, if I was free to dine with him. I was stupid enough not to save that first letter, but I well remember that my hotel was on the rue Casimir-Delavigne in the 5th arrondissement of Paris. At 8 o'clock I waited in the hotel lobby, for there was no telephone in my frugal room. At 8.15, I was still waiting in the lobby. By 8.30, I wondered whether Beckett had second thoughts about meeting a stranger, for I had read about his shyness. It was nearly 9 o'clock when Beckett rushed into the hotel lobby. I recognized him at once from his picture on the Grove Press editions, and I introduced myself – in English. He mumbled that he had mistakenly driven to the rue Casimir-Périer in the 7th arrondissement, instead of the rue Casimir-Delavigne in the 5th. Only later was I to learn how prompt he always was, and how rarely he found himself in the wrong place.

In spite of that inauspicious start, I date my friendship with Samuel Beckett from that evening in June 1962. The evening began suitably with silence. He was shy, and I was intimidated. We got into his 2 Chevaux [Citroën] and drove the short distance to the Closerie des Lilas. He asked whether I would have a *coupe*, and, not knowing what it was, I replied, 'If you're having one.' Only after-wards did I learn that he didn't like champagne, but thought that was the drink for an American. After the third *coupe*, we both began to talk, and I could never remember about what. I think we may have also eaten something. What I do remember is Beckett telling me to be sure to write him whenever I was coming to Paris. I didn't have to be told twice. Thereafter we met at least once a year, up to and including 1989, the year of his death. In the interim he sent me many letters, usually complaining about the translation or theatre work in which he was involved. They are now in the Beckett Archive at the University of Reading, founded by Jim Knowlson. Beckett also sent me signed copies of his French books as they were published by Les Editions de Minuit.

Technically, I kept my promise of not asking him to interpret his work, but I gradually learned which questions would not irritate him. For instance, when I read the phrase 'the great Cham' in one of his letters, at our next meeting I asked who that was. Astonished at my ignorance, he explained that it was Dr Samuel Johnson, who had obsessed him for years. Beckett told me ruefully: 'I bothered all my friends about Dr Johnson for a long time.' The next morning, on 23 April 1966, to be exact, my Paris hotel concierge informed me that while I was out, a Monsieur had left a package for me. I recognized Beckett's scrawl on the thick manila envelope, which I took to my room to open. It contained three notebooks full of quotations from and about the works of Dr Samuel Johnson, as well as Beckett's abortive effort to translate the Dr Johnson–Mrs Thrale relationship to the stage. Even after a single rapid glance, I knew that such a treasure should not be in my private possession. I rushed to a post office to telephone Beckett – in the 1960s he could still be reached by telephone. I protested: 'Sam, I shouldn't have this; it should go to a library.' Beckett snapped back: 'I don't want it in a library. If you don't want it, return it to me.' Again I protested: 'Oh, I want it; I cherish it.' Beckett added: 'I'd rather you didn't say anything about the wretched thing.' I did not say anything about the Johnson material for a few years, but when I was writing my book *Back to Beckett* in the 1970s, I asked Beckett whether I might mention his Johnson research, and he responded: 'Yes, of course; why not?' I don't think I answered that question. Then, in 1980, working on my third Beckett book, I asked Beckett whether I could print his Johnson scene entitled *Human Wishes*, in which Dr Johnson is awaited and does not appear. Beckett consented readily, without even rereading the material.

Let me back-track now from 1980 to the summer of 1968. Beckett had written no plays since he completed *Play* in 1964, and over a glass of wine in a Paris café, I asked whether he had nothing new for the stage. He answered almost angrily: 'New? What could be new? Man is born – vagitus. Then he breathes for a few seconds, before the death rattle intervenes.' I may not be quoting Beckett's exact words, but I remember 'vagitus' because it was a new word for me – Latin for crying or squealing. Pushing aside our wine-glasses, Beckett noted on the paper table-cover the timing for his 35-second play, *Breath*. I was so saddened by Beckett's despondency that I never thought to retrieve the paper table-cover. Nor do I know whether that was Beckett's first spontaneous rendition of his dramaticule, *Breath*, or whether he had already brooded about it. However, I do not think that he wrote it *for* Kenneth Tynan in 1969, as is sometimes claimed.

Beckett's bleak view of the human condition was expressed in the symmetrical form of *Breath*, but at other times he despaired of finding form for his sadness. In my appointment books over the years I noted very few of his spoken phrases, but one exception occurs in 1971, when he told me: 'Being is not syntactical'. Then he remarked that his play, *Not I*, composed as it is of fragmentary phrases, was released too soon, and he brushed aside my stuttering admiration of that piece.

My most sustained rapport with Beckett occurred in the winter of 1975, when he allowed me to attend Berlin rehearsals of his production of *Warten auf Godot*. Not only did I daily watch him in action, but we often walked around Berlin together after rehearsals. In the street, in a museum, in various buildings, he would sometimes stop stock still and listen to people's footsteps; only the next year would I realize that his listening formed and informed his play, *Footfalls*. However, Beckett in Berlin could speak as well as listen. To my ears Beckett's German sounded wonderful, and I once asked him: 'Is your Italian as good as your German?' 'MUCH better,' he replied. It is the only time I ever heard Beckett boast.

Rehearsals for the German *Godot* had already begun when I arrived in Berlin in February 1975, and although I was relatively unfamiliar with the German text, I immediately noticed an addition to the dialogue of the last scene. In the French original and in Beckett's English translation, Vladimir asks the Boy about the colour of Mr Godot's beard: 'Fair or . . . *he hesitates* . . . or black?' In German Beckett added: 'Or red?' After the rehearsal, Beckett asked whether I knew why he had added the third possible colour for Mr Godot's beard. At that time I still thought foolishly that he might pop out with a reason embedded in Descartes or Kant or Schopenhauer or even Dante, but of course the answer was obvious: 'To balance the three colours of the whores' hair in Estragon's brothel joke.' It was also Beckett who told me that joke, which I didn't know.

Unsolicited by me, Beckett offered the information about Mr Godot's beard, so I dared to ask him why he had made Atlas the son of Jupiter in Pozzo's mockery of Lucky: 'Atlas, son of Jupiter!' His eyebrows went up: 'Isn't he the son of Jupiter?' Pedantically, like the academic I now was, I taught Beckett that Atlas and Jupiter were brothers, and not father and son in Greek mythology. When next rehearsed, Atlas had become the son of Iapetus. That's my contribution to *Godot*, so I've come Beckettianly full circle.

5
Growing Fame

Beckett in 1964.

Biography, 1955–69

With the success of *Waiting for Godot* in so many countries and the
publication of his novels and later plays in dozens of languages,
Beckett's fame spread fairly quickly. He was the recipient of a
number of international awards, most notably the International
Publishers' Prize in 1961 (shared with Jorge Luis Borges), and then
the Nobel Prize for Literature in 1969. This growth in literary

celebrity did not, however, make him in the least complacent or satisfied with his achievements and his ways of seeking to express being in both his prose (e.g. *Comment c'est* [*How It Is*]) and his drama (e.g. *Play* [*Comédie*]) continued to be innovative and radical. (See in particular the notes on his conversations in the early 1960s with Lawrence E. Harvey on the following pages.) He also wrote plays for radio and, later, for television.

He had taken up important friendships again after the war: with his old friends, the Irish writer and art historian, Tom MacGreevy, and the Trinity College, Dublin lecturer, 'Con' Leventhal; with the Dutch painter brothers Geer and Bram van Velde; with the French painter Henri Hayden and his wife, Josette, whom he had first met in Roussillon; and with Georges Belmont, his former student, previously Pelorson. New friendships were also initiated: with the painter Avigdor Arikha; with the composer Marcel Mihalovici and his wife, the concert pianist Monique Haas; with the theatre director Roger Blin, with whom he worked on several productions of his plays; with the script editor at the BBC in London, Barbara Bray, who encouraged him to write for the radio and became first a close friend then a lover, moving to Paris to be near to him; and with numerous actors and directors in Paris, Berlin and London. He also became friendly with a number of writers, broadcasters and thinkers: Robert Pinget; Harold Pinter; Edward Albee; Aidan Higgins; at the BBC, Donald McWhinnie and Martin Esslin; and the Romanian-born philosopher Emil Cioran. He had a remarkable gift for friendship. Some of these friends speak or write about him either in this chapter or later in the book.

Lawrence E. Harvey on Beckett, 1961–2

Lawrence E. Harvey (1925–88) was Professor of English at Dartmouth College. He became a very good friend of Beckett in the 1960s when he was preparing his book, *Samuel Beckett: Poet and Critic*, Princeton, NJ, Princeton University Press, 1970. At one time he was considering writing a biography of the writer. These conversations, which took place in Paris in 1961–2 are reproduced by kind permission of Sheila Harvey-Tanzer and the Library of Dartmouth College, Hanover, New Hampshire, where Harvey's notes are held. The notes were written down immediately after his meetings with Beckett.

Being and Form

Beckett thinks that 'being' is constantly putting form into danger. He aspires, he said, to what he recognizes is the impossible task of eliminating form – not just breaking it down or working against it but eliminating it. He said that an ejaculation would perhaps be the most perfect expression of being. In a sense Beckett made clear that he is anti-form, if form is considered to be order. He spoke of

having come to feel the need for a disordered form, a broken form.
The great task of the artist is to express being and he sees being as a
collection of meaningless 'movements'. Being is chaotic – the
opposite of ordered form. He thinks in the antinomy 'being-form'.
He is aware of the paradox of trying to eliminate form when
language itself is form, but this viewpoint lies behind his breaking
down of the traditional forms of language.

His vision of man is of *inadequacy*. Form expresses adequacy; so it
must be broken. He realizes that there are techniques of expression
but he brushes these aside as being mere *trucs* [gimmicks], as forms.
He mentioned how much greater the unfinished sculptures of Mi-
chelangelo are than the completed works like the *David*. The accent
thus falls on the creative act as unfinished, as portraying man's
inadequacy and his flawed nature. I mentioned the themes of exile
and Eden in his work. But he felt that these were simply stereotyped
literary ideas and over-simplifications. Instead he preferred to speak
of just a series of 'movements'. However, we agreed completely on the
idea of man in exile as being inadequate, suffering and disordered.

Art and Being

Beckett feels that until now art has sought forms and excluded all
aspects of being that there were no forms to fit. 'If anything new and
exciting is going on today, it the attempt to let being into art', he
said, 'to let in chaos and what is not ordered'.

He then spoke of depths of being where all is mystery and
enigma. 'We don't know what our own personality is or what
our being is', he said. (The nostalgia for knowing remains, of
course, even in the midst of the despair of ever knowing.)

The function of the critic – all he can do – is to say 'There is a
poor devil in this situation'. And even if this particular artist in this
particular situation is the only one, 'yet it is still a human situation'.
He himself makes no claims to universality and senses the isolation
of each individual and the precarious nature of communication.
'We can't say this is truth. We can't even say that this is what is
happening in the twentieth century. We don't know.' The logic of
his position, he appreciates, leads to silence (to anti-form). But he
feels none the less a real necessity and an inner urge to write. He
must write. He yearns to achieve the freedom so that he has just a

'white page' in front of him so that he can write. Instead, as I speak to him, self-translation confronts him.

He mentioned the tremendous desire to write 'I' and yet the impossibility of doing so. He is an artist who yearns to really portray 'being'; but he believes that he has merely scratched the surface. However, he believes that someone will someday find a way. He thinks that his best effort to date is *Comment c'est (How It Is)*. He doesn't think that the theatre is the best medium to do what he is attempting. There are too many conventions (i.e. forms) that must be accepted and that restrict. He thinks that painting being does not lead to doctrine and form but that [Alain] Robbe-Grillet's negative stand does.*

[The name of Robbe-Grillet came up again at another time in conversation.] I spoke to him about the Robbe-Grillet/Resnais film *Last Year at Marienbad*. Beckett feels that Robbe-Grillet has a *doctrine*; i.e. he has a form [so] that his anti-plot, his anti-character and so on quickly becomes a convention. He felt that the love-story in this film was traditional and banal. It was merely expressed differently. He objected especially to actually seeing the two people on the screen. There is being but *individual personality* remains a mystery.

Art = strength, creation, ego, form.

Man = weakness, surface illusions, words, accumulation/accretion from outside chaos, *le néant* [nothingness], abortive being.

But how can these two then be combined? Solution; sometimes it seems like *le néant* and sometimes it seems like *abortive being* (Freud). But abortive being is at least something. One should try therefore to discover 'a syntax of weakness'. The problem is that he feels that he has tried everything. So what now?

Note; the double sense of *le néant* [nothingness] and a hard core self (abortive) is well expressed in this passage from *The Unnamable* cited by Blanchot, where he is, on the one hand only '*poussière de verbe*' [dust of words] and, on the other, '*une chose muette, dans un endroit dur . . .*' [a wordless thing, . . . in a hard . . . place] ('*une cage de bêtes*') [a caged beast . . . born in a cage].

---

* Alain Robbe-Grillet, published like Beckett by Les Editions de Minuit, was one of the leading figures in the *Nouveau roman*. Considered as a radical innovator in the form of the novel, he was the author of *Les Gommes, Le Voyeur, La Jalousie, Dans le labyrinthe* and *La Maison de rendez-vous*. He also wrote the film script *L'Année dernière à Marienbad*.

He said that in his work he had been searching for a 'syntax of weakness'. For form is an obstacle, a 'sign of strength'. Beckett said that this represents a 'clash of two incompatible positions. This will come to an end long before life comes to an end.'

'I don't know any form that doesn't shit on being in the most unbearable manner. Excuse my language!'

Restlessness and Movement

[Lawrence E. Harvey asked Beckett further about the sense of *le néant* (nothingness) in his work.]

Beckett responded that it is more – or at least he moved directly into this related theme – a sense of 'restlessness, of moving about at night'. Much of this is to be found in my work, he said. There is none the less the sense of having to go on (cf. *Comment c'est*). Beckett mentioned that Molloy, even when he is really beaten down, feels that he must keep on moving. By contrast, he mentioned a great desire just to lie down and not to move. This is apparently balanced and perhaps even determined by the above restlessness, the opposing compulsion to move on.

When I mentioned the Eden–Exile tension that I found in his work, Beckett objected and described life as being 'just a series of movements'. He no doubt objected to the meaning that I tried to introduce into what he described as essentially senseless moving about. (Compare the circular motion in *Waiting for Godot* that gets one nowhere.)

His Life and His Art

Beckett said that in his view his life had nothing to do with his art. He didn't at least see any relation. But later in speaking of the Irish place names that occur in his poems, *Echo's Bones*, he said, 'Of course, I say my life has nothing to do with my work, but of course it does.' The word that he used repeatedly was 'materials' to be used.

I suggested that I wanted to steer a line between the extreme of art for art (with no relation to life) and autobiographical art (art and life as one). I added that it seemed to me that art could be a reality that was just as real as existence. He seemed to acquiesce with this and replied: '*Molloy* was begun in order to find oxygen to breathe – to make my own miserable existence.'

Later he said 'Work doesn't depend on experience; it is not a record of experience. But of course you must use it.'

He feels, he said, 'like someone on his knees, his head against a wall, more like a cliff, with someone saying "go on".' Later, he said, 'The wall will have to move a little, that's all'. He also said, 'It's not me; it's my work that has got me into this position.' I suggested that theatre was still possible for him, because of links between life and the void. He agreed.

'Children build a snowman. Well, this is like trying to build a dustman.' I forget how this arose but the point is that it [what he was trying to write] would not stay together. There was his sense of destruction and of the futility of words. And yet at the same time there was the need to make too.

Revolt

Beckett said that there was 'no revolt at all' in his work. When pressed, he conceded that there was a little revolt in the early poems but that this was superficial. He used the terms 'complete submission' and said that he was 'revolted but not revolting'. He was using the word in its etymological sense of turning away from but not active opposition to. He sees the individual as having been the subject of a form of destruction and is more passive than active.

Aidan Higgins on Beckett in the 1950s

Aidan Higgins (1927–). Irish writer whose first novel, *Langrishe, Go Down*, won the James Tait Black Memorial Prize and the Irish Academy of Letters Award. It was later filmed for television with a screenplay by Harold Pinter. Other works include *Balcony of Europe* (1972), *Lions of the Grunewald* (1993) and the trilogy, *Donkey's Years* (1995), *Dog Days* (1998) and *The Whole Hog* (2000). He is also known for his shorter fiction and travel writing. The interview with JK was revised by Aidan Higgins in 2005.

We were living in Greystones, County Wicklow in the late 1940s, and Samuel Beckett's uncle Gerald and his wife, Peggy, were next-door neighbours. I met their son, John, and he lent me four books, among them Beckett's *Murphy*. The others made no impression on me, but *Murphy* raised the hair on my head. *Murphy* was the business.

Peggy Beckett said, 'If you like it as much as that, you must go and see uncle so-and-so in Donnybrook'. This was Walter Beckett, a musician – all the Becketts were musicians. We had a drink or two and he went upstairs and came running down with a brown paper parcel and in it was *More Pricks than Kicks*, a rare book which you couldn't get in those days. He said, 'This is for you,' and I said 'I can't possibly take it off you'. 'No,' he said, 'Sam means something to you which he will never mean to me and you are welcome to it.' None of the Becketts had any notion what he was up to. If he'd been a musician, they would have understood, but not being serious readers, they had no idea. And then I read *Proust* in the National Library, which was also unavailable elsewhere. It made a very powerful impression.

I wrote Sam a fan letter about *Murphy* and John Beckett said it's no use writing to Sam, he never replies. But he did reply, though it was no use to me because I couldn't make out the handwriting. The calligraphy was a beast: the hasty hand of a hard-worked doctor firing off prescriptions. Eventually Peggy Beckett, the mother of John, deciphered it as: 'Despair young and never look back.' In the same letter he wrote, 'For wisdom, see Arland Ussher'. So, through Beckett, I met Arland Ussher, and, through Arland Ussher, I met Arthur Power and Joseph Hone. This introduced me in my early twenties to a whole new world.

I remember having tea with the Hones one day and they said what a difficult guest Beckett was. He had come round one evening and Mrs Hone said, 'Sam, the dogs have pupped'. And Sam said, 'I'm not interested in dogs'. 'The cat has . . .' 'I'm not interested in cats'. No matter what subject came up he wasn't interested in it and he relapsed back into a heavy silence which they were doing their damnedest to break up, and it wasn't having any effect whatsoever. Anyway, at the door he gave a limp hand to Mrs Hone and said, 'Friede, Friede', and she said of course, 'My name isn't Freda', but Ussher happened to be there and said, 'It's the German for peace'. So the young Beckett was getting very difficult to entertain and when he said something that was pleasing, they didn't understand what he was saying.

[It was somewhat different with Arland Ussher, whom Beckett had known in the 1930s.] Ussher was an academic and he had no connection with life as we know it. Sam, although he was very academic in a way, had been, after all, in the Resistance and was very much in life. I remember once Ussher saying to me, 'You know, I had an evening with Sam and it got very sticky indeed,' and eventually it relapsed into silence in some bar or other and then he heard that the Sinclairs, the relatives, were upstairs carousing and they went up. 'And Beckett immediately changed. He became quite different.' Now something like that would affront Ussher greatly. If he and Sam were together, he thought they should be buddies. If they can't talk, he wouldn't like it. But the reason he wouldn't like it is because Sam lives in two worlds, he lives in the rough, tough world very much and he lives in the abstract world, too, and there he was bored. Sometimes he gets bored with the abstract world and he wants to join the rough stuff.

I first met Beckett some years later in London, during the Criterion Theatre production of *Godot* [at the beginning of December 1955] which had effectively bowled me over. He was coming down from Godalming with Peter Woodthorpe (Estragon) and a lady who had been at Trinity College with him. John and Vera Beckett were then living on Haverstock Hill, and invited my wife and me over for a supper (silverside of beef, as I recall, done quite rare), to meet Beckett.

The party from Godalming arrived maybe an hour late. I wondered whom I would meet, Democritus or Heraclitus. Well, in the event, neither. It must have been Sunday. The murmurous Dublin accent was lovely to hear; he was not assertive, taller than I had expected, carried himself like an athlete. He had a copy of *Texts for Nothing* in French on the mantel, stood with me after the meal, asked my wife's name and inscribed this copy.

The following evening we accompanied the Becketts and Michael Morrow to Collins Music Hall in Islington, where the young Chaplin had performed in Fred Karno's troupe. A nude chorus girl was pushed across the stage on a bicycle, but what affected Sam Beckett was the row in stitches at Mr Dooley, who gave a rapid-patter monologue on what the world needed, which was apparently castor oil. It was in essence Lucky's outpourings at the Criterion. Beckett was leaning forward, looking along the row. On the way out we ran into Mr Dooley, and introduced him to Beckett, of whom he had never heard; Mr D. was chuffed that Monsieur B. had liked his patter. It was all good clean fun.

The austere playwright, thought to be so reclusive, wasn't so reclusive after all, as close and enduring friendships with actors and actresses testify; as did the business of conducting much of his social life in bars and cafés. He seemed to be well aware of what was going on in the world at large, lived in no ivory tower.

He himself was not cold and inspired warm affection in others.

'When you fear for your cyst think of your fistula. And when you tremble for your fistula consider your chancre.' (*Murphy*)

Beckett in the Luxembourg Gardens, 1956.

Avigdor Arikha on Beckett and Art

Avigdor Arikha (1929–) is an internationally renowned artist whose paintings, etchings and drawings hang in galleries throughout the world. But he is also a distinguished scholar, having written catalogues for exhibitions which he curated at the Louvre (Poussin) and the Frick Collection (Ingres) and articles for many art journals. He has made documentary films on Velázquez, Poussin, Vermeer, David and Caravaggio and given talks on the radio for the BBC, France-Culture, Deutsche Welle and Kol-Israel. He was a close friend of Samuel Beckett from 1956 until the latter's death in 1989. Contribution written especially for this volume.

In spite of his great erudition, Beckett refrained from theorizing – even concerning Dante. Unlike erudition, theorizing stops at the white page. His knowledge of lives past telling how it was made them his hidden companions to say *how it is* – '*essayer encore une fois de dire un petit peu ce que c'est que d'avoir été là*' ['to try yet again to say a little of what it is to have been there'], as he formulated it in a letter.*

---

* Letter from Samuel Beckett to Avigdor Arikha, 18 Nov. 1958.

He was early on attracted to erudition which sustained his interest in art. This interest started even before Beckett lived at 6 Clare Street, Dublin, next door to the National Gallery of Ireland. Simply looking at paintings without knowing what he was looking at did not satisfy him. He had a passion for scholarly catalogues and acquired them avidly. They accompanied him from painting to painting, in the museums and galleries he frequented, wandering through London, Florence, Hamburg, Munich, Berlin, Kassel, Leipzig, Dresden, Braunschweig, Erfurt, Vienna, Milan, Dijon, to mention but a few.

He sometimes annotated these catalogues by a mark or a note such as the one in the 1928 edition of the NGI [National Gallery of Ireland] catalogue (cat. n° 443) next to the entry concerning Hendrick Gerritsz Pot, *Portrait of a Man*. Beckett inscribed in the margin '*at same time as Ter Borch*', and underlined in the entry the line *England 1632* (the year Pot painted the portrait of Charles I, now in the Louvre). While living at 34 Gertrude Street, London, SW10 [1934–5], Beckett inscribed, on one of his visits to the National Gallery, the NG [of London] catalogue (edition 1929), near the mention '*Butinone see Milanese School* n°2513,' printed without surname or referred work: '*Adoration of the Shepherds: given to Mantegna, then to Parenzo*' and added in the margin n° 3336. Beckett's attribution was right. It is not a Mantegna, nor a Parenzo, and was ascribed, by Martin Davies (1956) to Bernardino Butinone under n° 3336. He sometimes marked an analogy, such as the one inscribed in the catalogue of the Staatliche Gemäldegalerie zu Dresden, on the margin of n°958 (cat. 1930), entry Rubens' *Old Woman with Ember*, *c.*1616–1618: '*Honthorst*'. Or emphasizing a particular detail of the work seen, such as the note on the margin of the entry to Caravaggio's *Christ on the Mount of Olives* in the Kaiser Friedrich-Museum, Berlin: '*Peter's foot*.'

It is amazing that his qualitative discernment was there from the start, not simply looking for celebrated works but for pictorial qualities. His discernment sharpened along with the widening of his visual culture that spanned past and present. He was aware that the visual experience differs from the literary one. 'Art and literature can't mix, they are like oil and water' he said, adding 'I don't know which is which'.

His visual sense was as intense as his musical one. In later years he often sat gazing at a painting, print or drawing a long while without uttering a word. He would simply gaze, marvel, nod, and sigh.

Martin Esslin on Beckett the Man

Martin Esslin (1918–2002). Writer and radio producer. He was appointed the Head of the Radio Drama Department at the British Broadcasting Corporation in 1963. Author of many books, including: *Brecht* (1959), *The Theatre of the Absurd* (1961), *Brief Chronicles: Essays on Modern Theatre* (1970) and *Pinter: A Study of his Plays* (1977; first published in 1970). Interview with JK.

I was trying to write a book about the theatre of the absurd in 1960 and felt I wanted to interview the writers concerned. Through Cecilia Reeves, who was the BBC representative in Paris and who knew Beckett, I managed to get an interview with him in the rue des Favorites at the beginning of 1961.

I had, of course, looked up all the cuttings about him before-hand so that I was well prepared. But there was very little in the BBC cuttings library, except for a long *Observer* profile, which contained some rather sarcastic references to his being very much under the sway of his mother and all sorts of things and the suggestion was that he might well be homosexual.

He was there all by himself. He said, 'How very nice to meet you. You can ask me anything about my life but don't ask me to explain my work'. We got on like a house on fire. He gave me a copy of *Echo's Bones* with an inscription. It was a numbered edition, 148. Then he told me all about going to Germany before the war and wandering through Europe and how it left him feeling. And [we talked about] Trinity College, Dublin and so on. And all this time I was wondering whether I could ask him about women, about whether he was married.

He opened a bottle of whiskey and I thought my goodness, what a wonderful man. The most attractive man I'd ever met, in a way, and what a nice friendship was developing here. Then I thought, my God, can I ask him 'Are you married?' or 'What about women?' He was so scathing about this article in *The Observer* that I thought he would get furious and throw me out. And so I was in this Racinian conflict of conscience, between my duty as a researcher and my duty as a potential friend. In the end my friendship won and I didn't ask him.

He said, 'Well, send me what you have written. I can see whether there is anything I can help with.' And I was very happy but when I walked down the street, I said to myself, 'My God, now I've done it.' I already saw the review in *The Times Literary Supplement*: there is this snotty-nosed urchin from Vienna who pretends to be a biographer and he doesn't even know whether his subject is married or not! The same evening I went to the theatre with a friend of mine. It was very late; we were having dinner after the theatre in a little Chinese restaurant in the rue François Premier and we came out about 2 o'clock at night. It was a wonderful spring evening. The Champs-Elysées was completely deserted, when, suddenly from the other side, I heard a voice saying, 'Mr Esslin, meet my wife,' and there was Beckett with Suzanne. This stumpy little woman was then introduced. And I said to myself: 'My God, virtue has been rewarded'. Anyhow, so I met her. Then I went back to London and wrote my piece.

The chapter on Beckett for *The Theatre of the Absurd* was about forty or fifty pages long. I sent it to him and it came back with little red corrections of some of the biographical details, together with a

Beckett at Greystones, 1960s.

letter which said, 'I like this because you raise many hares without pursuing them too far'. So that meant that he gave me his blessing and that was very encouraging for me. Just at the beginning of 1961, I had got the job as Assistant Head of the Radio Drama Department of the BBC, and this of course meant that I was the successor to Donald McWhinnie. Val Gielgud, who was the head of the department, took me out to lunch and he said to me, 'I hate Brecht, I hate Beckett, I hate Pinter. But I know what my duty is. That's why I've appointed you to deal with those people'. At that time John Morris was still the Controller of the Third Programme and he had been instrumental in getting Beckett to do *All That Fall* and *Embers*, but also the first readings from *Molloy* and *Malone Dies* by Jackie MacGowran and Pat [Magee]; *From an Abandoned Work* also. And so, because Val didn't want to have anything to do with this, it fell to me.

The connection between the BBC and Beckett was that Donald McWhinnie was detailed to do the directing of *All That Fall* and he went to Paris and saw Sam about it and Sam immediately took to him. He really fell in love with him, and vice versa. They became the best of friends and that of course established a connection that went on and on. In a way I inherited that because I was the successor to Donald and fate luckily had meant it that I'd just met Beckett and he'd seen what I'd written about him. So he took to me in the same way, although perhaps not so passionately, as to Donald McWhinnie.

Beckett worked very much that way, with friendships. He wanted people whom he could trust and with whom he could work. So the next thing that happened was that there was some sort of jubilee, the fiftieth anniversary of the BBC or something like that, and we were told, again by the Third Programme, that we ought to have something by some big name, a world première, so that we'd get into the papers to celebrate this anniversary. So I wrote to Beckett and said, 'This again is a possibility, would you like to do something?' And he wrote back saying 'Not really, I don't work like that'. But then, I think he actually came into the office and said, 'By the way, my cousin John is in such a bad way [for he had had a horrific motor accident], I have had an idea which would give him some work.' So that is how *Words and Music* came about and he wrote something where the music was of equal importance to the words. I remember even when we were doing *Words and Music*, I went to the editing channel, he was in the editing channel and he said, 'No that six seconds should only be five'. He was very, very meticulous, very precise.

He was very, very technical and the interesting thing about it was that his interest in the purely craftsmanship side of things was absolutely fascinating. Because he was not at all an airy-fairy poet, you know. He was really down-to-earth. 'How do you do it?', 'How do you do it?' He was asking people how does one cut the thing and what's the best way of doing it and so on. He himself said, 'It's a matter of fundamental sounds. No pun intended.'

I retired from the BBC at the end of 1976 but, during that period, I did a lot of stuff with him, and always got on very well. What is wonderful about him was that if he disliked anything he always said, 'It's my fault, it's the text, not the production'. He was the most courteous and considerate of people, never wanting to hurt anybody. To give you an example, my daughter was born in 1961, roughly at the time when I started at the BBC. Beckett was in London shortly after she was born and came to our house and met her – she was a baby-in-arms – and ever since then, whenever I met him he said, 'How is Monica?' He remembered her name; extraordinary. He had the old-fashioned English, or Irish, gentleman thing. He was very meticulous about that, but he was very warm.

It was Sam who got in touch over *Lessness*. It had appeared in the *New Statesman* and then he said he wanted this to be done on the radio. It was really for the radio. And I then went to Paris to discuss it with him, I remember in the boulevard St Jacques under the Jack Yeats picture. He said, 'Well, this comes out of *Imagination Dead Imagine*. It was all an enclosed space which is like a womb, you see, which is then broken open and now you have this wilderness in which there is only the little body standing up. That's the only thing that's still standing up'. So I said, 'Well how do you want this to be read?' So he said, 'I'll read you a bit'. And he started reading out: 'Grey, everything grey, little body only upright, fallen over', etc. And I said, 'Sam, allow me to record a little bit so that I can tell the actors to pick up the tone'. He said, 'No, no I never record anything'. I said, 'Listen, I swear to you I'll never use this, only to play it to the actors'. And he read a few minutes of it for me and I've got that on the tape.*

The story goes on. I had this recording of Sam and I cast the six voices with Pat Magee, Nicol Williamson, Harold Pinter, Donal Donnelly (a great Irish actor), Denis Hawthorne and Leonard Fenton. And so I recorded this. I played them the recording and said, 'You take up the tone', and they all did it and of course Beckett had specified that each person be recorded separately and then we cut this together. And on the recording that he did for me he also indicated the pauses; it had to be exactly that. Now the interesting thing is that they'd recorded these and we'd cut these all together and I thought it was terrific and then we played it to him and he said, 'No, no', and I said, 'Why?' He said, 'Too sentimental'. And, of course, his own voice was extremely sentimental, so that he disliked his own sentimentality; he shuddered from it, from his own voice.

Sam told me (and I know he's told other people) that he remembers being in his mother's womb at a dinner party, where, under the table, he could remember the voices talking. And when I asked him once, 'What motivates you to write?' he said. 'The only obligation I feel is towards that enclosed poor embryo.' Because, he said, 'That is the most terrible situation you can imagine, because you know you're in distress but you don't know that there is anything outside this distress or any possibility of getting out of that distress' – and, if you remember, in *Endgame*, the question of the little boy that is being seen, Sam had an absolutely mystical obligation towards that poor, suffering, enclosed being that doesn't know there is a way out. But if you look through his work you find it confirmed over and over again. And the whole complex of *Imagination Dead Imagine* and *Lessness* and all these others always relates to this enclosed space from which there is no way out. He even describes how the body is bent and all sorts of things. So he had this terrific imagination or dream or reality of this memory of being enclosed. And that self is self-enclosed. You can't really get to the others.

---

* Thanks to Martin Esslin this recording was placed, after Beckett's death, in the Archive of the Beckett International Foundation at the University of Reading.

Eileen O'Casey

Eileen O'Casey *née* Carey (1900–95), singer, dancer and actress who married Seán O'Casey in 1927. Mother of Niall, Shivaun and Breon. She wrote a biography of her husband, *Seán* (1971) and her own autobiography, *Eileen* (1976). These memories of Beckett are published with the kind agreement of her daughter, Shivaun.

Seán O'Casey never met Samuel Beckett, although there was mutual admiration. When Seán had his eightieth birthday in 1960, Beckett wrote in *The Irish Times*: 'I send my enduring gratitude and homage to my great compatriot, Seán O'Casey, from France, where he is honoured.'

I was introduced to Samuel Beckett's work on the stage when I took my young son, Niall, to see *Waiting for Godot*. We were enthralled. The first time I met Beckett was on 19 November 1963. I was with Jackie MacGowran and his wife, Gloria, and we went to see *Uncle Vanya* at the Old Vic Theatre. I liked Beckett immediately and I knew he liked me. Jackie had told me that Beckett did not usually go out to supper after the theatre, so it was a pleasant surprise when he asked us to join him at a restaurant called 'Chez Solange'. We were in the restaurant upstairs, and it seemed to me that Beckett was well known there. We stayed there a long time; there was so much to talk about. Of course Seán came into our conversation a great deal. He was at our home in Devon, and when I was in London I used to telephone him each evening. On this particular evening, I telephoned him from the restaurant and, when he answered, I said, 'I am here having supper with Samuel Beckett.' Seán said, 'What is he like?' I remember replying, 'He is like you in appearance. He has a great sense of humour, like you have – but different.'

After Seán's death, I visited Paris and met Beckett there. From then on he became one of my dearest friends. I remember on one occasion I had gone to Paris to see Seán's publishers, and also another old friend, Tom Curtiss, the theatre critic of the *Herald Tribune*. The weather was fine and Beckett took me to a restaurant where we ate outside. Then he took me for a walk around Paris. I told him I wanted to do some shopping: clothes for my son Breon, and for the husband of my daughter Shivaun. Beckett said he would go shopping with me, as he knew the places to go. He took me to my hotel and we arranged to meet the following day. I was dead tired after so much walking. To my dismay, at 9 o'clock the next morning the telephone rang and the receptionist was telling me in an awed voice, 'Madame O'Casey, Monsieur Samuel Beckett is below waiting for you.' I am afraid I had to tell Beckett that I would not be ready for an hour. He was as good as his word and took me to all the best shops, where I could get what I wanted: the shop for the lovely thin jerseys and the shop where he bought his own shirts. He told me that he wanted to buy a present for Shivaun. He met Shivaun when she was fourteen years old [more likely to have been sixteen from Shivaun's own account below] and they struck up a friendship that has lasted to this day. I suggested he buy her some scent. He was very shy in the Parfumerie where he bought her a large bottle of 'Jolie Madame'.

After that, whenever I went to Paris, I saw Samuel Beckett. I felt completely at ease with him. Like Seán he enjoyed talking to people he liked. We used to outdo each other with conversation. On one of my visits to Paris I was taken ill, and Beckett was wonderfully kind to me. I have always found him one of the kindest of men, very understanding and a great friend.

Shivaun O'Casey

Shivaun O'Casey (1939–), Irish actress and director; daughter of Seán and Eileen O'Casey. Founder of the O'Casey Theatre in Newry, she has directed plays in Ireland, England and the USA. She also directed the film *Seán O'Casey: Under a Coloured Cap* (2004). Interview with JK.

I met Sam Beckett just before going to the Gibsons.* I was going with Jackie MacGowran and John Gibson. It was when *Waiting for Godot* was on at the Criterion Theatre [1955–6] or it might have been just after, so it was when I was at the Central School of Arts and Crafts. I was about sixteen at the time – or maybe a little younger. We got on the tube at Chiswick to go to the Gibsons and there was Sam. Amy and John [Gibson] stayed with him in his house, when they went to France. It was in his house in the country [Ussy], not in Paris.

---

* John Gibson was a producer with BBC radio who, with his French wife, Amy, became friendly with Beckett in the mid-1950s.

It was prior to dinner. We were on the way and poor Amy was only expecting Sam and John but there were a lot more people. I think John Calder was there, too, and another woman. Anyway, the little girl wanted me to bath her, I remember that, and I was as shy as Sam – you know, we were both very shy. But we shared a taxi back and that's really where we became friends, talking about the theatre and his work. We had a long chat. He was such a sweet man and very interested in what I thought about theatre. I was living in St John's Wood at the time, so it was quite a long talk and we sat outside a bit and chatted in the taxi. Then he went off. He said to look him up in Paris and he'd write a play for me, but I never did. I did look him up in Paris but that was quite a bit later, in the 'sixties.

I went over to Paris with my boyfriend at the time. I think we were on our way to Venice in this clapped-out old car, in the early 'sixties. And we met Sam. He gave us a meal in Montparnasse. I think I went to see him alone and we talked again about theatre and he told me what he was doing, trying to become more and more minimalist, if you like. He was beginning to think about staging just a face – even in those early days he was thinking about that. I do remember a nice incident though when I was in Paris with him. A young man came up to him and asked him something. And Sam really got quite cross because the boy persisted. He was very polite at first, you know, 'I really would rather not talk round here'; 'I'm having a private meal; it's very nice to meet you but . . .' Still the young man insisted, so Sam stood up and said: 'Go away. Don't you dare interfere.' So the guy finally went. I remember that, because Sam was such a polite man. He didn't like people being rude.

I think he was pessimistic in his philosophy but comic with it too. I found him very charming and funny. Not a bit dour; very sweet. I never felt miserable, I always felt uplifted after being with him. He loved young people and when I introduced my son Ruben to him, I'd said earlier to Ruben, 'Now you've got to go at a certain point; he'll get tired and that.' But Sam really didn't want Ruben to go at all. So poor Ruben was caught in the position of having made this pact to go and Sam looking at me and saying, 'Why is he going?' 'Because I told him to!' Laughter.

I wrote and asked Sam what of his could we do to go with my father's play, *Figuro in the Night* and I said that it would be good for us if it were a première of something because *Figuro* had never been done before. It was a première evening and that's how we were selling it. I said that *Figuro* is a certain length, so yours doesn't need to be too long . . . It was then that Sam suggested that we might do [an adaptation of his prose text] *From an Abandoned Work*. It was his suggestion. I think he even sent me the script or he told me where to get it. And he sent a letter suggesting how we could do it. It's a long typed-out letter, which for him is very unusual. It's very clear. The nice thing about it is that he described – you know, it isn't like, 'Walk three steps here and three steps there', it's not detailed like that. All it suggested generally was that this old tramp comes on, rummages for food in a bin, finds this bit of old paper, sits down on the bin, or beside it, whatever, reads it out loud, then finishes and thinks, 'Well, I don't think much of that' and crumples it up, which is very humorous, I think, and chucks it back in the bin. Sam gave it to us. We didn't pay any royalties, nothing; he didn't expect that because he gave it to us as a gift, really.

Our meetings were very infrequent. In Paris we would go out to dinner. I think I met him twice and Eileen never met him with me because I never went to Paris with her when meeting Sam. She would meet him separately. She went to Paris and I said you ought to look up Sam and she did. She didn't go over many times either, really. She must have met him about two or three times. It wasn't a great, close friendship but somehow it was in a funny way. I always felt and I suppose many people did because he gave you so much of himself when you met him. You always felt you could go to him for advice. He was very *sympathique*. I always felt he was there, and that was why his death was such a loss. And the feeling that you've got to keep going, you know you are right, do it. He always gave me that advice and that was nice. 'Bon courage', he said. In a way he took over from Seán, being positive like that.

After Sam died, I wrote a little article and it described him as being birdlike, very similar to Seán. They both had this birdlike quality about them. They had these very piercing eyes that looked right into you. Funnily enough, they both had trouble with their

Beckett with his cousins, Sheila Page and Mollie Roe,
at Sheila Page's house, Sweetwater Cottage, *c.* 1959.

Beckett on a seat at Sweetwater Cottage, *c. 1959.*

eyes. Even at the very end, when he was clinically blind, Seán still had these piercing eyes. They were both skinny and they both had this way of walking, and the grasp. They were from very different backgrounds: one upper-middle class and the other very low class. They were both brought up Protestant, I suppose, and they both had this great empathy and love of other people.

6

Beckett as Director

Beckett directing Klaus Herm and Carl Raddatz in
Warten auf Godot at the Schiller-Theater, Berlin, 1975.

Biography

Samuel Beckett took a keen interest in productions of his plays from
the very beginning of his career as a dramatist. In the mid-1950s
and early 1960s, he attended rehearsals with Roger Blin and Jean-
Marie Serreau in Paris and came over to London to help the
directors of several productions at the Royal Court Theatre: George
Devine, Donald McWhinnie and Anthony Page. Then, from the
mid-1960s on, he began to direct his own plays, in London and
Paris, but especially at the Schiller-Theater in Berlin. He also
directed his television plays in Stuttgart with Süddeutscher Rundfunk, ending his career as a director of his own work only at the age
of eighty.

In the first part of 'Beckett as Director' we publish interviews with some of those with whom he worked at the Royal Court Theatre. Two of them, Billie Whitelaw and Jocelyn Herbert, were to become really close friends.

In the second part, we look at Beckett through the eyes of some of the major German actors, the Schiller-Theater's dramaturg, Boles-law Barlog and Beckett's theatrical assistant, Walter Asmus. We also print the memories of a doctor friend, Gottfried Büttner, who attended a number of rehearsals at the Schiller-Theater.

In the third part, we explore a surprising aspect of Beckett's life when he went on to direct his plays with a small theatrical company called the San Quentin Drama Workshop. This came about through a strange friendship which evolved over the years with the founder of the Workshop, a former prisoner, Rick Cluchey. Cluchey received a life sentence in 1955 for a kidnap, robbery and shooting incident and served twelve years in the notorious maximum-security prison of San Quentin, until his sentence was commuted to one which allowed for the possibility of parole. He was later given a full pardon. While in prison, Cluchey had become heavily involved in drama and acted in several of Beckett's plays. Then, when he came out on parole, he travelled to Europe with his own play, *The Cage*, and met Samuel Beckett, who, intrigued by the man and his background, agreed to direct him in *Krapp's Last Tape* at the Akademie der Künste for the Berlin Festival in 1977 and went on to befriend him for the next twelve years. He worked with the group again in 1980, directing *Endgame* in London, after advising them on an earlier production of the same play in Berlin, and then directed – 'supervised' was the word that Beckett himself used – *Waiting for Godot* with them at the Riverside Studios in London in 1984, a production which Walter Asmus had begun in Chicago. We bring together here for the first time the memories of four members of the San Quentin Drama Workshop with whom Beckett had extremely relaxed, cordial relations. With them he became once again one of 'the boys' and, in spite of the big age difference between them, had genuine fun.

THE ROYAL COURT THEATRE, LONDON
Brenda Bruce on *Happy Days*

Brenda Bruce (1918–96), seen here as Winnie in the British première of *Happy Days* at the Royal Court Theatre, London, November 1962. Beckett had come over from Paris for three weeks to assist George Devine, the director and founder of the English Stage Company. Winnie is buried in a mound of earth, up to her waist in Act I and up to her neck in Act II. Interview with JK.

I'd never met George Devine, but he rang my agent and said that he had this play by Samuel Beckett and would I read it quickly, as he would like me to do it and my agent said: 'Yes, when is it starting?' And it was within about ten days, so I immediately thought 'I see, so who is sick', you know, that's to say I clearly wasn't the first choice. They sent me the script and I read it, having seen *Waiting for Godot* and so on, but I'd never studied these works at all. And I read it with all the dot, dot, dots . . . dot, dot, dots and so on . . . 'she lifts hand . . . puts hand to bag . . . opens bag . . .' and I thought: I do wish authors wouldn't do that, you know, it's so maddening. They don't need to. It's like Bernard Shaw who says 'She blushes scarlet'. But I thought this is extraordinary, having shown it to my then husband and he said 'Well I think you'll have to do that'. It was only later that I discovered that Joan [Plowright, Lady Olivier] had been asked to do it and then found she was pregnant and said: 'I don't want to sit on that lavatory stool, you know, for hours.'* So that's why it was such a late call. I only had about four days of preparation and didn't rehearse with George at all alone until we got rid of Sam. [Beckett left rehearsals for a few days because he found that he was putting too much pressure on the actress.] And if I ever said to Sam: 'What does that mean?' he used to say: 'Tis of no consequence'! And just when I thought I'm not getting anything that he wants me to do, one day, I finally burst into tears. It was rather like, you know, if you're about to have a bit of breakdown or be ill and someone says: 'How are you?' and you go 'Oh, boo-hoo . . .' And I went into rehearsal one day and George said: 'Hi, you OK?' and I went 'Aaaaahhhh' and out it all came. And I remember getting myself into a terrible state and saying to Beckett: 'You should get Peter Sellers and then he'd do an imitation of you doing an imitation of Winnie, and then you'd get what you want.' I mean, I was in such a state. Sam couldn't understand that because I'd read it I didn't necessarily know it. He did not understand the acting process.

George Devine could see increasingly that I was trying terribly to get everything right but as to giving a performance, I mean, I couldn't work. I couldn't explain to Beckett that it has to come out of one's working of the part. I was so alone. If I said: 'What do you think she's thinking here, Sam? Why is she reacting? Why does she suddenly go into "Fear no more the heat of the sun"? Answer: 'Tis of no consequence.' I think that nowadays as an older person I might say: 'Well then, why the hell did you write it?' you know. I wouldn't actually. I would still be terrified of him, I'm sure. He wasn't giving me time to work. I daren't open my mouth.

It wasn't that he wasn't nice to me. Very early in rehearsal I discovered that he hadn't seen Joan [Plowright] either, so then I didn't feel quite so bad. He was lovely though. One fell in love with

* Joan Plowright writes about George Devine's proposals for her to play the role of Winnie and the obstacle of her unexpected pregnancy in her autobiography, *And That's Not All. The Memoirs of Joan Plowright*, London, Orion Books, 2001, pp. 103–4.

him, you see, and this angelic smile and you thought 'Oh'. Then he took me to buy the glasses [that Winnie wears], so we had quite a jolly couple of hours buying the specs that had to be absolutely right. And then this hat which was nothing like the other girls wore at all because they all had little Saatchi hairdos and little flowered hats. No. I've still got it at home, with feathers coming out of it but the brim's cut off and a sort of gingery felt crown. Then one had the sort of evening dress, a boned thing. But acting Winnie was a terrifying experience. Because if you dry with that stuff, you see, you can't just go back and pick it up. If you drop a line with Sam's stuff, you are lost.

During the run I used to ring Sam because people would walk out and it always amazed me because he was right there in Paris and the receiver was picked up immediately; you know, you got straight through to him and I would say, 'Somebody walked out last night' and he would say: 'Good, that's great', you know. He loved it. So I never got any sympathy about that.

Jocelyn Herbert

Jocelyn Herbert (1917–2003). Influential British theatre designer, daughter of the writer A. P. Herbert. A very close friend of Samuel Beckett, she worked extensively at the Royal Court Theatre in London, designing all of Beckett's productions staged there. She also worked in opera and film. After the breakdown of her marriage to Anthony Lousada, she lived with the founder of the English Stage Company, George Devine. Interview with JK.

It was a bit difficult, I remember, our first meeting because Sam didn't like the colour of the set [Jocelyn Herbert was responsible for getting Jacques Noel's set made in England for the première of *Fin de partie* (*Endgame*) in French at the Royal Court Theatre, London, in 1957]; it was a kind of dark grey. I must say it seemed quite suitable. I remember that, once I had read *Endgame*, I said to George [Devine, the Royal Court director and her partner], I don't know how anyone could go on living having written this play. And at some point, I don't know whether we were having a drink, we talked about the play and I remember repeating this to

Sam, with some trepidation. I was very nervous of him, of his reputation.

George had this immense respect and love for Sam. And gradually we both did; we came to love Sam, as you do automatically, you can't help it. I became less frightened of him, as I got to know him better, and was able to say if I didn't think something was right or I didn't agree with him.

The thing was that, always with *Endgame*, I think it was terribly difficult to retain that certain strange black humour and keep the rhythm. And that was one of the things that George [who played Hamm] and Jackie MacGowran [who played Clov] did. They used to rehearse it in the car. I used to fetch them sometimes. And they had elements of it that were hilarious in a strange way. But when Sam came over, that was all stopped, completely stopped. And in a funny way it put a bit of a blight on that show. I know George was always utterly petrified [when he acted the role of Hamm]. I used to go and put the rug over him and the handkerchief over his eyes and he would be absolutely shaking like a jelly . . .

I think a lot of [Sam's relationship] with Suzanne [his wife from 1961 until her death in 1989] was gratitude and loyalty and I think that he felt remorse for the fact that he had so many friends whom he got drunk with. She didn't drink. And he had after all endless other women. And when people say to me he was a saint I say: 'Oh no, he wasn't a saint at all. And thank God he wasn't.'

[An evening spent with Beckett and Eugène Ionesco in Paris.] It must have been Boxing Night, we – Sam and Ionesco and my daughter and George and I – all had dinner at the Coupole, and we must have had it rather early because then we went on to see [Ionesco's play] *Le Roi se meurt*. And Sam came and Ionesco and we were all there and in the first interval Sam whispered to George: 'I think I'll go and meet you at the end'. So he disappeared and we all sat through this play. It wasn't very well done, to be honest, and then after we came out Sam said: 'Come on, let's all go and have a drink,' and Ionesco said: 'Ah non, je ne peux pas' ['Oh no, I can't']. So, rather sadly, we said goodbye to Ionesco and we all set off. It was Boxing Night and Sam said: 'I know a good bar,' and we went to one bar after another until they closed and we ended up about six in the morning at the Falstaff. We got there by taxi, finally, and there were all these iron bars up and I said: 'But it's shut.' Sam got out and rapped on the windows and the door opened and the *grilles* opened and it was crowded with people drinking and eating bacon and eggs. And all this evening, all the night through, the conversation had been as to whether it was possible to write a play with no action. Could you be only dramatic in words? And out of that came *Not I*. That was what he was thinking about at that time. I can't remember what date that was.

Billie Whitelaw

Billie Whitelaw (1932–). British actress known for a wide variety of stage and film parts, who worked on many occasions with Samuel Beckett, being directed by him in *Footfalls* (1976), which he wrote with Whitelaw in mind, and *Happy Days* (1979). She also acted in *Play* (1964) (when she first got to know Beckett) and played Mouth in the British première of *Not I*, directed by Anthony Page, with much help from Samuel Beckett. The photograph shows Beckett rehearsing Billie Whitelaw in *Footfalls*, Royal Court Theatre, 1976. Interview with JK.

Not I

[In *Not I*, Royal Court Theatre, London, 1973, directed by Anthony Page, assisted by Samuel Beckett, Billie Whitelaw was covered in a hood, except for her mouth, shrouded in black and placed high up in a chair on a podium. It was a very demanding role to play and one day she collapsed.]

Anthony used to say to Beckett, 'Go and talk to her next door.' He knew when I wanted to talk to Sam. Sam and I used to work in the afternoon at home – at my home. We used to go back and say it together, all the time. But he didn't know it word for word I'm delighted to say! He would sometimes make mistakes and I would say, 'No, there you are, you see,' even though he thought he did, with great moans and cries. But in fact it was the perfectly normal theatrical trauma that goes on when you're doing a difficult piece. I don't look back on the rehearsals of *Not I* and say, 'Oh my God, how dreadful', at all. It was just getting the damned thing on its feet. You have to get the damn thing right and I don't care which way. Now I would break any rule, if there are rules, to get what Sam wanted; even my back would break to get what he wanted.

My son, Matthew, was recovering from meningitis. Sometimes he developed night terrors which were quite awful and sometimes I was up all night; it was no secret. Sam's first question in the morning was, 'How's Matthew?' Always the first question: 'How's Matthew?' And he would bring little presents for Matthew. He gave him – this seven-year-old child – a Meccano set meant for a boy of thirteen and his own chess book, because Sam was a great chess-player. 'Does Matthew play chess?' And he gave him his chess book turned down at the corner. I said, 'Well I don't think he's actually as good as this.'

I'll tell you what, in my emotional memory, happened when I collapsed at rehearsal. It was nothing to do with Sam, nothing to do with *Not I*; it was to do with sensory deprivation. If you are blindfolded and have a hood over your face, you hyperventilate, you suffer from sensory deprivation. It will happen to you. And I hung on and hung on until I couldn't any longer. I just went to pieces because I was convinced I was like an astronaut tumbling out into space. And I thought I can't be tumbling out in space, but I am tumbling out in space and that's when I fell down; I couldn't go on. They lifted me down and, I think Jocelyn [Herbert, the designer] or Robbie [Hendry, the stage manager] or somebody, got me a brandy and milk and I remember Sam walked down the central aisle of the Royal Court saying, 'Oh Billie, what have I done to you, what have I done to you?' And I drank the brandy and the milk and said, 'OK, that's another barrier cracked. Back up in there, but can we have a little slit in there and a little blue light so that I know I'm here, because I can see that?' So the reason for the breakdown had

nothing to do with the play or the rehearsal, it had to do with the
pure technicality of being blindfolded, hooded, speaking at great
speed and hyperventilating.

Footfalls

[In *Footfalls*, Royal Court Theatre, London 1976, when she was
directed by Beckett, she played an isolated, tormented young
woman, a ghostly presence who paces relentlessly up and down
on the stage.]*

In *Footfalls*, there were no vast, extravagant movements: the
slightest little thing had an effect. We spent hours on the walking
up and down, and hours getting the relationship of the arm and the
hand and the bringing down of the hand from the throat and how
far this should go to the elbow. It was all very carefully done. What
is interesting is that what Beckett is doing requires far more
concentration from the actor, to add to his own enormous concentration.

When I was doing *Not I*, I felt like an athlete crashing through
barriers, but also like a musical instrument playing notes . . . In
Footfalls, I felt like a moving, musical Edvard Munch painting – one
felt like all three. And, in fact, when Beckett was directing *Footfalls*,
he was not only using me to play the notes, but I almost felt that he
did have the paint brush out and was painting, and, of course, what
he always has in the other pocket is the rubber, because as fast as he
draws a line in, he gets out that enormous india-rubber and rubs it
out until it is only faintly there.

Not so Happy Days

[In *Happy Days* at the Royal Court Theatre in London in 1979,
when Billie Whitelaw was once again directed by Beckett, she

---

* Billie Whitelaw's account of working with Beckett on the world première of *Footfalls*
is borrowed from James Knowlson's unscripted interview with her recorded on 1
February 1977 for television by David Clarke and the University of London Audio-
Visual Centre. The interview was first printed in the *Journal of Beckett Studies*, Summer
1978, no. 3, pp. 85–90.

Billie Whitelaw in *Footfalls*, Royal Court Theatre, London, 1976.

played Winnie, incarcerated in her mound of earth – up to the waist in Act I and up to the neck in Act II. Beckett changed the text after Billie Whitelaw had already learned the role and this put a great strain on their usually close relationship. Duncan Scott, who was involved with Jack Raby in lighting the production, offers an insider's view of Beckett's reactions to the controversy.]

Duncan Scott* The rehearsals for *Happy Days*, according to Sam, had been going badly from the beginning. He thought he had been pushing Billie too hard and too fast. Now she seemed unduly nervous and was complaining that she couldn't cope with what she was being asked to do. Even worse, she was accusing him of confusing her, of giving her too many notes, and of contradicting himself. 'I don't understand', he said, 'and I don't know what to do to help her.' He paused, then exclaimed incredulously, 'Me! Contradict myself!' But added, almost immediately, in an exaggerated Dublin accent, 'So I thought: keep your trap shut. Let them get on with it.' And so he went for a walk around World's End, past the Royal Hospital, as far as Thomas More's orchard, and finished up in a quiet pub in Old Church Street, intending to stay away from rehearsals altogether for a couple of days.

We went on to discuss the possible difficulties Billie was having. I told Sam that she had confided in me that she would rather be doing *Not I* again – which I found difficult to believe, in view of the terror she felt during each performance – but Sam said that he too thought *Happy Days* was the more difficult play. He attributed her nervousness to the fact that it was the first time she had appeared in a play of his that had been presented before, and that she was probably dreading the inevitable comparisons. She was said to be continually ringing up her predecessors, notably Peggy Ashcroft and Brenda Bruce, to discuss the play with them.

Now that he had been able to express his hurt, Sam seemed anxious to take the blame himself: 'I've always been aware of the imperfections of *Happy Days*, but it is only recently that I have realized how much I dislike it: particularly the first act.'

---

* Duncan Scott's memories of *Happy Days* are published for the first time with the agreement of his widow, Bernadette Scott.

Billie Whitelaw in *Happy Days*, Royal Court Theatre, London, 1979.

Billie Whitelaw   At the end with the Waltz from the *Merry Widow*, I said to Sam one day at rehearsal, 'I can't think how it goes'. So Sam sang it to me and I just copied the way he sang it from then on. His quavering, weak, reedy voice sounded so marvellous, I thought 'I'll use that'.

Eh Joe

[*Eh Joe*, filmed for television with Klaus Herm as Joe and Billie Whitelaw as the Voice in 1988.]

Billie Whitelaw   For *Eh Joe*, I went over to Paris [to rehearse Voice with Beckett] and saw Sam. We read it together. I found it unbearably moving but we read it and he kept on hitting my nose – which is neither here nor there, very sweet – and we read it through and he kept on saying as always, 'No colour, no colour' and 'slow', I mean slower than I've ever known him want me to go before, even slower than *Footfalls*: absolutely flat; absolutely on a monotone. And when he was saying it himself, he actually corrected himself, 'No, no, too much colour, too much colour', to himself, not to me. 'Like the title of a book about Samuel Beckett', I said, '*No, No, Too Much Colour!*'

Sam's chief characteristic as a director was his compassion, a general love of his fellow human beings, the feeling that he very much wants you to get it right. He will not let you go out and give a sterile performance – this is marvellously comforting. And, although he is very particular and meticulous and insists that it be right, he is the only director with whom, when he is in the theatre, I feel unafraid and safe. I wish he would be there sometimes on a first night, but I know that he never sees one of his plays in front of an audience. It might seem as if his precision and insistence on the minutest detail should totally restrict the actor; but it doesn't. It gives you a marvellous freedom, because within this meticulous framework and I suppose surrounded by this feeling of compassion and safety, there is freedom to experiment.

I think a lot of actors and a lot of people think that Beckett ties the actor up, that you are not allowed to move, that you just have to obey him. Obviously you listen to him, but within this framework, you can expand. Certainly I feel a marvellous freedom working with him. With Beckett, you can't cut corners. It is an immense privilege and good fortune to have worked with the man. But the most productive thing of all is to work within a context of love and compassion. That is the most fertile thing in the world.

THE SCHILLER-THEATER, BERLIN

Beckett with (*from left to right*) Horst Bollman, Stefan Wigger,
Klaus Herm and Walter Asmus, Schiller-Theater, Berlin, 1975.

Warten auf Godot (Waiting for Godot)

Produced at the Schlossparktheater, Berlin, September 1953, directed by Karl Heinz Stroux.

Boleslaw Barlog [Boleslaw Barlog (1906–99) was a distinguished
German theatre director, later Intendant General of the Schiller-
Theater in Berlin. He directed dozens of plays at the Schlossparkthea-
ter and the Schiller-Theater in Berlin from 1945 to 1972. Author of
Theaterlebenslänglich (1981). This and all other interviews with the
actors and directors of the Schiller-Theater are by JK, kindly assisted
by Walter Asmus or Dr Walter Georgi.] *Godot* was first played at the
Schlossparktheater and *Godot* alone would have been reason en-
ough to keep the Schlosspark open. It was a small theatre of the
Schiller, a lovely theatre with about 450 seats.*

* The Schlossparktheater: built in 1804 as the stables and garden-hall of the neigh-
bouring palace, 'Guthaus Steglitz'. In 1920–1 converted into a theatre. From 1935 to
1945 it was used as a cinema. Reconstructed in 1945 after the war and reopened on 3
November 1945. From 1950, it was operated by the city of Berlin, from 1951 as part of
the 'Staatliche Schauspielbühnen Berlin' and used as the 'Kleines Haus' [the small
house] of the Schiller-Theater.

Rosemarie Koch [Rosemarie
Koch was the Assistant Dra-
mautrg of the Schiller-Theater
for many years, advising Albert
Bessler and Boleslaw Barlog.]
We heard some rumours about
this play which was on in Paris,
so I got hold of the original
French version and read it. I
talked so warmly about the play
that Albert Bessler [the chief
dramaturg] became curious
and went to Paris to see Roger
Blin's production. Then he was
enthused. I thought it was wonderful, a great piece of literature

Boleslaw Barlog.

– but I said you can't play it on stage; it's impossible, I think. Bessler
met Elmar Tophoven in Paris. Then a rough translation came from
Tophoven to Bessler and Barlog read it. Barlog was a 'juicy'
character, a theatre man, not an intellectual. I think he read the
play but intellectually he couldn't understand very much of it. But
he was a theatre man and instinctive and he said, 'Yes, we'll do it'.
The final decision lay with Barlog. But Bessler exercised an enormous influence on Barlog from an intellectual point of view. He
was the shadow boss, as it were.

Boleslaw Barlog In the beginning I got the play to read from
Bessler. 'I would like to direct it myself', I said. 'I would make a
lovely Chaplinesque production of it.' But then Karl Heinz Stroux
came along and said, 'But I am your main director. I have the right
to do it. I must do it.' But he directed it, not, as had been done in
Paris, as a 'Chaplinade', but with German metaphysical depth.

Rosemarie Koch Barlog said, 'OK, I'll do it'. But at the same time
he saw how difficult it would be. It was not such a hard decision for
him to give it to Stroux because he felt instinctively that he was not
the man, the director, for this play. That was Barlog's strength: to
give in in difficult situations, you know, to listen to people who

could convince him, and then, instinctively, he would say, 'You are right'. And he would accept other people's opinions – because he knew where his capabilities lay, you know, and where they did not, in the end. That was his strength, I think, as a theatre leader.

It has been well documented, of course, that Beckett didn't agree very much with this first production. It was 'too German' for Sam. It was so deeply serious. Roger Blin had done more or less a clown thing with it. . . [But in Germany] some said, 'It's Nietzsche: "God is dead" '. And another said, 'No, it's Nietzsche: "God is dead", but underneath it says "God is alive" ' – you know all the Catholic newspapers and so on. There was much speculation about the nature of Godot. 'Who is Godot?' It was even attributed to the character in Balzac, 'Godeau'.*

Sam came to Berlin to see it. He came alone – with his translator, Elmar Tophoven. He was very polite but a bit confused about the production . . . irritated in fact.

Boleslaw Barlog   At the première, Sam wanted to leave. He took his coat but they brought him back again and pushed him on to the stage to bow. One could see that he was very unhappy with that kind of production, although Stroux was an excellent director. Sam felt that he didn't have the right approach to the play.

Rosemarie Koch   We expected a scandal at the time but there was no scandal. The main critics were capable of understanding the play and doing it justice. They felt that the play was important, and, even if they didn't really understand it, they said it was an important piece for the theatre to do. And, in contrast to that, there was the general opinion that . . . some people made it into a joke, but they didn't know what was going on, in spite of the production. So, it was good for the German public that jokes were directed at it in this way because the German public always wants, of course, this metaphysical approach and so they said, 'Oh no, it's not some crazy author who is playing a joke on us; it's a serious play. We have to think about it.' That production was good for the reception of the play. Otherwise, if it had been a light thing, you know, they

---

* Honoré de Balzac's *Mercadet* (also known as *Le Faiseur*), produced in 1848 and published in 1851, had a character named Monsieur Godeau, who was Mercadet's absent one-time business partner.

would have said, 'Oh no, it's just a vaudeville piece or something.' And this error helped to make the play successful. It was really courageous to do that first German production because there were many people who said, 'You are crazy to do this'. And remember the Schiller-Theater had an important position in Germany and the play spread inexorably all over the country, in all these theatres.

Boleslaw Barlog   The best Pozzo we ever had was Walter Franck in this first performance at the Schlossparktheater. A great actor. He was excellent. But there is this story in my book: a woman stood up in the audience and shouted to Herr Franck, 'You want to be a State Actor and you are playing such shit!'

Beckett as Mediator

Warten auf Godot (Waiting for Godot)

Produced again at the Schiller-Theater, Berlin, February 1965, directed by Deryk Mendel, with help from Samuel Beckett.

Klaus Herm (Lucky)

[Klaus Herm (1925–) Distinguished German stage and film actor. Born into an acting family, Herm worked extensively in Munich and Berlin theatres. He played Lucky in both the 1965 and 1975 productions of *Waiting for Godot*, directed in the second production by Beckett. He also acted in *Damals* (*That Time*) and *Spiel* (*Play*). At Süddeutscher Rundfunk, he played in television productions by Beckett of *Ghost Trio* and . . . *but the clouds* . . .]

There were great difficulties with the 1965 production of *Warten auf Godot* [*Waiting for Godot*] when Deryk Mendel was directing. Mendel simply could not explain the sense of it; he could not get the actors to work together on it. He also had difficulties telling Bernhard Minetti [who played Pozzo] what to do.* Minetti was an egomaniac, an excellent actor but very much on the edge, with a very big ego.

---

* Bernhard Minetti (1905–98), a leading German actor of stage and screen but with whom Beckett (as well as Mendel) had some problems.

Beckett did not take over. He just tried to listen, then suggested how Minetti could come down a little from his exuberant self-projection. Until his arrival, they were searching and digging to get at the deeper sense of it and Beckett said, 'But why? It's so simple. It's just a play'. This helped them very much to accept it as such – as just a play. The fact that Beckett was present helped us all so much. And it also calmed down Minetti. It went on to be a good production and they were all happy.

After the première, there was a party and Beckett also came and said, 'That was very nice – but one day maybe I would like to take over myself, and direct it myself, not today, not tomorrow, but whenever, and if you would play Lucky again that would be wonderful.'

Horst Bollmann (Vladimir)

[Horst Bollmann (1925–) Distinguished German stage, film and television actor who was directed by Beckett at the Schiller-Theater in Berlin on several occasions in *Waiting for Godot* (twice) and in *Endgame*.]

When Beckett came the sun was rising for us, everything became so clear and we were altogether very content, you know. Ohne Metaphysik . . . genau richt [No metaphysics . . . that's right]. The first night was a huge success. The press were happy. We were all happy. During the party after the première, Sam said, 'Shouldn't we do it again? I think we should do it again.'*

Beckett as Director

Endspiel (Endgame)

Produced at the Schiller-Theater, Berlin, September, 1967, directed by Samuel Beckett.

Horst Bollmann (Clov)   You have to be courageous enough to give in to Beckett's way of doing things. It's a matter of trust. He is a

---

* The play was indeed put on again at the Schiller-Theater in 1975, this time directed by Beckett, with Horst Bollmann (Estragon), Stefan Wigger (Vladimir), Klaus Herm (Lucky) and Carl Raddatz (Pozzo).

musician, preoccupied with the rhythm, the choreography, the overall shape of the production. [In this play] the sound of the steps can be used as a form of percussion, an additional instrument, adding another language to the dialogue. Every now and then Beckett would talk in particular about the silences, the long pauses. We asked him, 'What does it mean? What are we supposed to do during the pauses?' He told us, 'Act as if you are in a boat with a hole in it and water is coming in and the boat is slowly sinking. You must think of things to do; then there is a pause; then you get the feeling you have to do something else and you work at it once more and the boat goes up again.' This is a direction which any actor can understand. In *Endgame*, 'imagine that the relationship between Hamm and Clov is like flames, glowing, roaring flames and ashes. The flames are roaring, then they sink, by and by, into ashes. But beneath the ashes there is still the danger of the roaring flames flaring up again at any time. What holds your attention is that at any time they can blow hot again.'

With Ernst Schröder [who played Hamm] there were problems. There were personal things and also he had these long monologues and when Schröder did these monologues for the first time Beckett

Beckett with Ernst Schröder (Hamm) and Horst Bollmann (Clov), rehearsing *Endspiel, 1967.*

was . . . well, he didn't know what to make of them. At the beginning there were two worlds, Schröder's and Beckett's. Schröder had apparently said at one point that Beckett was not really a theatre man. The opposite is true [but] that is the way of the theatre when somebody is so dominating, domineering even, as regards his personality and Beckett was just the opposite. And, of course, Beckett was not brought up in the theatre. I remember one evening we all went to Schröder's house by the Wannsee. After the reception, Beckett said, 'Now we must go for a beer!' It was such a relief after all the formality.

Gottfried Büttner

[Dr Gottfried Büttner (1926–2002) medical doctor and author of *Absurdes Theater und Bewusstseinswandel* (Berlin, 1968) and *Samuel Beckett's Novel* Watt, Philadelphia, University of Pennsylvania Press, 1984. We are most grateful to Dr Marie-Renate Büttner for allowing us to use extracts from her husband's memoirs, in which he offers an outsider's view of a late rehearsal of *Endspiel*.]

There was a relaxed atmosphere, although there was obviously a lot of respect for Beckett. The work was wonderful. One actor said, 'It is all so friendly, but we also know exactly what we are doing in the way we could only have with somebody who was a very important figure like Beckett.'

Beckett took off his jacket, rolled up his sleeves, leaned over the table where the prompt was sitting and, with some notes in his hand, went through a series of details with the actors. To Herr Bollmann [Clov] he said, 'When you are speaking with Hamm about the word "grey", you must at the end speak so quietly that nobody hears you. Nobody must hear the word. You must whisper it.' The performance was almost perfect, almost without mistakes. Beckett was obviously very satisfied. In a very few places he stopped, corrected a false word, a position or an attitude that was not quite correct. He watched with great attention, leaning or sitting on the edge of the table. Obviously he knew the German off by heart because he noticed every little mistake and could correct people without having the text in front of him.

We were very impressed by the density of the action. The two main actors were bathed in sweat after one and three quarter hours. I asked Beckett whether Clov should not, after he had put on his travelling clothes, whether he could not give up his bent attitude and stand up a bit more upright when the curtain falls. Beckett was very strict and said, 'No, it must remain open as to whether he is going away or not.'

He didn't appear to know much of what was going on in the theatre in Berlin. He didn't seem terribly interested either. For example, he didn't even know that at that time a play by Audiberti was being performed in the Workshop of the Schiller-Theater (that is in the very same house where he was doing *Endspiel*). He didn't seem to be aware of this. He seemed simply to be doing his own work and going to rehearsals. Although one can imagine that he must have had a lot of discussions with artists and people and that took up a lot of time, he seemed to avoid as much as possible any kind of formal gathering. [This visit to a rehearsal at the Schiller-Theater took place on 11 September 1967; the first night was 26 September.]

Das letzte Band (Krapp's Last Tape)

Produced at the Schiller-Theater, Berlin, October 1969, directed by Samuel Beckett.

Martin Held (Krapp)

[Martin Held (1908–92) Famous German stage, film and television actor. His performance in *Das letzte Band* (*Krapp's Last Tape*) was recorded on film by Westdeutscher Rundfunk. This interview was conducted by Ronald Hayman, translated by Helen Watanabe, and revised by James Knowlson. It was first published in *Samuel Beckett: Krapp's Last Tape*. Theatre Workbook 1, ed. James Knowlson, London, Brutus Books Ltd, 1980. We are grateful for the publishers' kind permission to reprint it here.]

In the beginning, he seems to have felt that he had to tell me a lot of what he could remember from the first production [at the Royal Court Theatre, London, 1958] and that was, of course, not such a happy beginning, especially since Beckett was not really a director. If he had been a director, he would have translated what the earlier actor had done for me, but because he wasn't a director, he couldn't do that.

At first he was a little like some directors who are not very sure of themselves but to whom someone has said, 'Don't let the actors ride

Beckett with Martin Held, 1969.

rough-shod over you; get your own way'. This was the case for about three days of the four weeks we rehearsed and then he gave me my head a little. There were stretches when he left me a completely free hand right up to the last day. For example, the actual last tape which I recorded, he said practically nothing about that; I just did it. We'd talk in the evenings over a bottle of red wine. He'd sit there in that chair and we wouldn't by any means speak exclusively about the play. He talked a lot about James Joyce, whom he knew well, and from there we got back again to the play.

For me among the best things in our collaboration, and something I always like to do, was that he sometimes said, 'Let's save this situation up for the last few days of rehearsal. We haven't got so far yet that we can be completely clear about this'. This was a beautifully flexible way to work. I find this the ideal method of direction. He often went into detail, for example, in those glances to the rear, when Krapp is listening or he wants to switch the tape on, and he jumps and turns slowly round. He rehearsed these things exactly. They were more than just stage directions.

Beckett speaks very good German and we got on very well together right from the start, in so far as I knew immediately what he meant, for example, when he said that Death the Reaper, whom Krapp has been looking for unconsciously, is standing behind him or that, when he listens, he switches off and sinks into dreams; Krapp is eaten up by dreams. But this is without sentimentality; there is no resignation in him. It is the finish, the end. There is nothing more to say about it. All these three things are treated without sentimentality.

The encounter with Beckett gave me a lot of happiness. It belongs to those encounters in life which can help one to develop inwardly. I knew the play already and I'd seen the première ten years previously, the first performance in Germany. But I read *Krapp* only once and then put it away in order to go into rehearsal without preconceived ideas. This was all the easier for me in that, strangely enough, not very much of the previous production stuck, although I know that it was good. Beckett once said something very beautiful about this play. He said that Krapp is not a way of looking at the world (*keine Weltanschauung*), and that in fact answers everything. No, this is just Krapp, not a world-view. It is not valid for everyone.

I did something once where I was afraid I might hurt his feelings. When I have my hand on the table [and here he crooks the knuckle of one finger] – then this is Beckett. He can't move his hand. I gradually worked towards it and made it more each time. And he looked at it once and just said, 'Good'. There is an amazing amount of Beckett in Krapp. Even though he always said, 'Don't act any resignation', I still think that in him – he'd be at my throat if he heard me say this – there is resignation. For example, in that chair he once said something which shook me very much, it shook me so much that I have difficulty in repeating it – perhaps it is even very indiscreet of me – but I asked him what he was working on and, with a movement of his hand, he said, 'I have written myself out'. That is Krapp. But that doesn't have to be true, for heaven's sake. When a writer of the stature of Beckett says he has written himself out, then that can be the valley before the next peak.

Glückliche Tage (Happy Days)

Produced at the Schiller-Theater, Berlin, September 1971, directed by Beckett.

Gottfried Büttner [describes a talk that he had with Beckett in September 1971] Beckett spoke about his current work. The actress who was playing Winnie [Eva-Katharina Schultz] looked very young and had only played parts up till then in which she had really been able to let it all out as it were, but here, as Winnie, she had to hold back very much. He was very keen to get the musicality of the movement across. This is how the play had been conceived: as music and movement, very economical, conscious, clean move-ment; nothing superfluous was meant to be happening. For ex-ample, when one was putting on a pair of glasses – he demonstrated this – you only need one hand; you don't need to use two hands. Today they had the first lighting tests. The actress had needed eye drops because most of the time she is staring at this very bright light, but she is not allowed to blink. It is very demanding on her. Turning the head; the movement of the eyes; everything must be exactly studied. 'Time is too short', said Beckett. The actress was still a little bit unsure about the text. When I asked whether Madeleine Renaud, who had played the part in the French première and played it hundreds of times since, whether she was not a very good

Beckett with Eva-Katharina Schultz, 1971.

embodiment of this role, Beckett said she played very well in her way, but in a very French style. There was a lot of self-presentation going on there, whereas here in Berlin he was very keen to get the presentation of exact movement right, to focus on the musicality. Selfless presentation? In the sense of Kleist's essay on the marionette theatre. Movement must be like marionettes, objectively moved as if by a God. Beckett expressed doubt about whether the performance would come off because of the difficult circumstances. To my question as to whether he was interested in criticism, since the critics had always been very kind, or very favourable about his Berlin productions, he just made a sort of dismissive gesture, 'Oh critics! So much hot air' as if to say he didn't care about that. He said it was possible that it was important for the actors.

Eva-Katharina Schultz (Winnie) [Eva-Katharina Schultz (1922–). German stage and film actress. A regular member of the Schiller-Theater repertory company. She performed Winnie in Beckett's production of *Glückliche Tage*. Interview with JK.] I was already cast in the part when Beckett arrived, to his great surprise because I looked young. But I said to him, 'With my make-up and my wig and everything it will be OK'. It was a big problem because I was in seven [actually five] productions at the same time . . . Playing in the evening, almost every evening, and big parts. It was very difficult to cope with learning the lines as well as . . . cope with the lines and the props in *Happy Days*, at the same time. Beckett said, 'Don't worry, don't worry, it's not necessary to rehearse every day' and I didn't. I was so busy with thinking about my performances in the evening, and apart from not having time and being too busy playing elsewhere, I didn't feel that I deserved it.

Working with Beckett was not difficult because all the time he was very patient and he said from the very beginning, 'Don't ask me for any meaning in the thing; it just is what it is'.

I was very much in despair very soon with the whole thing and he said, 'OK, I'll read it for you.' He had his notebooks . . . But he was the best Winnie he ever had. When he was reading it, it was very flat, he didn't have any modulations. Yet it was so lively in a way in which I would have liked to have been capable of. During the first night I had the feeling that I had played it in a trance and it just happened. When I came back to my dressing-room afterwards, I broke down in tears because I thought it was not enough.

With colleagues at the Schiller there was a family feeling. My dominating remembrance is that all women, including myself, in that production and around us at that time had the feeling that they had to shelter him, to embrace him; they were full of love towards him. As a human being, not necessarily as a man. He was so patient and on his part there was a sort of love vibrating towards the stage, towards the actors.

Warten auf Godot (Waiting for Godot)

Produced at the Schiller-Theater's main stage, Berlin, March 1975, directed by Beckett.

Horst Bollmann (Estragon) Beckett was mostly on stage; he had a chair on stage, sitting very close to the actors, up against them and looking at their mouths, you know, when they were speaking . . . with a book. It was difficult with the English and German but we could very much rely on Tophoven's translation, of course, and once there were difficulties, let us say in the rhythm or something, he would change the translation. I remember I did not turn up to rehearsal once and Sam played the part of Estragon, word by word on stage, with all the movements and so on, and he was so shy with it, looking down at the ground all the time, you know, like a boy and looking up at Stefan [Wigger, who played Vladimir] to see what he thought of his acting.

Despite Beckett's very precise directions, there is still room for invention. Within a given situation the actor has to find a way to invent. Beckett would reinforce things, would correct things. But with him I never felt restricted, I felt free. He made you feel free in that his personality was so rich, so fully developed. He could communicate with you in a very simple way, so that you never had a complex about his being a genius and you being just anybody. I consider that my encounter with Beckett is reward enough, in itself, for having been an actor all my life.

Walter Asmus (assistant director) [Walter Asmus. Distinguished German theater director and close friend of Samuel Beckett. He worked with him on many occasions, first as assistant director on

Walter Asmus.

the 1975 Schiller-Theater *Warten auf Godot*. He later directed the play again several times for the Gate Theatre, Dublin. He is Professor of Theatre Studies in Hamburg.] In the beginning I spoke exclusively with Beckett in German. It was only later on, I think, when I went to Paris to see him, for example, that I started to speak in English with him. Certain people were quite overawed by him, you know, and I was quite shy and withdrawn. Being with the actors was different and being an assistant meant that I was not intruding. I could just be in the background and watch and listen and be there if needed. That, I think, was part of my success in doing this job. The actors were the important people for me, and for the director, of course. What can't be over-stressed was that there was an atmosphere of mutual respect and understanding, with every-body trying to make it a fine production.

Beckett knew the play by heart. He knew it line by line and he used, for example, to block it out himself and instead of explaining it, he used to show it – 'you go to here; then you say this sentence, this word; then you go on' – and so on and so forth. It would normally take him one or two years to prepare for it. That means he had to learn it, really, in German, by heart. He had to sit down and learn the lines.

Of course he was a perfectionist. He was always dissatisfied and would say, 'It's still a long way . . .', because he was a perfectionist.

He saw it as it should be, all in his mind, so clearly, and, because he did so, it was natural that at times he was uptight, impatient, and wondered whether he would ever get where he wanted to go. When he said, 'It's still a long way' it soon became a joke. He would say, 'Yes, it's very good' and someone would say, 'But it's still a long way, Sam, isn't it?' I exaggerate a little, perhaps, but that was the spirit of the thing. At times Sam tended to be – with the actors I'm not sure, but certainly with himself and with the whole situation, in his perfectionist way – an impatient man. It's normal to have an actor struggling with lines. It's a very painful, annoying process at times for a director. But, on the other hand, it's hell to learn these lines. And even the dialogue in *Godot*, you know, the little bits, the musical echoes, the little variations – the lines all have a similarity, but there's a little twist, a little difference.

At the beginning the actors are insecure with the words. Then it gets a little better, but they still need the prompter's help. Sam isn't interested in all that. Sam expects a great deal. He wants them to be word-perfect immediately and nobody can do that. But when they are word-perfect, then, at first, they try to show that they are word-perfect and that means that they just say the words. They concentrate on that and for whole stretches of time it becomes mechanical. So, it would happen, every now and again, that we would be sitting there listening to this beautiful, witty exchange, but nobody would laugh, nobody was amused because what they were doing was mechanical. It didn't have any heart. For example, the boot business, at the beginning, with one of the tramps, with his finger feeling inside it, bending down; it's a very fast thing, and when it was mechanical, it was not funny at all. But when they had finished working on it, it was. It was such an artistic thing. And in the end Sam was sitting there, as curious as a schoolboy, his eyes twinkling, and he'd say, 'That's it, that's it.' Everybody felt it. And he just stayed there like a spectator.

Underlying tensions are always there, in any production. It is the normal thing. So it was nothing specific to this Schiller production. Beckett had this feeling all the time: 'It is not enough'. It's the 'not enough' syndrome! I remember him sitting there and I was taking notes and he said, 'I know it so well' and he complained. But one needs that in this world, this striving to get there and if somebody says, 'Oh you will', you are happier. You need somebody to comfort you. And he always did. You always had to comfort him. He said all the time, 'I want to stop doing theatre.' On various occasions, he's said, 'I can't do it, Walter.' He blamed himself. Later, at the Riverside [the Riverside Studios in London],* where he was not so well prepared, it was exactly the same. He was sitting next to me during rehearsal, with people there. And he was sitting silently and I felt certain vibrations and I said, 'Sam, it will be OK. It's quite good Sam. It's coming, you know', just comforting him because I knew what was going on in his mind. He turned to me and his eyes glittered as he said, 'Walter, I *hate* this play!' Just like that. I was scared. He looked at me so wildly. But that was just the way he worked.

Let there be no misunderstanding. That had nothing to do with the Schiller, or with the actors. That was Sam Beckett's own way of getting there, and in that he was indispensable. I know so well from my own experience of the theatre that all theatre people have this as well. But at times he seemed almost to have a complex about not being a trained theatre director. He felt not in command because he was not a theatre man, because he thought there was a deficiency in him. He thought theatre people could do it in a better way because they knew how actors function. But basically they can't, or hardly any can. You always have to go this same cruel way.

Damals (That Time)

Produced at the Schiller-Theater, Berlin, October 1977, directed by Samuel Beckett.

Klaus Herm (actor) Having all the details, the information, imagining stories about these simple sentences and then, little by little, peeling it away and reducing, this seems to me an important way of working. But you can't reduce right at the beginning. Rehearsals were rather short, at the utmost, three and a half hours, but with pauses. In the pauses there was always a lot of smoking. It was like working in a mathematical or logarithmic way but all the same we never had the feeling of being corseted. Beckett always asked,

---

* This occurred when he assisted Walter Asmus with the San Quentin Drama Workshop production of *Waiting for Godot* in London in 1984.

Klaus Herm in *That Time*, 1977.

'Would you agree with that? Would you be able to do that?' He never said, 'You must do this' or 'You must do that.'

Spiel (Play) and Kommen und Gehen (Come and Go)

Spiel was produced at the Schiller-Theater, Berlin, October 1978, directed by Samuel Beckett, and *Kommen und Gehen* was directed by Walter Asmus (same location and date).

Walter Asmus (director)   Beckett gave me more or less his *Regiebuch* of *Come and Go*, something like that, and we talked about it and I made little changes in the text, I think. We rehearsed separately. He rehearsed *Play* in the morning and then afterwards I rehearsed *Come and Go*. I rehearsed *Come and Go*, of course, in my own way. He came to a few of my rehearsals. We had made plans to have a fan on the stage for the dresses in *Come and Go* to move in the wind; things like that. He suggested that at a certain point. I don't know whether it was his idea then or whether he had had it before, but in the end we dropped that for technical reasons. I remember one thing which was quite enlightening for me and very typical. We were experimenting with the three actresses, because actors always want to know 'Where do I come from? Why am I here? What is my intention? What am I going to do?' – big 'W' questions which are important in acting, and the actors' situation. So we had fantasies about these three ladies coming to meet after shopping, for example, to give them some social context. So, as they were sitting on the bench, we gave them plastic carrier bags, and we did the normal discussion. Then Sam turned up at the rehearsal. I don't think we had arranged it; he was just there. It was dark in the room with only the light of the stage. Sam was standing there in his parka and it was cold and he was watching and getting used to the light and peering around, having a close look at everything, at every detail and then he saw the plastic bags at the foot of the bench. He looked at the bags. Then he looked down at the ground. He had this way of looking, when he got tense and uptight and he looked at the bags again and you really could have cut the atmosphere with a knife. Finally I said, 'Oh Sam, don't worry, don't worry, we'll take it all away. It's just for ourselves, you know. We need this to help us do this.' And he said, 'Yes, Walter, yes Walter, I trust you.'

THE SAN QUENTIN DRAMA WORKSHOP

Rick Cluchey

Rick Cluchey (1935–), seen here in *Krapp's Last Tape*, 1977. Founder and animator of the San Quentin Drama Workshop. Formerly an inmate for many years at San Quentin prison before being released on parole and receiving a pardon. Worked with Samuel Beckett as an assistant in Berlin, he then played the roles of Krapp in *Krapp's Last Tape*, Hamm in *Endgame* and Pozzo in *Waiting for Godot*, all directed in Berlin and London by Beckett. This is a revised version of an essay in *Samuel Beckett: Krapp's Last Tape*. Theatre Workbook I, reprinted by kind permission of the publishers and Rick Cluchey.

I first began to act in Beckett's plays in 1961 while serving a life sentence at San Quentin in California. Although many other of my fellow convicts had a similar interest, as early as 1958, we were all, none the less, required to be patient and wait until the

Warden of that day decided to allow us the special sanction of an experimental workshop, where such plays might be performed. So, in 1961, with the advent of our own small theatre, we began to produce a Beckett trilogy, as the first works to emerge from this little workshop.

Thus our first effort was *Waiting for Godot*, then *Endgame* and, lastly, *Krapp's Last Tape*. In all we gave no less than seven productions of Beckett's circle of plays during a three-year period. All of the plays were acted and directed by convicts for a convict audience. And so every weekend in our little theatre at San Quentin, it was standing room only for imprisoned Americans; and rightly so, because if, as Beckett has stated, his plays are all closed systems, then so too, are prisons. I, personally, can say that San Quentin is a closed system, a very tightly closed system!

If the critics are right when they proclaim that all of Beckett's characters are drawn from his early life in Dublin – that is, the streets, bogs, ditches, dumps and madhouses – then I can only add that the most informed, knowledgeable and qualified people to portray Beckett's 'characters' would be the inmates of any prison! For here more than any other place in the world, reside the true Beckett people: the cast-offs and the loonies, the poets of the streets, and all of the 'bleeding meat' of the entire system; the real folk of our modern wasteland.

And may I say that it was of special interest to us at the time, that while all over the world audiences were puzzled and fascinated, the critics astounded by the plays of Beckett, we, the inmates of San Quentin, in fact found the situation perfectly normal. Yes, and we did understand about waiting, about waiting for nothing! Our 'affinity' with the works of Beckett has perplexed many critics, but never our audiences.

During my work with the Beckett plays at San Quentin the first role was that of Vladimir in *Godot*. I was then, and am now, struck with the simple situation of a man waiting in 'fear and trembling'. Certainly that was my own situation at the time in San Quentin prison. Yet too, I was reading Kierkegaard and we knew the old philosopher's idea of a God beyond reason. All I really knew for sure was that *Waiting for Godot* is like waiting for God. And, needless to say, in places like San Quentin, the possibilities of Him making an appearance seemed highly unlikely. In short I had no real idea who Godot might really be. However, it was never a problem, I just felt very close to the character of Vladimir and that too seemed natural and harmonious. Between 1961 and 1963, two productions of *Godot* were given and in both I was to play Vladimir.

Yes, and in my own mind I wondered about the man who could create these plays which seemed so much about my own life. I was being driven mad by my own calendar maker, the Warden and the State of California. So of necessity I took up the mask of Beckett's people: Watt and Murphy, Molloy and Malone and the Unnamable. In [Beckett's] works I was to feel secure with the characters, perhaps, in many ways because they were so like the people of San Quentin: extensions of disconnection, decay and uncertainty. 'Can it be we are not free? It might be worth looking into.' Well in the end it was Beckett and not the Warden, who gave me my freedom, a freedom of mind if not of body. Yet the passing of time, the playing of games and the telling of stories was to continue.

So, in mid-1963, I decided to re-stage *Krapp's Last Tape*. I had previously directed a production and one of my associates had directed one; so now I felt compelled to try acting Krapp. It was to be our third production in two years. San Quentin never had it so good, all that stroking of bananas before sex-hungry convicts, a Freudian tease. If Krapp, as I performed him at San Quentin, is a frustrated man, so was every convict in our audience. If Krapp seemed to reject his burden of past misery as being too heavy, so had these poor, bitter convicts! 'All the dead voices', a line from *Godot*, seems to speak of the situation Krapp is in. He is trying to redeem time, the lost time, his past time; and so were the convicts. Krapp wants to recall a girl in a punt. And the convicts' reality as audiences has never been as close to that same desire. The symbols were clear: those bananas, the girl in the punt, the lost time, the light and the dark, and the need to relive the past somehow. At San Quentin, my Krapp was in a trap; but then so was the audience.

The truth is I never had the slightest notion I would ever meet Samuel Beckett, Yet I knew the man or felt that I did. When eventually I was to realize my parole, I decided to come to Europe and, quite by chance, met Beckett in Paris. It was the beginning of a long and lasting friendship; one which in due course would bring me into greater artistic contact with Beckett the director. The road from San Quentin to Paris was a long hard one for me, but the rewards have never been more worthwhile.

In December of 1974, the San Quentin Drama Workshop gave a special performance of *Endgame* in Beckett's honour at the American Cultural Centre in Paris. Again quite by chance, I was able to be invited to Berlin to direct a play at the Forum Theater; and as fate would have it, permitted to work with Beckett at the Schiller-Theater on his own production of *Godot*, during January, February and the first week of March of 1975. Beckett, as a director, inspires awe. He is so much his own master, completely in control of his stage, knowing each step of the way exactly where it is he is going. He seems in command of a special art form; one must observe his work with actors in order to realize how simply he unlocks the difficult problems inherent to the staging of his plays.

Beckett with members of the San Quentin Drama Workshop, 1984.
Back row: Walter Asmus; John Jenkins; *seated, middle row:* Bud Thorpe; Samuel Beckett; Rick Cluchey; Lawrence Held; *seated on floor:* J. Pat Miller; Louis Beckett Cluchey.

Theatre legends abound with warnings to the writer who would attempt the direction of his own plays. Yet with Beckett these admonitions are meaningless. However, I agree that it is a rare occasion when one finds an author who can place his work before the public in its most dramatic context, and Beckett is that man. In the hands of other directors, his work appears untidy, flat, too realistic and unpoetic. With actors other problems are manifest; perhaps it is mainly the fault of a lack of understanding of Beckett's special form, which has caused his work in other hands to seem so ponderous upon the stage. Perhaps it has been this lack of understanding more than anything else, which seems to have so maligned Beckett's theatre plays. Certainly the critics would agree now that these plays which in years past have caused controversy and hard criticism, have become more recognizable and fluent to the public. Maybe we had to catch up with Beckett? I believe Beckett rightly knows his own work and in this he is unique. But then so are the characters of his drama unique in all of modern literature.

His Schiller-Theater production of *Godot* set standards for all other productions, many of which are now being produced in other parts of the world by people who came to Berlin to discover how Beckett did it. His *Godot* succeeded finely because it was Beckett the artist in full control of his canvas. The shape and style of his *Godot*, with its musicality and mime, the beauty of tone and sound, its movement and silent landscape merging, flowing richly, gracefully like the form of a fine mobile at play in the wind.

I know of no other dramatist who could do this with his own work on the stage. Following the Schiller production, I went to Paris to observe Beckett's work-in-progress with a young French actor, [Pierre] Chabert, who was then doing Krapp. But after some days in Paris my good fortune ran out and I was forced to return to the USA. I vowed, however, some day to do the role of Krapp again. [And he did – on many subsequent occasions.]

Alan Mandell

Alan Mandell (1927–) has worked as a producer, director, actor and manager on and off Broadway and throughout California and Europe. He was general manager for the San Francisco Actor's Workshop and for the Repertory Theatre of the Lincoln Center, for whom he also acted and directed. He co-founded and toured with the San Quentin Drama Workshop, performing in *Waiting for Godot* and *Endgame* directed by Beckett. He also performed in Beckett's *Stirrings Still* and starred in the English-language première of *Company*. He has appeared in numerous films and television series and is the recipient of many awards for his work. Contribution written especially for this volume.

Meeting Beckett reduced me to silence. My first experience of working with him was in 1980 with the San Quentin Drama Workshop production of *Endgame*, in which I played the part of Nagg. Although clearly in awe of him, he quickly put me at ease by telling me that we were colleagues and I was to call him Sam rather than Mr Beckett. During our rehearsals of *Endgame*, I was fascinated by Beckett's description of actions in musical terms. As a director, he seemed to conduct with both his hands raised like wings at about chest level, and to signify the end to a pause or silence, he would raise the ring finger and the pinky on either hand. These for him were the equivalent of musical dynamics – a pause was a beat; a silence was a rest.

Beckett described *Endgame* to me as a chamber piece in eight movements and when I took over from Greg Mosher, who had been carrying the book and keeping Beckett's notes, I began marking the script as Sam had indicated with eight distinct movements. I also incorporated his directorial comments. In the opening of *Endgame*, Clov says, 'Finished, it's finished, nearly finished, it must be nearly finished.' Beckett asked for these lines to be done *legato*, slowly. Rick Cluchey played Hamm. Beckett asked that he pronounce the word 'wonderfully' in four distinct syllables, which took Rick quite some time to perfect to Beckett's satisfaction.

I recall asking him if he could tell me something about Nagg's character, who he was and what had brought him to his current situation, on his stumps in an ashcan. Beckett stared at me intensely and with a long sweep of his hand said, 'He's greeeyy!' It wasn't the response I was expecting, but I jumped back into my ashcan thinking 'Grey'. Later, when Beckett asked me to work with Tere [Teresita Garcia] Sauro, who was playing Nell, I asked him if he could tell me something about Nell's character. After a pause he said, 'She's not there.'

Beckett was a tireless editor, making many cuts and changes in the text during the rehearsal period. 'There's too much text,' he would say with irritation in his voice, and then he would make a cut. It had to do with the way a line scanned, so that a change in a line, though minor to the actor, was major to the playwright. For example, Nagg's line, 'Your sand then. It's not important', was changed to, 'It isn't important'. With Nell's response, 'It is important', it created a better rhythm and, also made the moment clearer.* He would stop an actor who said 'it is' when the text read 'it's'. He never needed to consult the text; he knew precisely what he had written.

At the end of the rehearsal period we gave a party at our London

---

* The changes made by Beckett are recorded in *The Theatrical Notebooks of Samuel Beckett*, vol. II, *Endgame*, ed. S. E. Gontarski, London, Faber and Faber, and New York, Grove Atlantic, 1992.

flat. I asked Sam what he thought it would be like when we opened in Dublin at the Abbey Theatre. He told me he wouldn't be going, which quite surprised me. 'But we'll need you there when we mount the production', I said. 'No', he replied, 'you'll be fine, just make a tape of your performance and send it to me. I'll know just how it's going.' I asked him why he wasn't coming to Dublin with us and, in his wonderfully musical Irish voice with a slight lisp, he said, 'They'd eat me up alive.' After I'd been in Dublin for a couple of weeks I understood what he meant, for Dublin was a small town where everyone seemed to know everyone's business, and presumably he preferred more privacy. When I asked what he was going to do now that the play was over, he said he was going back to France, to a 'shack' he had in a place called Ussy, where he would write. Apparently, he had not been writing for some time. I said I thought it was wonderful that he'd begin writing again and he said, 'No, no, it's very painful, very difficult.' 'Why?' I asked. 'Because it gets harder and harder to write a line that's honest.' His response had such an impact on me that I found myself unable to write to him for almost a year, questioning the honesty of the words I put on paper.

Long before meeting Beckett, I had played Lucky in *Godot*, Krapp in *Krapp's Last Tape* and Nagg in *Endgame*. In 1957, I had arranged for the San Francisco Actor's Workshop production of *Waiting for Godot* to be presented at San Quentin Prison directed by Herbert Blau, who had introduced me and many others to the work of Beckett. But much later, when returning from Spain where I had been performing *Stirrings Still* and *Company*, Beckett and I arranged to meet for a coffee and a chat at Le Petit Café, along with Pierre Chabert and two others whom I can't recall. Someone suggested I see the new all-star production of *Waiting for Godot* at the theatre in Montmartre and, since I had one more day in Paris, I said I would go the next day and get a ticket. Someone said that would be impossible as the show was booked solid. I remarked that perhaps for a single ticket I might be able to get in, and that I would go and wait in line, to which Beckett said, 'Alan, do you have a card, a business card?' I took out an old business card, on which he wrote, 'Une place, s'il vous plaît, pour mon ami. Merci', and signed his name, with the date 9/05/85. 'Show them that,' he said. 'Maybe it will help.' The next day I went to the theatre early. There was already a very long line of people waiting for cancellations, but when I showed the rude box-office person my card, he cried 'O, mon dieu!' and I was told to wait. After a few minutes I was presented with a seat, fifth row centre, although what I really wanted more than I wanted the ticket to the play was my business card back with Sam's note on it.

His many kindnesses and his generosity to me, to members of my family and to so many others will always have a special place in my heart, in my thoughts.

Lawrence Held

Lawrence Held (1948–), seen here as Estragon. Australian writer and former actor with the San Quentin Drama Workshop. The son of a Russian-Polish father and an Australian mother, he was born in India and raised in Australia. He acted Nagg in *Endgame* and Estragon in *Waiting for Godot*, when he was directed by Samuel Beckett. Contribution written especially for this volume.

My first image of Beckett, the one that has stayed with me most clearly over the years, is of a tall, angular, somewhat mysterious figure who had the ability to appear and disappear at will: both before and after rehearsals and meetings at that large, very un-Beckett-like American hotel near his apartment in Paris. [The PLM Hôtel Saint-Jacques.] The fact that he was not particularly tall and was made of flesh and blood has in no way diminished my sense, in the intervening years, of his loftiness and ethereality.

I first met Sam the day after a performance of *Endgame* at the American Cultural Centre in Paris in the early 1970s. I had recently joined the San Quentin Drama Workshop and the one and only performance of *Endgame* was presented 'for and in honour of' Beckett. Needless to say he didn't turn up, but instead sent his niece.

(If he doesn't – or didn't – have a niece, then it is my memory that is at fault, but as far as I can recall someone with access to Beckett was sent to see the performance and reported back favourably on it.) The following day he turned up at our hotel with a present for Louis Cluchey, the workshop director's son, and an invitation to Rick Cluchey to join him in Berlin for rehearsals of *Godot* at the Schiller-Theater.

It was not until the late '70s that I actually got to work with Sam on a San Quentin Drama Workshop production of *Endgame* at the St Matthäus church in (West) Berlin, which he graciously agreed to 'clean up' for the *Festwochen* theatre festival. Before starting on the renovation, he asked us to perform it for him. I was playing the part of Nagg, the irascible old man in the barrel. All of us I think were a little nervous, but because I had been sealed in my barrel prior to my first 'entrance' I had been denied the surreality of the situation. On emerging, I looked out to see the wraith-like figure of Sam sitting alone in the middle of the church, his head tilted a little to one side, as if in deep contemplation. I did my best to entertain him with the tailor's speech while he sat perfectly still, in that same contemplative pose. It is another very powerful image I have of him: his remarkable aptitude for stillness.

After the performance he suggested a few areas of concern, adding (in that barely audible, gentle, Irish-accented voice of his, but – as I recall – with a twinkle in his eye), 'Otherwise I'm afraid your run will be dull, flat and unprofitable.' He knew, I think, that we relied upon the box office to pay our way, and that therefore an unprofitable run would be as unappealing as bad reviews. In the event, the reviews were excellent and the houses full. The vision of Sam sitting trance-like in the church as I hurled the tailor's speech at him was only equalled by the droves of serious young Berliners who sat in the church night after night with the scripts of the play in their hands in which they followed every word being said on stage.

What I hadn't realized during the course of the rehearsals (I was an unworldly young man, recently out of drama school) was Beckett's intense dislike of discussing his work. This being the case I asked him what *Endgame* was about. (I should mention that a world championship chess tournament was at that time underway, and it was not until later that I discovered that Sam used to return to his atelier at the Akademie der Künste every evening and replay the moves from that day which were included in the newspaper.) Beckett looked pained for a moment, then said, 'Well, it's like the last game between Karpov and Korchnoi. After the third move both knew that neither could win, but they kept on playing.' I was satisfied, and went away feeling that I had uncovered a secret – that a secret had been shared with me! – that was beyond the ken of most other mortals. Later, on the way to Sam's atelier in Rick Cluchey's old Mercedes, I asked him what he most liked about Berlin. I had heard that he felt drawn to the city, which I also had come to like very much. Once again there was a pause. 'I like the spaces between the houses', he said. I had never particularly noticed the spaces between the houses, but now I started to see them as just as much a part of the city as the architecture. It also occurred to me then that Sam's liking of the spaces between the houses said something about his writing: the spaces he allows between the bits of dialogue, the spaces between the bits of the set, even the spaces between the characters (also the characters and the set, the characters and the audience), which are as much a part of the characters as their own corporeal existence.

Skip to 1984. Some friends and I in Australia put together a production of *Waiting for Godot* to be directed first by Walter Asmus in Chicago and then by Beckett in London. During discussions at that same very un-Beckett-like hotel in Paris between Sam, Rick Cluchey and myself, Sam begins recounting a story told to him by a friend. The punchline of the story relates to an American academic saying of Beckett, 'He doesn't give a fuck about people. He's an artist.' At this point Beckett raised his voice above the clatter of afternoon tea and shouted. 'But I *do* give a fuck about people! I *do* give a fuck!'

Skip to rehearsals for *Godot* at the Riverside Studios. I am sitting by the Thames, thinking about my part (Estragon). Sam appears mysteriously out of nowhere. 'Hi Sam', I say, 'what are you doing?' 'Watching the mud and the gulls', he replies; then – he disappears! Perhaps it was simply that I had returned to my ruminations. I am sure it was that. How else can I explain it?

Sam as a director. It is not news that he was different. This, also, I think, is why he had Walter Asmus begin the work. Walter understood what he wanted on stage. This was not method acting, not Stanislavski: when the characters (if they could be called characters) left the stage, they left the stage. They went nowhere but backstage. They ceased to exist. Later they came back on and began to exist again. Both Sam and Walter, I think, liked the fact that we understood this. Perhaps it was simply laziness: it is relaxing to be off-stage and not have to worry about whether you've gone to a shop for a packet of cigarettes or to your mother's funeral. The acting is at times more vaudevillian, certainly less cerebral. It is also more precise. During one of the rehearsals of *Godot* at the Riverside Studios, Sam took Bud Thorpe (who was playing Vladimir) and myself aside and said, 'When the moon rises at the end of the first act, I want you to talk with the tone of moonlight in your voices.' We knew exactly what he meant.

Bud Thorpe

Bud Thorpe (1951–), seen here as Vladimir, acted with the San Quentin Drama Workshop and was directed several times by Samuel Beckett, twice in *Endgame*, then in *Waiting for Godot*. He was also lighting designer for the San Quentin productions of *Krapp's Last Tape* and *Waiting for Godot*, and stage and lighting designer for *Endgame*. Interview with JK.

The first time I ever met Sam Beckett was with Rick [Cluchey] and Rick's boy, Louis, who was, what, two or three: still in his arms. We were going to meet Sam after a show at the Schiller-Theater. I don't know what was playing, I couldn't tell you, but Sam was working at the Werkstatt. Off we went, and as we walked down one of the side-streets near the back entrance, all of a sudden we saw this figure come out of the stage door. Sam was always at places at specific moments; I was aghast that he would walk in as the bells were chiming six, and he was supposed to be there at six. He goes under a pool of light and lights up a cheroot. All you can see is the shadow of a man with his hands as he lights up a cheroot, and, as we walk up, Rick goes, 'Sam', and all of a sudden Sam says to Rick, 'Louis'. Sam picks up Louis, and Louis starts to comb Sam's hair. I was introduced to Sam: it was very short. He did not know who I was.

[Because of his growing friendship with Cluchey, Beckett then agreed to help the San Quentin group with the production of *Endgame* in the St Matthäus Kirche in Berlin. Thorpe recounts first his experiences playing the part of Clov and then the advice that Beckett gave him at rehearsals.]

In the beginning, it took a little bit of time to realize that he was not going to be Elia Kazan! He was not going to be one of those directors who would give you a lot. But I was very surprised at how much he wanted to participate as an actor in the production. He would go up on this little podium area, a little raised area more accustomed to a grand piano concert than to a production. So he would go up there and say, 'Bud, now, it's the attitude, it's the attitude'. He'd sort of take his hand, and, say, 'move aside'. We got that quickly enough. And he would do it. He would sit there and go: 'Is it not time for my painkiller?', doing it in an Irish accent. 'That's not enough for ya?'; never 'you', never 'not enough for you' but 'that's not enough for ya'. You saw, even before he really directed it in 1980 that the cadences were Irish, and they connected better with Irishness to them. So, he would go up there and say, 'Bud, Bud, don't lose the attitude. He [Clov] is a dog; he is a beaten dog. He has his place: the wall, the kitchen, his light. That's his haven.' Mainly he was going for attitude, and he said, 'You are subservient to Hamm, but you can retaliate.'

[When he was directing in a regular theatre,] Beckett loved to go on little adventures in the theatre, especially up in the catwalks and in the basement and things: he was fascinated I think because he was an author, not a craftsman and a theatre person. But he was absolutely enamoured over the technical things.

[Thorpe then speaks of his experiences with Beckett directing the San Quentin Group in *Endgame* at the Riverside Studios in London in May 1980.] He was actually moving his hand up and down to the beat of the poetry. It was a symphony he was conducting. It was all rhythm and music and he said to us that because we had done *Godot*: 'Now I am going to fill my silences with sounds' and 'For every silence there will be sounds, be they the shuffling of feet, steps, the dropping of things.' Beckett would walk the steps for you, and then check, just because he was a bit shorter, no more than an inch shorter, but his steps were shorter than mine, and then we would measure steps. Incredibly mathematical: now he's hitting things that I never thought of as a young craft actor before. He was making a ballet out of it, and he said, 'If you follow the mathematics, if you follow the sounds, if you follow the repetition of sounds, if you then put the repetition of sounds with your feet to the repetition of sounds that you make, then put them all together, you are then going to have' – and he didn't use the term 'building blocks' but I do – 'you will have building blocks of sounds that surround the words.'

At an early rehearsal, Alan [Mandell, playing the part of Nagg] comes in; Teri [who was to play Nell] is late. So Beckett said 'I'll play Nell.' So, there he sat next to Alan and, again, it was almost the Clov character. He put his head to the left shoulder, and sat there, and put his hands up, as though they were on the edge of the bin, and he said: 'Nell is a whisper of life. Just a whisper of life.' And so he sat there, and both he and Alan mimed that they had their hands on the edge of the barrel, and Sam did not move. He went through this whole thing. I was standing there, with my hands on the top of my head, watching Alan and Sam, because Sam *was* Nell. Put a wig on him, and he would have driven . . . The two of them combined were the best, the best. Oh boy, it was just . . . it was frighteningly beautiful, and both of them without a script. Extraordinary. Sam lisped a little bit, so he had the little 'yeth' [Nell's repeated 'yes'], and it sounded like 'y-e-t-h'. And he had this lilting whisper about him, just being on the brink of life and death.

I caught on very easily and very quickly over the fact that there are musical tones and canters to what we're doing in this. You don't have to play-act, but you do have to find it from the inside. And he kept on saying, 'Tone, tone, tone, we have to hit the right tone'. And we also learnt about mirroring, fore-shadowing, re-shadowing, and doing mirror-images of what we had done earlier. He just said, 'we want a mirror-image of what you had done earlier. We want you in the same place, the exact same position, the exact same amount of time.' I use the term 'ghosting', that is if something happens and Clov has to take five steps, and Hamm is sitting there, then we try to do the exact same thing, not once, but two and three times during the course of the play.

There were all of these people who did it before us. We did it, when, quote, 'Sam was an old man', and things had changed, and his philosophy towards the theatre, his way of looking at the productions had changed, etc., etc. And to this day, too, recognition will never be there because of the stigma of the San Quentin Drama Workshop. We had done it after the initial performances had been done years ago, in the 'fifties and the 'sixties, and we will – and I will take this to my grave – we will always be considered third-class citizens because it was . . . Sam in his ageing years had decided to help this group, because of love . . . And because of love, we were hated.

7

Memories of Beckett in London and Berlin

Beckett in Berlin.

Biography

From the late 1950s Beckett used to come over to London fairly regularly to attend rehearsals of his plays, especially when they were being put on for the very first time. In Berlin, as we saw earlier, he started to direct his own productions at the Schiller-Theater from 1967 onwards. Later in the 1970s he also directed a few plays at the Royal Court Theatre, London, in addition to advising the directors, Anthony Page or Donald McWhinnie, on others. In London, with so many friends and family eager to see him, his social life often became incredibly hectic. In Berlin, where he stayed quietly at the Akademie der Künste, it was still busy but less pressured.

One of his characteristics was to take a keen interest in the technical side of a production and he became friendly with some of the crew, often going for drinks with them after rehearsals. One technician involved in lighting the plays at the Royal Court Theatre was Duncan Scott, who set down his memories of Beckett in London. For Berlin, we have assembled a collage of the memories of some of those who spent time with him there.

LONDON

Duncan Scott

Duncan Scott (1940–2000). Lighting engineer at the Royal Court Theatre, London. He became very friendly with Beckett during the productions at the Court of *Footfalls, Endgame* and *Play* (1976) and *Happy Days* (1979). He was the board operator for the lights on *Not I* (1973) and operated the interrogating light in *Play*.

Duncan Scott*   After a rehearsal of *Endgame* with the San Quentin Drama Workshop at Riverside Studios, Sam is asked, why only two yawns in this production, whereas previously there were three? He shrugs: it is not important. *La literata* however, insists that an explanation is crucial to her understanding. (Of what?) With his usual courtesy, Sam offers her one. Then he confides to me, *sotto voce*, 'Maybe it was for fear of inducing another in the audience.'

---

* These notes were made at the request of James Knowlson when he was writing his biography of Beckett. Only two anecdotes, however, were used there. See *Damned to Fame*, p. 627. These are omitted from this collection of revealing notes, which is published for the first time with the agreement of Duncan's widow, Bernadette Scott.

But [Scott adds later] it is easy to scoff at the interest shown in the question of the yawns in *Endgame*, but it would be a mistake to do so. Beckett always had a good reason for the changes he made, however slight. In the case of the yawns, I think that he had indeed seen that, in performance, three could produce tedium, while two were sufficient to express it. His aside was not then entirely a joke. His attention to every detail of a performance is well attested to: lighting, sound, movement, the text in all its aspects, props and scenery, make-up, eye movements, breathing and silences. Whatever else I may not have listed too. Nothing was left to chance, the whim of the moment, or the discretion of the performer. Though this is not to say that suggestions from the performers, or anyone else, did not receive his consideration: they did, and he welcomed them. That this method of working produced creative masterpieces, no one can deny.

We spoke of Schönberg, Berg, Bartók and Wagner. He said he did not like Wagner in general, only *Tristan und Isolde*. When I suggested that *Parsifal* was Wagner's definitive statement, he showed interest, but said he didn't know the music. He had been very upset by Patrice Chéreau's design for *Lulu* in Paris. He said he couldn't understand how Boulez could 'let somebody fuck such an opera about' except that Boulez and Chéreau were 'cronies'. A water-closet on the set particularly upset him. He called it a 'Lulu loo'.

Music was a constant topic in our conversations. He once said that if he had been unable to be a writer, then he would have become a composer: if not a composer, then nothing. And there is no doubt that he treated words musically when composing his sentences, and directed his plays as if they were musical compositions. I witnessed a striking confirmation of this during the San Quentin Drama Workshop rehearsals at the Riverside Studios. The rehearsals were in an advanced state and were proceeding with little or no interruption from Beckett, who was standing in the auditorium, half-turned towards the prompt side, checking the speed of delivery, the timing, the duration of the pauses, and so on. As he did this, he mimed the words, and during silences, he could be seen measuring beats. What was remarkable, was that, although the actors could only see the back of Beckett's head, and he did not once look at the stage, the synchronization of the words and Sam's lip movements was so precise, there was no perceptible difference between them.

I think it is worth noting that, at Riverside, Beckett was reproducing the performance he had wrested from Patrick Magee [who played Hamm] at the Royal Court a few years earlier, though Beckett's actors were not automata working to a rigid, pre-arranged programme. As a fine conductor enables his orchestra to realize its full potential, so Beckett led the interpreters of his scripts to ever more masterly expressions of his intent.

He suffers from excruciatingly painful cramp in the legs at night. He had to get up and stomp around the room. Even so, the circulation takes a long time to return. He sighs wryly: 'Incontinence! Tunnel vision! Dodgy lung! If I had control of my body, I'd throw it out of the window.'

'*Look at the world, then look at my trousers!*' [from Nagg's 'the tailor and his pair of trousers' story from *Endgame*.] We talked of Giscard d'Estaing's 'little problem' with the Emperor Bokassa [i.e. gifts from Jean-Bédel Bokassa, the military ruler of the Central African Republic from 1966 to 1979, to d'Estaing] and I told him about the French-made documentary, *Amin Speaking*. From this we went on to the state of the world in general and he said he would have preferred to have lived in the eighteenth century. I muttered something about 'distance lending enchantment' and, by way of apology, quoted a journalist in The *Guardian*, who argued that young people watching television and reading newspapers 'might get the impression that the world was a violent place'. 'Whereas . . .!' said Sam, with a smile.

Would he mind telling me, I asked, where he found those arcane words he used, such as 'cang'? Of course not. He got them from his extensive reading, and when he came across a word that appealed to him particularly he would jot it down in a notebook. 'To use such words in one's writing is a fault of youth', he said. 'Nowadays I strive for the complete opposite.'

'Ah, yes!' I replied. 'Look what you have achieved with "ping". '

'From "cang" to "ping"', he said.

'It's like the game where you have to change one word into another by successive alterations of one letter, each time making a new word. "Cang" to "ping" in three throws.'

'Throes!' he cried. 'There's another good word.'

He wondered if I had ever detected the influence of Burton's *Anatomy of Melancholy* in his own works.

A quotation from Mallarmé he liked to cite: 'Le vide papier que la blancheur défend' [from Mallarmé's poem 'Brise marine']. 'It is that "blancheur" that I wish to attack. I can't wait to get back to the blank paper.'

Foolishly, I thought it would be an abuse of his friendship to ask about his work, but once I asked him if, while writing *Watt* [written 'for company' in the village of Roussillon d'Apt, in the South of France, after fleeing from the Gestapo] he had made himself laugh. He at once became extremely animated and with that hair-sticking-on-end look, and ultra-penetrating gaze, confessed that sometimes he had. He was keen to know which parts of it I had found particularly funny and hardly allowed me to finish describing the effect on me of the complex feeding arrangements of the famished dog before crying, 'Yes, but what about the family that owned the dog?' and then it was: 'What about this bit?' 'What about that bit?' with such enthusiasm that I wished I had asked him before.

[A propos of his prose text *Company*] 'It begins with a happy sentence' – pause for twinkling smile – 'Birth was the death of me.'* How's that for a beginning! The situation is a man, lying in a room, in the dark, he has no past and no future, and there is a voice suggesting various pasts to him. One of the questions is, is it his own voice? Or that of someone else? If it is that of someone else, is he in the same room or not? And so on. Of course, there's a lot more to it than that. Very complicated. 'I wrote about ten thousand words, then gave it up. It became bad company. I got out of me depth. Maybe I'll go back to it sometime. I can't finish anything these days. Perhaps I'll send it to the publishers unfinished, as I have with all the other stuff.'

[On speechlessness] A résumé of what Sam said: The ideas of speech arising from speechlessness and old age, or the imminence of death providing a kind of mental clarity whereby the definitive speech could be made at last, were inextricably intertwined. The

---

* This 'happy sentence' then became the opening line of a short play, *A Piece of Monologue*.

child on the threshold of speech, i.e. leaving his state of literal speechlessness for another state of figurative speechlessness, was compared to the man in his second childhood, i.e. himself, at the boundary he must pass beyond to gain the real escape from speechlessness before dying – that is to say, entering an eternal state of total speechlessness.

He fervently disagreed with Wittgenstein: 'Wovon man nicht sprechen kann, darüber muss man schweigen.' [When you can say nothing, then you must stay silent.] 'That's the whole point,' he said, 'We must speak about it.' He told me that one evening he had had dinner with Jocelyn [Herbert], and on the following day learnt from the newspaper that, on the day prior to their engagement, Jocelyn's sister had been found drowned in the Thames. Not once had Jocelyn made reference to this tragedy, and when he later questioned her about this omission, she replied simply: 'What was there to say?'

All examples of definitive statements were taken from music. The 'Vier letzte Lieder' of Richard Strauss, for instance. In some cases, he said, the imminence of death without the concomitant of dying was quite sufficient to produce it, as witness Schubert, who died at the age of thirty-two.

Once, during the rehearsal period of *Happy Days*, Sam asked me if there were somewhere we could go for a drink after the rehearsal at three o'clock. I suggested that we go to The Lindsay Club in Kensington Church Street, of which I was a member. The club was managed and staffed by three elderly ladies, one of whom had extensive experience working in films as an extra. Many of its members were also from the theatrical profession. Guests were required by law to sign the visitors' book, but did not have to provide proof of identity. It was not until the receptionist handed Sam the massively heavy book to sign that I realized that I had forgotten to suggest he adopt a pseudonym. Sam didn't hesitate however, but, unable to hold the register high enough to see properly, wrote at arm's length, in large, capital letters: SAMUEL BECKETT. The lady studied the signature closely, then, impassively, waved us inside.

Once downstairs, Sam took a seat while I went to the bar to order the drinks. It was the film extra's turn of duty behind the bar. She turned a deaf ear to my request. She stared at me, and then she stared at Sam. Her stare went to and fro, increasing in intensity and lingering longer and longer on Sam. Finally she snapped: 'Which one of you is the member?'

When we were leaving Sam said warmly, 'I like this place. Can we come here again?'

BERLIN

Ruby Cohn He stayed in Berlin in a two-storey room at the Akademie der Künste with the living area downstairs and bedroom and bath upstairs. It was very spartan – which is what he liked. There was a big writing table in front of a bay window and the bay window looked out on the woods, which he loved. He had binoculars and he would look at squirrels and birds. There was also a small end-table at the side of a sofa. In the winter it was incredibly cold there. He complained about it and I said to him, 'Why don't you go to a hotel?' But he wouldn't and I pleaded with him to be careful, many times, because it was so icy on the streets and so on. I was afraid he would fall.

Gottfried Büttner The first time Marie Renate and I visited Beckett in the Akademie was one evening in 1967. He was waiting for us, wearing his brown artist's suit with two polo necks on top of each other, one over the other, because it was unpleasantly cool in his modern, rather barely furnished atelier. Up on the third floor we noticed the view out on the tops of trees, dark green, the daylight having disappeared; it was grey as in *Endspiel* [*Endgame*].

We visited him there again in February 1975. The porter had

Beckett with Gottfried Büttner, in Berlin
at the Akademie der Künste.

said, as we came in at four o'clock, that Beckett was not there and they didn't know where he had gone. No answer on the 'phone. As we had arranged to meet between four and five, we waited for an hour, then I asked if I could go upstairs. There was Beckett sitting and waiting for us. The telephone had rung but by the time he got to the 'phone it had stopped ringing (in the room there is a staircase with twenty steps). The telephone is upstairs and the desk and a small writing table (everything made simply out of wood and to be folded together) are downstairs in the atelier area. During the conversation, the 'phone went twice, Beckett jumped up on both occasions and ran upstairs hanging on to the handrail all the time, which looked very funny but of course was necessary because of his poor eyesight. 'Quite a sporting achievement!' he commented, and smiled.

Beckett and the Cleaning Lady

Walter Asmus   Maria Wimmer, the actress, interviewed Beckett's cleaning lady at the Akademie der Künste and the headline was 'What Beckett's cleaning lady told me at the Akademie der Künste'! When he first came there, Beckett was always very serious and silent and he didn't talk to anybody and Miss Pietz, the cleaning lady, said [to Maria Wimmer], 'He doesn't talk to anybody, you must be careful. One day I cleaned his atelier and he came up to me and I said to him, "Now listen, Mr Beckett, do you believe in God?" "No," he said. "But you have a soul?" "No," he said. "But, when you're dead, what then? What's going to happen then?" "Nothing," he said. "That's not true", said I, "but you have a soul, you are a good human being." "I am not good," he said, "I wear a mask." "No, no, you are such a fine man, but so serious. And all your plays," I said to him, "why do you write all these gruesome plays? Men and daft things?" "*Ja*, that's my most vicious play." But, after all, he is such a fine man. When my mother was still alive, she was very old then, about eighty and ill, then he brought a bottle of wine for me every Saturday to give to her, or he always brought me something to give to her. And I talked to him about my mother and said, "But I have another mother, a second mother, the Virgin Mary. I always light a candle for her." And I talked to him about my parrot, about my dog and at that time I also had a canary, you know, and he always enquired about him. And when he came the next time my mother had died. One day he brought a beautiful bunch of flowers and he gave it to me and I said that I would put it by the picture of the Virgin Mary and the picture of my mother, next to it, and in church light three candles, one for the Holy Lady, one for my mother and one for him because he was ill. He was sick with toothache and bronchitis and he wasn't well at all. And he looked at me very seriously and said, "I hope it helps." And then he had to leave and I asked, "When do you return?" "I don't return", he said, "I don't want to return". After he had left and I cleaned his room, I found a cigar box on the window seat behind the curtain. It was very heavy and I opened it and there were lots of 10-*pfennig* pieces in it and a sheet of paper on top of it on which was written, "For the Mother of God and the other mother".'

Art, Music and Chess

Ruby Cohn   He knew what was in every gallery in Berlin. He made me go and see the Caspar David Friedrich [*Two Men Observing the Moon*] which he told me was the origin of *Waiting for Godot* and I'd never heard of it. And I always send a postcard – he and I would send a joint postcard to Kay [the novelist, Kay Boyle] – and I remember once getting a Manet vase of flowers and he said, 'Ah, yes' and told me which room it was in!

Gottfried Büttner   I asked about his favourite composer. 'Haydn at the moment', he said. And Bach? No. He is too violent, too large for him. Wagner? No, that seemed even more impossible to Beckett – too pompous. And which modern composers? To my great pleasure he immediately said, 'Webern' (Anton von Webern), which I found matched exactly my own sort of comparison between Beckett's work and the music of Webern.

Boleslaw Barlog   Sam loved chamber music, and he listened to music here [in Barlog's house] – he was sitting here and there is my gramophone and we used to play records together after dinner: Beethoven and Schubert quartets, which he loved. He came to this house many times. He always came when he was in Berlin for his plays . . . I wanted to invite him to concerts, but he said no; he didn't want to go out when he was at the Akademie. We wanted to invite him to hear Fischer-Dieskau, since he loved Fischer-Dieskau so much.

My relationship with Beckett was that of friendship – from my side great warmth. We were able to laugh about the same things and that is very important.

Horst Bollmann   He came to our house, too. He admired the pictures we had, but, in order to see them, he had to go right up close to the paintings [on account of the cataracts on his eyes in the late 1960s]. I know he was well acquainted with painting and so on and he asked me: 'Do you have a Schmidt-Rottluff?' and I replied: 'Oh, I can't afford a Schmidt-Rottluff'. Beckett also played the piano when he came to see me, Haydn especially, and he played on a piano in his apartment. There was one time I remember when he said: 'What remains is music'. Two years later, when he was here again at our home, I reminded him of this sentence and he said: 'Habe ich das gesagt?' ['Did I say that?'] and I said 'Ja, ja' and he thought again and then said: 'Yes, well I think that's right'.

Klaus Herm   Every time Beckett was here in Berlin I used to meet him. I played chess with him as well. I met Beckett one day walking back from the Schiller-Theater and I said to him, 'May I accompany you? What are you doing tonight?' It was a Saturday or something. And Beckett said, 'Oh, I don't know, maybe I'll play chess with myself'. And I said, 'Oh, I play also.' So we arranged to play. I don't remember exactly when that was; maybe after the second *Godot*. I don't know exactly. I played him once in the Akademie and neither of us was a winner. This bothered us at first, but finally we both started to laugh.

Compassion: A Disagreement

Walter Asmus I was sitting at the dentist's and Sam was sitting with me. It was before the opening hours of his practice, and we were sitting there and there was an old man sitting over there like this [he gestures – making his hand twitch]. I didn't say anything; Sam had toothache and we didn't speak. He was looking at this man for several minutes, like this. [He stares fixedly.] You know his look when he got interested in something; he was watching him, watching him – and you felt that something was going on in his head. Then he turned to me and in a whisper he said: 'You know my mother had Parkinson's disease.' He was so captivated by it, you know. That was his way of looking at the world. He always connected it to something to do with his compassion for people and always connected it to himself, to his own experience, his own life.

Rosemarie Koch   As far as I observed Beckett, I think it was always the cold interest of someone who has to write about human beings – the cold interest of the writer.

Walter Asmus   But that was just a way of protecting himself, I think.

Rosemarie Koch   There was a man in charge of the props at the Schiller-Theater, you know – the stage-manager – and he had eye trouble. And he had forgotten to do something and he said to Beckett: 'Oh, I'm sorry but I have trouble with my eyes; perhaps I'm going blind', and Beckett's answer was: 'Such is life'. That was his only response.

Walter Asmus   I think it was not vicious, not cynical; it was just a dry remark, not to get involved at that particular moment.*

Rosemary Koch   It was at the same time a literary remark if you compare it . . . to his writing. 'Such is life' [*Comment c'est* (*How It Is*)].

---

* There is, of course, another possible explanation for Beckett's off-hand, perhaps even callous reaction which could be his concern for the state of his own eyes and his own fear of blindness. He may well have considered that he was in a worse state than his complainant.

8

Beckett in the USA:
Tributes and Memories

Beckett on the set of *Film*, New York, 1964.

Biography

Beckett came to the United States only once, in the summer of 1964, to help Alan Schneider to film his script of *Film*, with Buster Keaton playing the main character. He already had a close knowledge of early American cinema from his youth: Chaplin, Keaton, Ben Turpin, Harry Langdon, as well as the Marx Brothers and Laurel and Hardy. And he read far more American fiction than has often thought to be the case, including Faulkner, Salinger and Bellow.

Beckett himself has always had a large and faithful following in the USA. Many American writers, artists and musicians have been inspired by his prose or by his drama.* Since its disastrous

---

* As examples we mention the writers Edward Albee, David Mamet, Paul Auster; the artists Bruce Nauman, Jasper Johns and Tony Oursler; and the musicians Philip Glass, Morton Feldman, Earl Kim and Roger Reynolds.

Beckett in the 1960s.

opening at the Cocoanut
Grove Playhouse in Miami
in January 1956, *Waiting
for Godot* has rarely been absent for long from the stage
of some large US city, with a
number of prestigious productions. *Endgame, Happy Days*
and *Krapp's Last Tape* too
have all received notable revivals, some with distinguished
actors playing the main roles
(among them Alvin Epstein,
Irene Worth, Hume Cronyn,
Jessica Tandy and David
Warrilow).

Beckett with Alan Schneider, Paris, 1956.

As well as directing the American premières of these four
main plays, Alan Schneider also premièred several of Beckett's
other shorter plays, mostly at the Cherry Lane Theater in New
York or at Arena Stage in Washington DC, but also in several
university venues, usually conferring closely by letter or by
telephone with Beckett prior to and during rehearsals. Then
there have been many experimental and highly innovative
productions such as those put on by Mabou Mines, described
here by one of the company's artistic directors and a good
friend of Beckett, Frederick Neumann, and some controversial
ones such as JoAnne Akalaitis' *Endgame* with the American
Repertory Theatre in Boston and André Gregory's earlier production of the same play.

It is worth stressing that (mostly through Alan Schneider) Beckett
took a lively interest in what was happening to his plays in the USA.
His New York publisher, Barney Rosset – who acted as his
dramatic agent for many years in the USA – and Schneider kept
him fully informed by sending him first-hand reports of the productions they had seen or copies of the plays' notices. It is not
surprising then that a number of our tributes and memories should
come from actors and writers in the United States. We have
excluded major players such as Rosset, Schneider and the actor

David Warrilow (who, though British, often acted in Beckett's plays in the USA and for whom Beckett wrote *A Piece of Monologue*) only because their correspondence or memories have appeared elsewhere.*

---

* See, for example, Alan Schneider, *Entrances. An American Director's Journey*, New York, Viking Penguin, 1986 and *No Author Better Served. The Correspondence of Samuel Beckett and Alan Schneider*, ed. Maurice Harmon, Cambridge, MA, Harvard University Press, 1998 and an extensive conversation with David Warrilow in Jonathan Kalb, *Beckett in Performance*, Cambridge/New York, Cambridge University Press, 1991, pp. 220–33.

Edward Albee

Edward Albee (1928–). American playwright. Among his best-known plays are *The Zoo Story* (1958), *Who's Afraid of Virginia Woolf* (1961–2), *A Delicate Balance* (1966), *Three Tall Women* (1991) and *The Goat, Or Who is Sylvia* (2000). Interview with JK.

I think there are perhaps four playwrights of the twentieth century that we could not have done without: Chekhov, Pirandello, Brecht and Beckett. I think if you've got those four, you've got the century covered.

I don't remember which of Sam Beckett's plays I experienced first. I don't know whether I saw *Godot* before I saw *Krapp's Last Tape* performed, which was on a double bill with my *Zoo Story*, first in Berlin and then in New York. It was done first at the Schiller [-Theater] Werkstatt, because there was no off-Broadway theatre at the time. You know, it must have been my first experience of Sam's work then, because I remember seeing that my play, *Die Zoo-geschichte* as it was called in German, was being performed on a

double-bill with a play that was called *Das letzte Band* by Samuel
Beckett. Maybe this was the first experience. What I found so
interesting about that production – I forget who was playing Krapp
[it was Walter Franck] – there was a huge loudspeaker on stage:
stage right. And what this guy did, and I knew it was not in the text
to do it, but when he started listening to the stories about two-thirds
of the way through the play (reeds, woman's eyes open), this actor
playing Krapp got up from behind his desk, took his chair, went
and sat by this huge loudspeaker, and put his arms around it. It was
beautiful, totally beautiful. So that may well have been my first
visual experience of Sam's work.

Why I get so confused is around that time in New York we were
beginning to see productions, not only of Sam's work, but of
Ionesco's and Genet's; it was all happening in the late 'fifties
and the early 'sixties, so I get very muddled as to what I saw when
. . . But, anyway, once I became aware of Sam's work and the
power, it was great. You don't find revelations like that every day.
The only terrible thing about being influenced by extraordinary
people like Sam, like Genet, like other people, is that you have to try
and keep your own voice. There is the danger that you can end up
sounding like a carbon copy of somebody else, and I think you can't
consciously fight it, but you've got to absorb the influence, take
what is nutritious from it, and at the same time realize that this
person did it that way but I must use, I must absorb and use it in my
own way, in my own voice. It's something that I think a writer of
any sensitivity would just do naturally.

I'm sure Beckett and I also saw each other in Paris and had a beer
together. I think Alan Schneider put us in touch. Because I'm a very
shy person and I wouldn't have done it without an introduction.
Both of us rather shy, I think. I went to Paris a fair amount. But I
don't think we saw each other more than two or three times in Paris
though. It was all very casual. We also wrote to each other [over the
years Albee sent Beckett copies of his plays]. I don't recall if he
commented much beyond generally encouraging enthusiasm: 'I
liked this very much; I was very moved by this.' I've got the letters
somewhere. Then when he came to New York in 1964 for *Film* with
Buster Keaton, I thought that Alan Schneider brought him out to
Montauk [to Albee's house there]. I can't remember whether he

came out; I know a lot of people did. Then I remember an extraordinary evening when the New York production of *Who's Afraid of Virginia Woolf* was put on in London. The company moved to London. There was Uta Hagen and Arthur Hill and George Grizzard and Melinda Dillon. After a rehearsal of one of Sam's plays [which Albee attended], Sam was with Harold Pinter and Patrick Magee. Everybody sat around and discussed the Marquis de Sade. And I was very interested to sit there listening to people who knew a great deal more about de Sade than I did. I was very quiet: I was a mouse in that conversation, pretty much.

Beckett and Chekhov taught me two things, something that I had known, I suspect, but maybe hadn't been quite able to articulate: the relationship between music and drama. I wanted to be a composer when I was young, and writing a play is very much like composing a string quartet; the psychological structures are the same: sound, silence, duration, all these are so terribly important. Beckett taught me that, if nothing else, when you write a play, see it and hear it as a staged piece, as a performed piece as you write it. Then when I end up after I've directed both my own plays and other peoples', after a certain point, I can just close my eyes and conduct, if the rhythms are precise. It's all sound and silence . . . relations, rhythms. Technically – from a technical point of view – I'm sure he probably taught me that more than anything else. The precision of language also, although I think I'm a bit more voluble in some of my plays. In Beckett everything is down to essence. Nothing beyond what is needed.

I wrote a line in a play, which I think I cut from a play of mine; it was in the text originally, and one of the characters says: 'The least dishonourable defeat is the only honourable goal'. And I think that's what Sam was writing about. It's the same thing as 'I can't go on, I'll go on'.

I've never felt Sam to be a pessimistic playwright. A pessimist does not try to write. The true pessimist wouldn't take the trouble of writing. Writing is an attempt to communicate, and if you're a pessimist you say communication is impossible: you wouldn't do it.

Paul Auster

Paul Auster (1947–). After attending Columbia University, he lived in France for four years. Since returning to America in 1974, he has published poems, essays, novels, film scripts and translations. He is best known perhaps for *The New York Trilogy*. He wrote a brief essay about Beckett's novel *Mercier and Camier*, and refers to Beckett or his work several times in his own writing. Based on a telephone interview with JK, this contribution was heavily revised by Paul Auster in 2005.

I moved to Paris in February 1971, a few weeks after my twenty-fourth birthday. I had been writing poetry for some time by then, and the road to my initial meeting with Beckett began with Jacques Dupin, a poet whose work I had been translating since my under-graduate days in New York. He and I became close friends in Paris, and because Jacques worked as director of publications at the Galerie Maeght, I met Jean-Paul Riopelle, the French-Canadian painter who was one of the artists of the gallery. Because of Jean-Paul, I met Joan Mitchell, the American painter he lived with in a house once owned by Monet in the town of Vétheuil. Years earlier, Joan had been married to Barney Rosset, the founder and publisher of Grove Press, and she and Beckett knew each other well. One evening, she and I happened to be discussing his work, and when she found out how important it was to me, she looked up and said, 'Would you like to meet him?' 'Yes,' I answered. 'Of course I would.' 'Well, just write him a letter', she announced, 'and tell him I said so.'

I went home and wrote the letter, and three days later I received a reply from Beckett informing me to meet him at La Closerie des Lilas the following week.

I can't remember what year it was. It might have been as early as 1972 – or as late as 1974. Let's split the difference and call it 1973.

I saw him only once after that – on a subsequent visit to Paris in 1979 – and over the years we exchanged a couple of dozen notes and letters. It could hardly be classified as a friendship, but given my admiration for his work (which bordered on idolatry when I was a young man), our personal encounters and fitful correspondence were exceedingly precious to me. Among a horde of memories, I would cite the generous help he gave me while I was putting together my *Random House Book of Twentieth-Century French Poetry* (to which he contributed translations of Apollinaire, Breton and Eluard); the moving speech he delivered one afternoon in a Paris café about his love for France and how lucky he felt to have spent his adult life there; the kind and encouraging letters he wrote whenever I sent him something I had published: books, translations, articles about his work. There were funny moments as well: a deadpan account of his one and only stay in New York ('It was so damn hot, I was hanging onto the rails'), not to speak of the unforgettable line from our first meeting when, gesturing with his arm and failing to attract the waiter's attention, he turned to me and said, in that soft Irish brogue of his, 'There are no eyes in the world harder to catch than a barman's.'

All that, yes, but one remark from that afternoon at La Closerie des Lilas stands out from the others, and not only does it reveal much about Beckett the man, it speaks to the dilemma all writers must live with: eternal doubt, the inability to judge the worth of what one has created.

During the conversation, he told me that he had just finished translating *Mercier and Camier*, his first French novel, which had been written in the mid-forties. I had read the book in French and had liked it very much. 'A wonderful book', I said. I was just a kid, after all, and I couldn't suppress my enthusiasm. But Beckett shook his head and said, 'Oh no, no, not very good. In fact, I've cut out about twenty-five per cent of the original. The English version is going to be quite a bit shorter than the French.' And I said, 'Why would you do such a thing. It's a wonderful book. You shouldn't have taken anything out.' Again, Beckett shook his head. 'No, no, not very good, not very good.'

After that, we started talking about other things. Then, out of the blue, five or ten minutes later, he leant across the table and said, 'You really liked it, huh? You really thought it was good?'

This was Samuel Beckett, remember, and not even he had any grasp of the value of his work. No writer ever knows, not even the best ones.

'Yes,' I said to him. 'I really thought it was good.'

Jessica Tandy

Jessica Tandy (1909–94). British-born actress, who married the American actor Hume Cronyn, and lived in the United States from 1942 until her death. She won critical acclaim for her creation of Blanche DuBois in Tennessee Williams' *A Streetcar Named Desire* (1947) and appeared in many films, earning an Academy Award and a Golden Globe for her performance (at the age of eighty) in *Driving Miss Daisy* (1989). Interview with JK.

[Jessica Tandy acted the part of Mouth in the world première of Beckett's short play *Not I* at the Forum of the Lincoln Center in New York in 1972. She met the author in Paris prior to this production.]

I was going to do *Happy Days*, Hume [Cronyn, her husband] was going to do *Krapp's Last Tape* and we were also going to do an *Act without Words I*. But we were missing another play. So Alan Schneider, Barney Rosset and I flew over to Paris to talk it over with Beckett.

It was extraordinary because we came there thinking that what we needed was not a long play, but something short to balance the programme. 'Could it possibly be that you have something new?' we asked him. [In fact, Alan Schneider had written to Beckett a few weeks earlier saying 'And I'd love to get something of yours for her (i.e. Jessica Tandy) to do on the bill with *Krapp*; perhaps you have a small piece or could write one.'*] And it was so funny because he said: 'Well, yes, I do as a matter of fact'. And he pulled out these few pages of closely typed script which we passed around. We all three read it and we all thought, 'Wow!' I read in the stage directions that there was just light on Mouth and nothing else. Then he said 'It is . . .' – he didn't use the word 'vomited out' – but it is as though there is no control, the mouth is not controlling anything, the sound is just pouring out: 'spewed out'. If you look at one of those stone lions in a fountain; the water gushes out of its mouth. And it was a wonderful thing to keep in my head. I found that you must not think what you are saying; it just has to come out. The difference was that instead of, say, an exclamation mark, there would be nothing – or else there would be four dots. But it all makes perfectly good sense, musically.

So we left that meeting in Paris with great exhilaration, because we all three thought it was a wonderful piece. But I must tell you also that, when we played the Beckett Festival, before I had to go on for that one, I would be dressed and walking in the corridor, saying 'God, could you just hurt me in some way? Can I lose my voice or break a leg, so I don't have to do it?' It was an experience that stayed with you. The production was in the Lincoln Center – a beautiful little theatre, not the main stage but the one downstairs [The Forum]. And God heard me one night because, as they wheeled this contraption that I was in across the stage, it went across some electric cables and disconnected the whole system. So there was no light and we couldn't do it!

But I thought it was a wonderful challenge; the nature of the piece was so compelling. I found the less I thought about it and the more the mouth was working on its own, the righter it was. I found the

---

* Letter from Alan Schneider to Samuel Beckett, 2 July 1972 in *No Author Better Served. The Correspondence of Samuel Beckett and Alan Schneider*, ed. Maurice Harmon, 1998, p. 272.

challenge exhilarating. But I didn't ever find it fun to do. I was terrified and didn't enjoy it.

With any play I do, I struggle to play what the author wrote and not give it a little twitch here and a little twitch there. Beckett doesn't mess around. He tells you exactly what he wants. And that's very good for actors. I know it's very unpopular with actors. They need to express themselves. But if you started in the theatre, as I did, by doing Shakespeare, you learned that you don't mess around, because he really knows what he is doing. So if he puts a comma there, he means a comma there. And Beckett puts his four dots in when you need to take a breath.

Hume Cronyn

Hume Cronyn (1911–2003), Canadian-born actor, who married in 1942 the British actress Jessica Tandy. Then, after her death in 1994, he married the writer Susan Cooper, in 1996. Often teamed with Jessica Tandy, he starred on Broadway (*The Four-Poster, A Delicate Balance, The Gin Game, Foxfire*) in a TV series (*The Marriage*, 1954) and in a series of 'old-codger' roles in *Cocoon* (1985), and *Batteries Not Included* (1987). In 1994, Hume Cronyn and Jessica Tandy won the first Tony Award for lifetime theatrical achievement. Interview with JK.

During the Beckett Festival, Jessica and I were staying in a small hotel, 'The Mayflower', which at the time was rather shabby. It was filled with elderly people with different ailments, so that the lobby had more than its fair share of wheelchairs and walkers and crutches. It was really quite depressing. But we came in one night, after struggling with a 'matinée day'. We had done two Becketts in the matinée and a different two in the evening.

I have to digress just a little to say that Beckett's belief in the resilience of the human spirit ('I can't go on, you must go on, I'll go on' [*The Unnamable*]) is very marked. However, the particular mountain top from which he views the world is pretty bleak. But, despite the defeats and the defeats and the defeats, the character still picks himself up and says 'I can, I can, I will' – the subject, by the way, of *Act without Words I*, which I acted in the Beckett Festival.

Anyway, Jessie and I came back to the hotel exhausted. We went to the elevator and pressed the button and there was a long delay. And we became conscious of two old ladies sitting on a bench right outside the elevator. The bench was there for a very good reason. The old people would come and press the button of the elevator and they would sit down while they waited. And we picked up this snatch of conversation. One old lady was saying to the other: 'But darling, what does one do?' And the reply from the other lady was: 'Dearest, there is nothing one can do – except, of course, to die young'! Well, after a day of Beckett, I expected to go upstairs, open the window and jump out!

While we were rehearsing *Krapp's Last Tape*, we came to a point in the script when one of Beckett's stage directions is 'Krapp curses'; then a few lines later it says 'Krapp curses louder'. And I got Alan [Schneider, the director] and I said, 'What do you suggest he says when he curses?' And he said, 'I don't know. What do you think is appropriate? I think it is a mutter anyway.' And I said, 'I think he is saying "Rubbish. Rubbish"; only it wouldn't be "Rubbish". I think it would be "Balls". He is a quite a randy old man. Then later on I don't know what he says there. He could repeat it, or he could say "great hairy clusters".' And Alan said, 'That's fine, that's fine.' Now we are playing in a four-, five-hundred seat house and it is a thrust stage, so the audience is all around you. And the first row is very close to the apron of the stage and one evening I was muttering 'balls' and 'those great hairy clusters'. Some weeks later – we were still playing – a letter arrived for Alan [from Beckett]. He didn't write to me. He wrote to Alan. And Alan was unwise enough to read me the letter over the telephone, which said: 'I understand from Harold [Pinter] that Cronyn is saying such and such and I object to that and please tell him to desist.' I said, 'OK, Alan, then what do you want me to say instead?' But Alan said, 'I don't want to change anything. You just keep it that way.' He was upset. I was upset. I thought I can't go on saying something that Beckett, who was very meticulous, objects to.

So I sat down and wrote to Beckett. I had written to him a number of times before. 'This is what we are doing; this is where we are in rehearsal; this piece appeared in the *New York Times*; this piece appeared in the *Post*; here's a copy of the photographs.' I didn't know the man but I thought I had been extremely attentive. And then suddenly this contretemps came up and I wrote to him and said, 'Very well, sir, I know what you don't want; now please tell me what you do want?' It was short and to the point and rather brusque. That is the one letter I have from him. He wrote back and he said 'Dear Mr Cronyn' – or something to this effect, so you cannot take this as gospel – 'any suggestions that I have in regard to the text will be made to the director of the production, Mr Alan Schneider. Sincerely. Samuel Beckett'* – which really put me in my place.

So the whole thing was never resolved. As I say, it was a very minor point. But obviously I had stepped out of line. It would not be like me to be directly rude, but my note to him may have had about it a brusqueness.† I felt that I had been responsible for getting the whole damn thing on, and we had received extremely good reviews. But it really put Beckett off me because I heard from some other source later on that, talking about the American production (which he never saw), Beckett said something to the effect that 'Tandy was probably OK, but that fellow Cronyn . . .'. I thought, 'Christ, he never saw it, he doesn't know.' Krapp was a wonderful part for me and the other part was also a wonderful part for me [*Act without Words I*]. And we had brought it off. It was a smashing success. Now that is Beckett. That is not the Cronyns. That's Beckett. It was a world première. Anyway years passed. And I knew about Alan's collection of Beckett's correspondence. So I wrote to him and I said, 'I have this priceless letter from Samuel Beckett and I don't think I am going to keep it, so let me send it to you.'

---

* This letter, which is alluded to, though not included, in the Beckett–Schneider correspondence, is part of Boston College's collection, since Cronyn did indeed, as he says here, give it to Alan Schneider with the note 'To Alan from H.C. with a touch of the forelock'.

† Hume Cronyn fails to mention here, as Deirdre Bair quotes in her *Samuel Beckett: A Biography*, that, after the question to Beckett, he did add: 'This minuscule point is balls and rubbish, especially at this time.' (Bair, *Samuel Beckett*, New York, Harcourt Brace Jovanovich, 1978, p. 626.) Beckett wrote to Schneider that 'he had an offensive letter from Cronyn dated Nov. 16 to which I replied briefly'. (*No Author Better Served*, p. 293.)

Frederick Neumann

Frederick Neumann (1926–), director and actor, seen here in *Worstward Ho*, 1986. One of the founder members of the theatre company Mabou Mines. Adapted and directed several of Beckett's prose works for the stage: *Mercier and Camier* (1979), *Company* (1980) – with original music by Philip Glass – and *Worstward Ho* (1981). He also acted in JoAnne Akalaitis's adaptation of *Cascando* (1976) and with Julian Beck and George Bartenieff in *Theatre I and Theatre II* at La Mama, New York. Interview with JK, added to by Frederick Neumann in 2005.

[It is widely believed that Beckett clamped down very firmly on adaptations of his work or on freer versions of his plays. We print this interview with Fred Neumann to show how, when he was dealing with people whom he liked and whose work he respected, he could accept some freely imaginative transpositions.*]

I think the first time Beckett and I really talked was in Berlin in 1976. We all met up in Berlin. In fact, Ruth Maleczech and Lee

---

* Neumann spoke in this interview about his other adaptations of Beckett's prose works. However, since this is not the place for a detailed analysis of such productions, we refer the curious reader to Jonathan Kalb's excellent discussion in his *Beckett in Performance*, Cambridge/New York, Cambridge University Press, 1991, pp. 117–43 and 206–11. We confine ourselves to *The Lost Ones* and *Mercier and Camier*.

Breuer [fellow members of the Mabou Mines theatre company] never met Beckett; they had hoped to meet him there, but they were somewhere else at the time. But David [Warrilow, the actor] was there and yes, JoAnne Akalaitis was there. In fact, if I'm not mistaken, it was JoAnne Akalaitis who slipped a note under his door at the Akademie der Künste and he responded rather quickly saying 'Let's meet downstairs in the coffee-house'. We were putting on two pieces of his at the time, *Cascando* and *The Lost Ones*, and we were also doing a piece by Lee Breuer called *B-Beaver Anima-tion*. Then, of course, later we met in Paris. I would go to Paris, and we would have very long talks at the PLM [Hôtel Saint-Jacques].

The Lost Ones

[This text, first written in French, largely in 1966, *as Le dépeupleur*, has many 'lost bodies' confined to a cylinder 'each searching for its lost one'. These figures climb up ladders in order to reach niches or alcoves or to find an egress. Frederick Neumann describes how these scenes in the cylinder were rendered in stage images with the British actor David Warrilow manipulating tiny, plastic creatures who represented the 'lost ones'.]

The adaptation of Beckett's prose text *The Lost Ones* was the first to be done by Mabou Mines. It wasn't I who asked for his permission to do that. It was Lee Breuer. Or at least I think JoAnne Akalaitis asked permission for Mabou Mines, and Lee Breuer did the directing, and it was not supposed to be anything more than a reading. So [when he saw the set in Berlin] Beckett said, 'My, you have adapted it, haven't you?' Lee Breuer directed it, and turned it into a rather brilliant stage production – which was far more than a reading, of course.

Everyone had to take off their shoes and pick up the binoculars as they went into the theatre, so that they could look at 'The Lost Ones', who were represented by tiny plastic human beings, naked, sunburned. David Warrilow narrated the story of *The Lost Ones* and used these little creatures, little plastic things, stage people. And David was functioning himself as a 'lost one', if you like, in the larger cylinder which was the theatre. And then there was this miniature replica of the cylinder in which he was located, of people not much larger than grains of sand, and which we were to represent, which you could rub in your hand, and they would . . . you could hear the dry crisp sound of the skin, you know that sound. And Philip Glass did this tinkling music, that *Time* Magazine said was music down in the molecules, or something equivalent. All this tiny, tiny, tiny percussion of . . . I think *The Lost Ones* established some kind of reputation for Mabou Mines.

I can't remember now whether I asked Beckett when we met in 1976 if I could do *More Pricks than Kicks* as a stage version. It took him four months to respond, and I can't find that correspondence. Four months later, Sam wrote to me and said, 'Dear Fred, Please leave the poor little thing alone'. Then I wrote back and said, 'But, you know, the piece I really wanted to do, but I didn't dare ask you, is *Mercier and Camier*. I would like to stage that.' And it took him a good, maybe four months again, to respond. And he finally said 'OK', and we talked about it, and I was going back and forth at the time, constantly going back and forth, from New York to Paris and back, and was able to talk a little bit about it.

Mercier and Camier

[*Mercier and Camier*, first written in French in 1946, concerns two characters, rather like Flaubert's Bouvard and Pécuchet, who are travelling with their bicycles on a journey in a hybrid countryside, part Ireland, part France. The novel looks forward to *Waiting for Godot* written two years later. Neumann describes the highly inventive, exuberant production that was put on by Mabou Mines – and Beckett's own reaction to it.]

Mercier and Camier is a kind of road play. 'It's a picaresque work, therefore you can move the text around, as you will', Beckett said. I must say, I was just amazed. And it seemed to walk through time, not just down a road, but through time, and through different spaces. Or time spaces. That of the First World War: a time of bicycles. In fact, I once used that as a kind of subtitle for it: 'A Time of Bicycles'. And there was a kind of slow, wheeling movement by human beings that seemed to allow for conversation and gaff between two buddies. There was a pub, which was like the main place, which was located in an Irish village, or it could have been a

French village, and there was a prostitute, who was upstairs in this pub. And, though it was not written in the text, I designed the pub to have a TV above the bar on which David Warrilow was a TV person who spoke a lot of the text from that piece. So I had everything sort of moving. There was a canal: as you know, in the text, there is the road, the canal, the pub, the house of prostitutes, and there were these allusions to the terrible things that happened in the First World War . . . and after the First World War, 'la belle Hélène', I think . . .

I have a card of something that's less than a square, a very narrow alley, a picture that Beckett sent me. It's quite a wonderful picture. And it just so happened that it corresponds somewhat to this Irish theme that one could see through the pub window, and the pub door, and the pub wall, because there was no wall. And there was no real window either: there was a glass in a frame, so that when it rained, it rained only in that window and it rained only in the doorway. So every time Mercier and Camier, or Mercier himself wanted to step out, it would rain. Every time he'd come back in, the sun would come out.

But the main thing about the whole production was this enormous acreage of scrim [a sort of fabric] that enveloped the whole audience. And I wasn't trying to be spooky or anything, but it was useful for me to use it as a screen, and also to have this tunnel effect . . . the black hole of the universe, if you like, that was represented right down stage-front, which was the door with the raindrops.

Philip Glass did the music again. It was called 'The Train Music', since they were also in the train, if you remember. And we had an actor with no legs; he pushed himself along. But there was a kind of fantasy of the text: I do not call it fiction, although it was somewhat fictionalized. I had people come in on bicycles, through revolving doors, from backstage, they would get up enough speed, or on roller-skates, which you could not see. They seemed to float: the bartender always came in with a tray . . . and the audience could not see that he was on a ramp, a long, slow ramp; first one direction and then the other. The waiter – he was called the Waiter, you know – could come through the revolving doors and glide across the whole stage without talking and you couldn't see that he had skates on. They were hidden. All of that was meant to show this in some kind of fantasy time.

I remember the bog, which is another element that was particular to Ireland, and a place for more than just getting your feet wet! But we had a real bog on the other side of the canal, and the canal was water about six to eight inches deep. We used it to reflect light, in their drunken moments, talking about stars and things like that. And, wallowing in the bog, Bill Raymond was a Mabou Mines person, who did this with me. We wallowed in the bog while David Warrilow waxed. Fiction, if you like; wonderful poetic fiction that Sam had written. Then the bartender glided back and forth, and then the hills of Dublin were represented by a structure that had been built by a sculptor. She devised the hills of Dublin all around the audience, so that we could go all the way up, and carry on . . . and it was just a device not to use a microphone, a device to be able to speak into the thing close to all sections of the audience about things. I and Bill Raymond, we went all around the audience, and across the heads of the audience.

It was all in a world that was set just after the Second World War or maybe just before it. We had a very, very good photographer, who had devised and had done the 35mm stills of the various visions of France, the various things out of the windows of France, but various things that you would have seen during the Second World War. Things about . . . where all the bones are, in the North Sea, in France, and other images that changed the world. This was something that Sam and I had in common, talking about the war, the Second World War, and I think that was one of the things that was something of a bond, about my relationship to his work. His work spoke for me of the devastation that that war [had brought] and what had happened to Europe, and that such a great cultural centre of the world would so destroy itself.

So look into the black hole of the universe and on stage-centre, you have projecting on either side of the audience, on this scrim, going all the way back, six windows, all of them because they are being projected from the back foreshortened, so that the audience had the impression of being in a train. And the projections were historical. Pre-war, and afterwards. And you could see Hélène through the scrim, and the men with her . . . and there was a huge projection of her above the bar. And there were like two little men; the apples of her eye, because the projection was so big that we were the small people in her eye, and then when she opened her mouth to have us, we were in her throat, and she could just snap her mouth shut, and we would be . . . but we were live and she was live, but she was also a small person in her own image.

I said to Sam when I saw him, 'I guess you must have received some reports of *Mercier and Camier*, and I have to apologize right away about it being over-produced. There was too much.' ('The simpler the better, Freddy', he used to say, 'the simpler the better.') Anyway, he said 'Yes, I've received good reports' – and he held his finger up – 'with reservations.'

Best of all, Beckett followed with the years, by allowing me to adapt *Company* for the stage, including a quartet by Philip Glass. To assist me with the trepidation I felt in asking to include music in that work, he said, 'I think there are the proper interstices'. Then again, towards the end, regarding the adaptation of *Worstward Ho* (which was handed to me by Ruby Cohn in San Francisco, with Sam's permission) '. . . with all due respect for Philip, no music for pity's sake; it's my last gasp.'

9

The Last Twenty Years

Samuel Beckett at the Royal Court Theatre, 1973.

Biography, 1969–89

Beckett's sixties and seventies were still highly productive years. He wrote several short, challenging plays for the stage in the 1970s and early 1980s, testing how far it was possible to go in the theatre (*Not I*, *That Time*, *Footfalls*, *A Piece of Monologue*, *Rockaby*, *Ohio Impromptu* and *Catastrophe*). He also wrote minimalist plays for television (*Ghost Trio*, . . . *but the clouds* . . . *Quad* and *What Where*) which have exercised a great influence on video and installation art. His prose works of that period (*Company*, *Mal vu mal dit* [*Ill Seen Ill Said*] and *Worstward Ho*) are powerful and thrillingly innovative.

Productions of his plays in London, Berlin and Paris kept Beckett actively involved in the theatre, in which some of his friends (e.g. Jocelyn Herbert, Billie Whitelaw, Donald McWhinnie, Pierre Chabert) worked. His support – both moral and financial – for members of his family and his friends was unwavering and he gave money away constantly to charities and institutions, as well as to numerous private individuals. Friendships with 'Con' Leventhal, his publishers John Calder and Barney Rosset, Barbara Bray, Josette Hayden (whose husband, Henri, died in 1970) continued unswervingly. Always deeply humanitarian, he began, in a new development, to take much more public stances on political issues: apartheid in South Africa, greater freedoms in Communist Eastern Europe, and human rights cases throughout the world (e.g. the house arrest of Václav Havel).*

His fame made many other demands on his time and his appointment diaries of this period reveal that he met a quite extraordinary number of people whom he knew scarcely at all to discuss new productions and publications or musical and dance works inspired by his writing. Tribute volumes tend to publish contributions only from those who knew their subject well. But how did he appear to his occasional visitor, anxious to glean as much as possible from meeting him? We have selected two sets of memories to answer that question: Michael Rudman speaks of his meeting with Beckett to talk about a revival of *Waiting for Godot* that he was directing at the National Theatre in London; Charles Krance also writes of his conversation with the author about preparing a critical edition of his manuscripts. Then, as an example of someone who never met Beckett but who was profoundly influenced by him, we print the film director Anthony Minghella's thoughts on Beckett and on filming his play *Play*.

Looking back at his work a hundred years after his birth in Foxrock, County Dublin, its impact on writers, artists and musicians, as well as on those who are none of these, seems likely to last for many generations to come.

---

* Beckett's personal concerns and his involvement in various campaigns for political justice and human rights are more fully charted in *Damned to Fame*, pp. 636–43.

James Knowlson

James Knowlson (1933–). Emeritus Professor of French Studies in the University of Reading, England. He is the author (with John Pilling) of *Frescoes of the Skull. The Later Prose and Drama of Samuel Beckett* (John Calder and Grove Press), the general editor of the four-volume series *The Theatrical Notebooks of Samuel Beckett* (Faber and Faber) and editor of two of the volumes. He wrote the authorized biography of Beckett, *Damned to Fame. The Life of Samuel Beckett* (Bloomsbury and Grove Atlantic). Most recently, he wrote *Images of Beckett* with photographs by John Haynes. Contribution written especially for this volume.

According to a recently rediscovered old notebook, I wrote to Beckett for the first time in March 1970. He had just been awarded the Nobel Prize for Literature and my letter was to inform him that we hoped to mount an exhibition at the University of Reading in England to honour him and his work. At his request I met him in his Paris apartment in September. I remember we drank whiskey (which I actively dislike) as we skimmed hastily through the broad details of his life. Although reticent at first, he was very co-operative, providing me with the names of people

who would help me as well as lots of factual information. Over
the nineteen years that I knew him, he was in fact invariably
helpful. In spite of his reputation to the contrary, I also found him
happy to talk about his work – provided you knew what to ask
him – but not to explicate it.

The May 1971 exhibition led directly to the foundation of what
was eventually to become the Beckett International Foundation, a
charitable trust, to which, for almost two decades, Beckett do-
nated virtually all his recent manuscripts and theatrical notebooks, making Reading's Beckett Archive into the richest
collection in the world. I was regularly invited to Paris to collect
his gifts and this led to a friendship which helps to explain why,
after publishing a number of books on his work, I became his
biographer.

Two things stand out clearly in my memory from our drinks or
dinners at the Iles Marquises, the Closerie des Lilas, the Palette or,
later, the PLM (Hôtel Saint-Jacques) on the boulevard of that name
near his apartment. First, Beckett was not just an excellent listener,
he also had a genuine talent for putting things into perspective. He
could distinguish between a real problem (and offer help and
support to solve it whenever possible) and something which, looked
at in a different light or seen in a wider context, was relatively
unimportant. For someone who was usually thought of as pessimistic, he was extremely positive and helpful when the problems
were your own, although he was often anxious and despondent
about his own concerns, especially when they were to do with his
health or the lack of progress he was making on his work. He was
not afraid of emotion either. I often recall him telling me about the
illnesses or difficulties of friends, sometimes with tears in his eyes. It
was only much later that one heard – from others – how 'Sam' had
paid for their medical treatment or helped them out with gifts of
money. His financial generosity is legendary. He gave so much
away: settling the rent of a friend's apartment; educating another
friend's children; sending regular cheques to members of his family
and helping out many hard-up writers or painters. What has been
commented on much less frequently was his willingness to be there
whenever his friends needed his time and his moral support.
Fortunately, I had to benefit from his offers of actual financial

help only once. This was when, having taken leave of absence to edit his Theatrical Notebooks, I was left high and dry without any income for a year by the late withdrawal of the promised fees on the strength of which my leave had been taken. Beckett immediately made over his percentage of the royalties as author to me and the other two editors so that we lost less money. Like so many of his friends, however, I had many reasons to appreciate his compassion and human concern. Our eldest son, Gregory, was badly injured in 1979 in a motorcycle crash and was in intensive care following an emergency operation, his life hanging by a thread for some days. Beckett called me every single night after we came back from the hospital to see how Gregory was getting on. Fortunately Greg survived and made a full recovery. But subsequently Beckett never failed to ask after his health.

Second, contrary to popular belief, evenings with Beckett were often lively, fascinating occasions. This was partly because he was so witty and could laugh at himself, as well as at funny things that occurred. I once knocked my empty glass off the table in the American Bar at the Coupole and, to my acute embarrassment, it broke into a thousand pieces on the tiled floor. 'It's not serious. The glass was empty at the time,' was Beckett's speedy rejoinder. He even treated the adversities of old age with self-deprecating humour. One day, in the last two years of his life, I leapt up from my chair to leave: 'Hang on a minute. Getting up isn't as easy as that, you know.' When he was living in a retirement home during the last few weeks of his life, the hospital he was taken into when he fell gave him a course of injections for vitamin deficiency, called 'Avitaminosis'. As a result alcohol was strictly forbidden. The problem was that Beckett liked his whiskey regularly. 'That must be a bit of a bitch, Sam', I commented sympathetically. Long pause. 'No Jim. It's not a bit of a bitch. It is a bugger of a bastard of a bitch!' – a distinctly 'cool' remark for any 83-year-old to make. He went on: 'I'll make up for it later'.

Dinners over the years were also lively affairs because his knowledge of literature, art, music and sport was so extensive and so discerning. He would quote W. B. Yeats, Joyce, Verlaine, Rimbaud, Chamfort, even Heredia at the drop of a hat, and always in context. We talked of French authors he admired (Marguerite Duras, Robert

Pinget, Fernando Arrabal) and of those he preferred to others: Camus in preference to Sartre, for example. We often spoke of the books he was reading. 'As you see, I am in the middle of Richard Ellmann's *Oscar Wilde*. It is good – but not as good as his *James Joyce*.' But he went on to say that he thought Ellmann was wrong to publish Joyce's 'dirty knickers' letters later. One day he confided to me, 'I didn't like Ernest Hemingway, you know, when I met him. He was very rude about *Finnegans Wake*.' On another occasion he advised 'You have to bring Yeats' "cold eye" to bear on anything you write'. 'Goethe and Yeats were old men when they produced their finest work', he judged. And in art it was the late work of his old friend Henri Hayden, that he admired the most, 'the paintings of the Mont-Moyens [in the Marne] in the 'sixties'. He offered precise memories when we talked about painting, such as 'I remember there is a wonderful Poussin hanging in the National Gallery [of Ireland]: *The Holy Family*.' In music, he judged that 'Schubert's music is the closest thing to pure spirit you could ever find'.

He liked to talk about the actors with whom he was working, often in personal terms, offering a striking verbal portrait of the French actress, Delphine Seyrig, arriving for rehearsals of *Pas* (*Footfalls*) on her motor scooter, her newly Afro-styled hair flowing in the wind: 'she is lovely', he commented. (Delphine later told me how intensely intimidated she had been by Beckett.) He positively glowed with pleasure as he described how 'wonderful' Billie White-law was. He frequently confided information about his latest plays: '*That Time* is on the very edge of what is possible in the theatre'; 'there is some [John Millington] Synge too in [the television play] . . . *but the clouds* . . .'. And he spoke at length about the difficulties he was encountering in staging them: lighting the Auditor in *Not I*, for example in London, finally abandoning the figure altogether in Paris; Madeleine Renaud's problem in speaking quickly enough in the same play; and so on.

In the quite different field of sport, Beckett asked me whether I had seen David Gower cover-driving that summer or Ian Botham ('Beefy' as, laughing, he referred to the famous England all-rounder) hammering the Australians at cricket. Harking back to his childhood, he said 'my great hero at cricket was Frank Woolley, the Kent player'.* We also spoke of the latest rugby matches between France and England or Ireland when he used to listen to the radio commentaries or when, in the last years of his life, he watched the games on television.

There were a few curious incidents at these meetings. I remember one evening during the early years of what I would then describe as our acquaintance rather than our friendship, we were having dinner at the PLM hotel when a lightbulb suddenly flashed close by. Beckett reacted with horror. 'What was that? What was that?' he asked with real panic in his voice. I realized with dismay that he might think that I had set up a clandestine 'photo-call'. So I hastily reassured him, commenting: 'You know I would not do that to you.' 'But they do, you know, Jim, they do', he replied. The sight of a waiter advancing with an enormous pair of steps to change a broken lightbulb on the high ceiling answered Beckett's question. But it made me realize how intensely he loathed and feared that kind of intrusion into his privacy. Much later on, when he was living in an old people's home, he used to go for a walk around the streets of the neighbourhood. One day, a photographer approached him and, thrusting a camera in front of him, took several flash pictures. As Beckett saw the camera raised and registered the flash, his arms went across his chest in a gesture of recoil, a reflex response to protect himself, just as he had done in 1938 on another Paris street when he had been stabbed in the chest by a local pimp. Memories of such intensity die hard.

My most poignant memories of Sam Beckett relate of course to those final few months of his life when I visited him every week in the old people's home to interview him for my biography. He was frailer, moving less easily across the room as he went to get the five-o'-clock Jameson or Bushmill's whiskey, which I liked no more then than I had nineteen years before. The oxygen cylinder propped up against the wall was a keen reminder of the emphysema from which he was suffering. Mentally, too, he was less agile, less sure of finding the right words, although, as the interviews published earlier in this book reveal, he usually found them in the end. His wife, Suzanne,

---

* Frank Woolley (1887–1978) an elegant left-handed batsman and bowler, he played in sixty-four test matches for England from 1909, until, amazingly, he returned to play against Australia in 1934–5 at the age of forty-seven.

died in July only three weeks after we had started our interviews. Yet he called me the day after her funeral to ask when we were going to resume our talks.

Perhaps even more than in previous years when he had been in better health, I was impressed in those final months by the traits that lay behind his genius. He had not focused on himself to the exclusion of others, as so many old people do. He stayed almost as involved in the world as he had always been, still reading, still observing, still asking questions. You were constantly aware that you were with one of the best-read writers of the century, who had absorbed what others had expressed and made it his own. And yet, alongside his intellectualism, I was even more conscious of the deep veins of feeling that he had so often tapped in his work. As we talked about his life, experiences that had touched him most deeply emerged with startling clarity: his deep love for his mother, with whom it is known he had such a difficult relationship, and about whom he could scarcely bring himself to talk; the guilt he experienced at letting his father down by quitting his academic post and the pain that returned sharply as he talked of his father's death; the huge debt he felt towards Suzanne, who had believed in his writing when all the French publishers had been turning him down. The sensitivity to pain and suffering that had always been a key element in his writing now seemed more starkly exposed. I felt how much his sensitivity, even his vulnerability were preconditions of his creative endeavour. And as we sat in his modest, austere, little room, I often thought of an earlier remark he had made that he was 'all feeling'. It made perfect sense.

S. E. Gontarski

S. E. Gontarski is Sarah Herndon Professor of English at Florida State University, where he teaches courses in twentieth-century Irish Studies, in British, US and European Modernism, and in drama and performance theory. His theatrical work includes guest directorships at the Los Angeles Actors' Theater, the Magic Theater in San Francisco and the Teatros del Circulo in Madrid. He is the author or editor of numerous books, most recently *The Grove Press Reader, 1951–2001* (2001), and *The Grove Companion to Samuel Beckett: A Reader's Guide to His Works, Life, and Thought* (with C. J. Ackerley) (2004). Contribution written especially for this volume.

Beckett in Performance

Paris, 4 November 1984. Nothing to be done. Technicians drop lights; microphones and speakers crackle; the huge black box in which the play's unnamed character will appear squeaks noisily as it lurches across the stage in spasms. The 'machine', as the crew calls it, was designed as an invisible frame, to mask the source of theatrical light and to subvert the audience's faith in its own perception. Within this black box, Pierre Dux (an institution in the French theatre), dressed in a black, neck-high cassock, will sit on the black chair, and the 'machine' will move his speaking head imperceptibly across the stage. At some point during the performance the audience will suddenly discern that the head has moved, although no movement, no sound, no change in the intensity or source of light is perceptible. The 'machine' is an ingenious contraption which swallows up the corporeality of the actor, as well as two-thirds of the production budget. But it should create some stunning theatrical effects: a levitated, speaking head, illuminated by a source-less light.

It is one week before the announced opening of *Compagnie*. Everyone knows that Beckett is to attend the afternoon run-through, and nothing is ready. He had come to earlier rehearsals, had discussed this adaptation of his novella with the director, Pierre Chabert, and the actor, Pierre Dux, over coffee and whiskey, but he has not returned for three weeks. Even I (who have been watching rehearsals as a disinterested party in preparation for directing the English-language première at what was then the Los Angeles Actors' Theater) am nervous.

Beckett arrives precisely at four o'clock at the back of the Petite Salle of the Jean-Louis Barrault/Madeleine Renaud Théâtre du Rond-Point, pulls a copy of *Compagnie* from the pocket of his greatcoat, and sits inconspicuously at the makeshift desk at the back of the theatre. He exchanges a few words with Chabert, who then mutters into his headset and turns on the masked reading lamp as the house lights begin to fade. With his wire-rimmed glasses perched on his forehead, Beckett follows the text with his finger, his nose nearly touching the page.

The run-through is flawless, but eerie. The lights fade and come up to total silence. It is theatre in a vacuum, a ghost performance, the only kind Beckett attends. Beckett sits silently with his head bowed, rubbing thumb and forefinger so deeply into his eyes that his sockets seem to be as empty as those of Rodin's Balzac. He is massaging his brain directly. Still no comment. He rises and begins to make his way towards the stage, but his eyes, failing him regularly now at seventy-eight, are slow to adjust to the light change, and he stumbles on the stairs. He recovers, moves to the edge of the stage and stares at the floor. Silence. Finally, hesitantly: perhaps the narrative cannot be staged at all. Four weeks into rehearsals, opening night is a week away. It is entirely my fault for consenting to the adaptation. It is too complicated, too theatrical. Beckett had been reluctant to attend rehearsals from the first. It was, after all, Chabert's production. Chabert persisted, and persisting, incurred obligations.

Beckett's theatrical vision is unsparing: making concessions to audience, friendship, or even finally self is an alien notion. Theatre, like politics, is an art of compromise, but somehow Beckett has failed to make any and has succeeded none the less. He has somehow resisted the collaborative nature of theatrical production. (I once asked Ruby Cohn to referee a grant application that I made to work in Paris with Beckett on an adaptation of his prose work *First Love*. I used the word 'collaborate' in my application, meaning simply 'to work with'; she snapped back, 'No one collaborates with Beckett.' In a very real sense she was right; somehow the word is inappropriate when one works with Beckett.)

Perhaps, if the character is fully lit and his costume simplified, Beckett resumes, looking down at the floor – just a bathrobe, say. Perhaps, if the 'machine' is discarded. Perhaps, if Pierre Dux's moving lips could be masked during the second-person, listening phase of the narrative. Perhaps, if Dux were surprised by the second-person voice, which he speaks but which is amplified through speakers at the rear of the theatre. Dux ought not to anticipate the voice. So he must begin speaking with his head still bowed and raise it to search out the source of the sound. There is no insistence; the suggestions are almost whispered. The cast and director, eager for an imprimatur, agree (as does the visiting American director). In good spirits despite a substantial re-staging a week before opening, the cast and crew withdraw to the dining room for drinks. Pierre Dux is buying, so we follow his lead, with Scotch all around. Everyone relaxes. They at least have a show! Beckett buys a second round and leaves.

The following morning I meet Beckett at the pricey, tourist PLM hotel that he favours for its convenience to his boulevard St Jacques flat and we discuss changes for the American production. Why aren't the second-person narratives taped, I ask? That would be preferable, Beckett responds. Should the American text follow the cuts in the French text exactly (I want to restore some of the deleted material)? Not necessarily, he says. He is unusually forthcoming today and is obviously trying to leave me some working room. 'What is the relationship between the two voices?' I ask. The third-person voice, he explains, is 'erecting a series of hypotheses, each of which is false'. The second-person voice is 'trying to create a history, a past for the third person'. We have spent an hour over one *double express*, and I have gathered enough clues for my staging. But would it be *my* staging of *Beckett's* play? Working with Beckett forces one to rethink the whole nature of the genre. Where is the theatre work, anyway? Whose work is it? It's Beckett's text, but whose theatre work?

In April of 1986 I was back in Paris, preparing to stage another play. The previous summer, Beckett had been in Germany, directing a television version of his play *What Where*. In the process he had rewritten the text, filmed it and offered the rewritten version to Pierre Chabert to stage in Paris. I was offered the English version and would as usual attend Paris rehearsals in preparation for the American staging. Beckett was again preoccupied with simplifying the visual imagery and his dialogue. In the original stage version, the voice of Bam was represented by a hanging megaphone. For his television version, he substituted an enlarged, diffuse image of a face. Such an oversized face was not possible on the stage, according to Chabert – at least at short notice – so Beckett suggested just the outline of a skull, a ring of diffuse light, an image with almost angelic overtones. Again we met after rehearsals, this time in the deserted restaurant of the Théâtre du Rond-Point. I suggested that I thought I could create a hologram to serve as the image of Bam. That was preferable, he suggested. Could we not restore the 'mime' as well, the wordless pattern of appearance and disappearance early in the play? The Paris version seemed to be over-cut. Yes, of course, if I wished, he said.

I staged the revised *What Where* at the Magic Theater in San Francisco in *Visions of Beckett: A Quartet of One-Acts*, and it was filmed for television by John Reilly of Global Village, who then took the tape to Paris to show Beckett. This would be the first production of mine that Beckett would actually see. He had of course seen photographs, listened to audio tapes and the like, but that was all. He watched *Rough for Theatre I*, as he later disclosed, for the first time, ever, and watched my production of *Ohio Impromptu*, and then *What Where*, about which he had most to say. Yes, yes, Beckett said, that's fine . . . but perhaps the lips could move when Bam speaks. And perhaps the other characters, Bim, Bem, and Bom, could be positioned differently. John Reilly, who was producing the piece for Global Village, returned to New York, and, through the magic of computerized editing, repositioned the images according to Beckett's instructions. He hired another actor, filmed his lips miming the dialogue, and electronically grafted those lips onto the computer-created face of Bam. Then he brought the videotape back to Beckett. Yes, yes, Beckett said, that's fine . . . but perhaps Bam's voice could have less echo. And so John returned to San Francisco to re-tape the voice with me and actor Tom Luce. To be safe we taped several versions of the dialogue and so brought Beckett several choices.

In 1989, I staged a revised script of *Endgame*, again at the Magic Theater. I had just revised the play myself for Faber and Faber, incorporating Beckett's cuts and additions for two productions he directed: one in German at the Schiller-Theater Werkstatt in 1967 and one in English with the San Quentin Drama Workshop at the Riverside Studios, London, in May of 1980. I sent Beckett the revised and fully annotated text of *Endgame*, and he reviewed and approved the changes and made a few additional emendations to the text and to my annotations, marking the more elaborate explanations in my footnotes with a huge 'X', which symbol he had established early to mean 'not intended'. I felt that I was approaching rehearsals with more information than the average director. I had spent, for example, two weeks watching Beckett direct the San Quentin Drama Workshop in London in 1980, and had just studied, translated and annotated Beckett's Schiller *Regiebuch* and his notes to the San Quentin production. I had also established a new text for *Endgame* based on Beckett's directorial changes and sent them to him for his approval. I was as prepared as I could ever hope to be for rehearsals, and I began knowing more about how Beckett conceives the staging of this play than I could have known about the work of any other playwright, including

Brecht, whose notebooks for the Berliner Ensemble were almost as meticulous. I had done most of my work, however, without the actor. Ronnie Davis, who played Clov, had his own ideas about revisions, Beckett's and his own. Why shouldn't Clov be blind and walk on all fours? If he's mentally unstable why shouldn't he periodically bang his head against the walls of the bunker, preferably in the midst of Hamm's monologues? Why can't we reintroduce scenes that Beckett cut? Why shouldn't the play represent the political realities of the period of its composition, the Algerian and Indo-Chinese crises, for instance?

The glib answer to these questions was that we were performing the play that Beckett wrote and then rewrote in productions. But the questions were not frivolous, or rather were not all frivolous. They represent a search for the art of the actor in Beckett's theatre. When Beckett is done paring down his minimalist texts, how much creative space remains for other artists: actors, designers, and director? Or is there only a single artist in Beckett's theatre? Beckett's contributions to theatrical performance have been extraordinary. He has shorn the theatre of theatricality, reintroduced metaphysics and indeterminacy into the confident, plastic art of theatre and reasserted the primacy of language, of narrative and poetry, of the playwright himself, even as the capacities of writer and narrative are simultaneously diminished and subverted. In a letter to his American publisher, Barney Rosset, Beckett expresses his diminished authority:

> . . . had a highly unsatisfactory interview with SIR Ralph Richardson who wanted the low-down on Pozzo, his home address and *curriculum vitae*, and seemed to make the forthcoming of this and similar information the condition of his condescending to illustrate the part of Pozzo. Too tired to give satisfaction. I told him that all I knew about Pozzo was in the text, that if I had known more I would have put it in the text, and that this was true also of the other characters which I trust puts an end to that star.

Similarly, in rehearsals for *Endgame* in London in 1980, Rick Cluchey, who was playing Hamm, asked Beckett directly if the little boy in Hamm's narrative is actually the young Clov. 'Don't know if the little boy is the young Clov, Rick', Beckett responded, 'simply don't know.'

Beckett has both extended the primacy of the playwright, and so authorial power, to an unprecedented extent, while simultaneously proclaiming authorial impotence, a diminished authority. That creates an ideological and aesthetic vacuum, which many a director and actor are all too willing to fill. It is a vacuum, however, that Beckett expects no one to fill, that, in fact, defines Beckettian performance, separates it from that of others. If actor or director fills that space, Beckett becomes Ibsen.

Charles Krance

Charles Krance (1937–) was Associate Professor of Romance Languages and Literatures at the University of Chicago. The author of *L.-F. Céline: The I of the Storm* (French Forum Monographs, No. 75), Nicholasville, KY, 1992, he also edited bilingual manuscript studies of *Beckett's Company, A Piece of Monologue* and *Mal vu mal dit (Ill Seen Ill Said)*, New York, Garland Press, 1993; 1996. Contribution is a revised version of Krance's memories set down shortly after his meeting with Beckett.

Meeting with Beckett, 1 September 1986. Our appointment was for 11 a.m. at the PLM Hôtel St Jacques, 17 boulevard St Jacques.

At 10.58, I entered the PLM from the main entrance into the lobby, busy with rich American tourists planning their day. Not seeing Beckett, I stood to one side and waited. At precisely 11.00, Beckett descended the four carpeted stairs into the lobby. There was no mistaking him for anyone else with his elegant stance, determined, though relaxed, stride and noble head slightly bowed with a hint of undisguised vulnerability. He was wearing a café-au-lait camel-hair jacket, rust-coloured turtle-neck sweater and light-grey flannels. I walked towards him and we met a few paces in front of the stairs. Beckett held out his hand with a gentle 'Mr Krance' and I responded in kind, 'Mr Beckett'. 'Shall we go up this way?' he suggested and we headed back up the four stairs and made our way to the Café Français. Beckett, in the lead, headed towards a rectangular table at the rear. While we traversed the room, several of the people inside nodded and smiled politely at Beckett's entrance and the waiters, mostly young, greeted him warmly and with knowing respect. Beckett pointed to the seat behind the table. 'Why don't you sit there, Mr Krance?' he suggested and moved to the seat opposite.

His voice was of a slightly higher and considerably mellower pitch than I had imagined it would be. I was aware of the gentle Irish lilt in his pronunciation. His pronouncing of my name was the most noticeable example, for it sounded like Mr 'Krentz', with a slight roll on the 'r' and an abbreviated vowel sound. As he spoke and listened, his light-blue eyes glowed with a subtle variety of expressions. He sat comfortably but very straight on his chair, with an occasional lean forward, especially when making a point. Occasionally he would half-swing to the left in a relaxed, but still straight, posture, to puff gently and gracefully on his cigar and momentarily reflect.

He told me about the short, one-and-a-half-page text he had just written for Barney Rosset to help him possibly start up again in publishing. He dismissed it with 'It's nothing, really'.* 'But sir, you've been known to pack a lot into a two-page text', I protested. Amused, Beckett chimed in immediately, 'I also pack a lot out', and we both dissolved into laughter. He described his lifelong commitment to writing less and referred to the principle of failure, 'to write things out, rather than in'. He also mentioned *Eleutheria* and *Dream of Fair to Middling Women* and said that when asked, he had looked at them again but judged them too poor for publication. 'They're really quite bad', I believe is how he described them. I reflected, 'So, we'll never see them?' Beckett smiled impishly, and replied, 'Well, not for a while, anyway . . .' which I took to mean not in his lifetime.

I then proceeded to describe the work I had been doing on his

---

* In extended form, this was to become *Stirrings Still*, illustrated by Louis Le Brocquy, New York, Blue Moon Books; London, John Calder Publishers, 1988.

manuscripts at the Beckett Archive in Reading University: my first experience ever in manuscript study. I quoted James Thompson, the Librarian, who remarked that my beginning manuscript study with Beckett was like going directly into the Olympics! Beckett then asked if I had any problems and I was able to say that in all I had been unable to make out only about twelve lines of manuscript in a week's work. He smiled admiringly and told me that he, too, sometimes could not decipher what he had written a year or two before. I informed him that after my week's work at Reading I was, in any case, confident of being able to decipher the concluding portion of his dedication to me in the copy of *Comment c'est* [*How It Is*] that he sent me in 1976. He laughed. My confidence, as it turned out upon my return home, was ill-founded, for I still can't make it out!

I had many detailed questions for him regarding the textual work I was doing and the way he went about translating his own work. In this connection, when we were discussing the whereabouts of the typescripts of *Company*, Beckett suddenly stopped short and, leaning rather anxiously over the table, he asked, 'Tell me, Mr Krance, did I write *Company* first in English or in French?' I was slightly taken aback but, after a couple of seconds' hesitation, I reminded him that he wrote it first in English.

It was by now about noon and the conversation turned to more general topics. When I told him that I had seen it quoted that he thought Céline's *Voyage au bout de la nuit* [*Journey to the End of the Night*] was one of the greatest works of the twentieth century, Beckett momentarily hesitated then said, with a grin, 'I don't remember ever saying that.' He was quick to add, though, his enthusiastic admiration for Céline's later works, the trilogy, *D'un château l'autre* [*Castle to Castle*], *Nord* [*North*] and *Rigodon* [*Rigadoon*], making a definite point of his high praise of *Nord*, which he found fascinating. Beckett praised Céline's art as a stylist, saying, 'Yes, he was a great artist', but immediately qualified this statement, almost as a knowingly understated aside, with, 'although he was a bit foolish' for a period. We both grinned in appreciation of the understatement. I then asked Beckett, although I was sure of his response, whether he had ever met Céline. 'No', he readily replied, adding with an impish grin, 'I was on the run from

'42 on.' I retorted immediately, 'So was Céline, a little later, in '44, but in the other direction . . . you were running in opposite directions.'* At this we both openly laughed and it was here that it dawned on me how freely Beckett had laughed on several occasions in the course of our meeting.

The conversation then shifted to Oscar Kokoschka's painting. Beckett was genuinely surprised and impressed when I told him that I had studied with Kokoschka for a six-week period in Salzburg. I asked him if he liked Kokoschka's work and he replied forthrightly that he liked his earlier works but the later works not so much. With keen interest he asked, 'What kind of man was he?' He seemed genuinely pleased when I described him as 'vital, lively and energetic' and smiled widely and approvingly when I told him that Kokoschka liked to end his day with some good bourbon.

It was now 12.15 and our meeting was coming to a close so I here interjected the lead into my 'closing remark': 'Let me tell you what happened to me on the last day of the Salzburg session. After six weeks of neglect, I was despairing that the Master would take any notice of my work. But on the last day of his rounds, with everybody in the room around my easel, which was full of watercolours, Kokoschka stopped short and began leafing through the top half-dozen paintings, saying "There! *This* is what I've wanted all of you to do for the past six weeks! Bravo! Who did this?" I stepped forward, with knees shaking, and identified myself. Kokoschka then inscribed the top painting with the following: "This is the greatest moment of your life. Repeat it often [followed by the date; probably something like the end of July 1959] OK." ' With Beckett smiling almost paternally, I went on to explain that, my head dizzy with joy, I had put all of my paintings in the (unlocked) locker overnight, with the intention of moving my things out the next morning. When I got there the next day, the signed painting was gone. Beckett and I both said almost simultaneously and with a shared resignation, that someone had stolen it for the dedication and the signature. I was now ready for my closing remark: 'In any

---

* Accused of collaboration, Louis Ferdinand Céline (1894–1961) fled France in 1944 to live in Germany at Sigmaringen and then moved in 1945 to Denmark. Condemned in his absence in 1950 to a year of imprisonment and declared a national disgrace, Céline returned to France after his pardon in 1951.

case, what I wanted to say was that I have had three great moments in my life: the first one was when Kokoschka signed my painting; the second one was when you sent me a signed copy together with a dedication, of *Comment c'est*; and the third one was meeting you today.' Beckett was pleased even if, perhaps, a touch embarrassed and I believe that he said something like, 'Well, thank you', and that I replied, 'Thank *you* . . . Sam.'

We got up from the table and walked back towards the entrance of the café. In the foyer Beckett turned towards me and we shook hands. I noticed more consciously than when we shook hands on meeting, how steady and solid his grip was, despite a gnarly hint of arthritis. I told him again what a great pleasure it was to meet him. He smiled warmly and, as we made to separate, said, with equal sincerity, these two words, 'God bless.' And I, after an instant's pause and slightly stunned, think I remember having said 'God bless, Sam' in return.

Michael Rudman

Michael Rudman (1939–). American-born director who has directed widely in the USA and in England. He directed *Waiting for Godot* at the Lyttelton Theatre of the National Theatre, in London, opening 25 November 1987. These notes, which appeared in an abbreviated form in the National Theatre programme, are reproduced by kind permission of Michael Rudman.

Notes for the National Theatre Staff on a Meeting with Samuel Beckett, 2 September 1987

The first impression was somewhat coloured by what I had been led to expect, but also became the lasting impression: an extremely courteous Anglo-Irish gentleman, living in Paris very near several hospitals and experiencing old age with grace but with considerable irritation.

He was prompt for our meeting, scanning the lobby of the very modern PLM Hôtel St Jacques, at about four minutes before the appointed hour and seemed pleased when I recognized him. He led me to a coffee shop [the Café Français in the hotel] where we took a 'quiet table' and we both ordered coffee. On many occasions he lowered his head onto one hand and looked slightly pained at his inability to remember either a name or a line or a place. But usually he did remember in the end or came up with some description that served well enough instead of the proper name. He had more interest in small things about me and the rest of the world than anyone I've ever met over the age of sixty-five.

The two things he seemed most interested in, to do with me, were my (then) forthcoming child and my interest in tennis and golf. Whenever I mentioned any of these subjects, his face broke into a warm smile and my memory is that he nodded.

His eyes are the brightest blue with what I would swear are black crosses in the middle of them.

He said he had no children which was 'fortunate for them'.

He remembered the prices of the theatre seats that he occupied at the Abbey Theatre in the late 'twenties and early 'thirties and he said that he had a weekly ticket, which contradicts some things I've read about him. Apparently he would go once a week and sit in the one-and-sixes which were just to the right or the left of the three-shilling seats in the balcony. He was full of praise for that period of the Abbey's history.

Beckett gave me a lot of specific comments on the play, most of which I've written down for use in rehearsal. The notes that I'm now dictating are mostly impressions which I don't want to lose.

As to the play [*Waiting for Godot*] he's not bored with it but he is almost certainly tired of it or at least tired of answering questions about it. After an hour and twenty minutes, I apologized for tiring him and he said, 'I would have got tired anyway.' One has to be very careful about quoting him because one wants to be exact. He makes one want to be that.

He seems very impressed with the fact that Mike Nichols is directing *Waiting for Godot* in New York at the Lincoln Center [with Robin Williams and Steve Martin as Vladimir and Estragon] and is using the Assistant Director from the production that Beckett did at the Schiller Theatre in Berlin in 1975 [Walter Asmus]. I told him that I had directed *Hamlet* at the Lincoln Center, but he wasn't impressed and, later, when I began to describe the auditorium of the

Lincoln Center and its difficulties to him he declared the interview at an end and called me 'Mr Rudman'.

Just as the play seems to want to break dramatic moulds, so he seems very resistant to any conversation about accepted theatre practices such as actors delving into the biography of characters or costumes representing the history of characters and he is particularly scornful of suggestions such as that Vladimir's carrot should teach us something about Vladimir.

He displayed a considerable amount of acting ability when I asked him if Estragon spoke the truth when he said that he was a poet. He demonstrated that Estragon was referring to his clothing in a graphic and slightly comical way. His acting ability was also apparent when he quoted lines from a play or sang either of the two songs. I suspect that like most playwrights he's an actor manqué, but in the sense that the profession is missing an actor rather than the other way around.

He liked the man who played Lucky in the San Quentin Drama Workshop production which he oversaw at the Riverside Studios in London. He couldn't remember his name but thought his first name was Peter [it was in fact J. Pat Miller] and reported to me that he had died recently of AIDS. He liked Jack MacGowran, who played Lucky with great success [at the Royal Court Theatre, London, in 1964], and of course the actors in the Schiller Theatre production which he had directed. He seemed very aware of how difficult it was to direct a play but seemed strangely innocent of how directors normally work with actors. He said he had spent months preparing that production, which leads me to my most important impression. What he would really like, I think, would be to see an English reincarnation of the Schiller Theatre production. He referred me to the Assistant Director from that production [Asmus], who is apparently willing to go anywhere in the world and help out, and I think that we should try to get this bloke to England.

He agreed with me that the play sounded good in Irish and that the Irish way of speaking, he said, was good because it enabled one to separate syllables. I think he would rather like it if all four of the actors were Irish.

He seemed to think that only a playwright could direct his own play with enough care and attention because only a playwright would take sufficient pains. I don't think he believed me when I implied that I would give it as much care and attention as he did.

I think that if it is at all possible we should take Lindy Hemming [the costume designer], Bill Dudley [the designer] and whoever is playing Vladimir and Estragon to Paris for one or two days and rehearse in that hotel which has large meeting rooms, and let Beckett walk down the street, about 300 yards, and look at some rehearsals. I can't see what harm it would do and I think it would do a great deal of good.*

This leads me to my main point which is that I'm more and more convinced that the play is like one man's dialogue with himself – rather like [the way] the two Byzantium poems of Yeats are a dialogue within the poet's head. I think this is why he is so resistant to and scornful of considerations of biography for the characters. It follows then that the most difficult thing is the most important, namely to get to know this man himself in order to realize his play properly. Really, it's a dramatic poem much more than it is a poetic drama. Everything he said to me seemed to bear this out and I'm certain that the reason he finds it difficult to talk about the play is the same reason he finds it difficult to talk about himself. In neither case is it impossible, if you ask the right question or a question that he finds comfortable to answer. For example on tennis or golf he is quite forthcoming about his childhood. His family had their own lawn-tennis court and he would sometimes spend 'all day playing golf by himself with two balls, one ball competing with the other'.

When Beckett refuses to answer questions on specifics I believe that he can't. I think that this play simply happened in his head and that that is the only possible landscape for it. I think that he wrote it (as he told me and has told others) to divert himself from a novel he was writing and that he has an unfulfilled longing to be diverted by it again. He wants the stage 'uncluttered' and he doesn't want much colour. He referred to other productions as 'cluttered' in a derogatory way.

My biggest single worry is that on the one hand he wants it to be funny (I think he wants it to be *really* funny and I think he *really*

---

* The parts of Vladimir and Estragon were played by Alec McCowen and John Alderton. Pozzo was played first by Colin Welland, then (after Welland had an accident) by Terence Rigby. Lucky was played by Peter Wight. In the end, the cast did not go to Paris to see Beckett.

wants it to be funny), but on the other hand he wants the movements stylized, maybe a little bit like mime. My worry is that the English audience won't find that kind of thing or that way of doing things funny. My worry is that the English audience (and I suspect most audiences, except possibly for the Germans) will find things funny that are rooted in character and, dare I say it, in time and place. Still I think we must try to give him what he wants.

Jan Jönson

Jan Jönson (1947–). Swedish director, actor and writer. He studied at the Academy of Dramatic Art in Stockholm, performing afterwards as an actor at the Royal Dramatic Theatre. He directed *Waiting for Godot* at Kumla maximum-security prison in Sweden, followed by a production of *Godot* at San Quentin State Prison in California, after consultations with Samuel Beckett. In 2002–3, he directed *Endgame* at ILA maximum security prison in Oslo. Contribution written especially for this volume. The translation, revised by the editors, is by Vibeke Kennair Ottesen.

Barefoot, dressed in a transparent shirt with long sleeves and a pair of pale trousers which ended just below the knee, at the age of fourteen, I stood in the wings at the Folketeatern in Gothenburg, Sweden, warming myself under the stage lights, and watching the actors perform the roles of Vladimir and Estragon in Samuel Beckett's *Waiting for Godot*. I played the part of 'A Boy', who came on twice per night, at the end of the first and second acts to say in one breath, 'Mr Godot told me to tell you he won't come this evening but surely tomorrow'. In time it became a ritual for me hiding behind the scenes under the warm lights, from curtain up until the very end. I wanted to listen to their feelings, to follow the story and feel the 'temperature' on the stage, before I carefully entered to deliver my message. Something had been ignited inside me.

A few years later, after performing Alan Drury's monologue, *The Man Himself*, at the Royal Dramatic Theatre in Stockholm, I was invited by the Department of Corrections in Sweden to perform it at Kumla maximum prison for men, as they found that the monologue captured the inmates' lives. After my performance the men did not applaud. They had, after all, just seen a play about themselves, which was not something to applaud. Instead, one man stood up from the front row and gave me a red rose, saying, 'Please, come back and teach us some drama'. His face reminded me of 'Estragon' in Samuel Beckett's *Waiting for Godot*. I responded, 'I can't teach you drama, but I can come back and read a play with you written by an Irish playwright called Samuel Beckett'. Another man called out, 'Beckett is my hero!' I told those men about my love for Samuel Beckett and his work. I also suggested that we should meet again soon and read *Waiting for Godot* together so as to experience what happens to the text when it is read by people who live in darkness. They answered, 'Come back soon – we're not going anywhere'.

I returned with several scripts of *Waiting for Godot* in English, Beckett's own translation from the French. I met the men and we read and listened to each other and found a way of doing this. For each scene we changed readers and, after about a week of this, one day a man suddenly got up from his chair with the script in his hand, and said in a clear voice, 'This is not a script. It's my fucking diary'. He continued, 'What Vladimir is saying, thinking, waiting for, laughing and crying about is almost identical to my life'.

Greatly moved, I felt I must show people this play and the prison management agreed to let me do a production. Of fifty men it seemed to me that five were identical to the five characters in *Godot*. After a year of rehearsing, we felt ready. The dress rehearsal, performed for the other inmates and the employees at the prison, was a mesmerizing meeting between the actors and their audience; the prison somehow was no longer there. The première was held for invited guests from 'the outside' and, more importantly, for the actors' families.

My actors received due recognition. The prison management saw something new; they did not see inmates standing before them; they saw human beings; and they said that this was the best correctional work they had ever seen. As a result the prison gates were opened and we went on the road in a comfortable van loaded with the costumes, the props, Estragon's stone and the poor-looking tree which we had stolen the night before from a farm behind the prison. We were invited to do a guest performance at the Stadsteater in Gothenburg. My actors got to experience freedom: sounds, colours and smells from which they had been banished for years. We performed only the first act, since we did not have the rights for the whole play. The audience listened to the actors with absolute respect and attention and there was a feeling of forgiveness in the air for these men. Afterwards we returned to the closed prison and, the next day, the actors woke up back in their cells, prisoners again without identity and without human worth.

Samuel Beckett was told about my work. I was delighted to receive a beautiful handwritten letter from him suggesting a time and a place for a meeting. When we met he asked me questions like, 'What happened to my play when you gave it to people who live in darkness? What happened with the silences in the play? What happened with the rhythms?' I answered that, when we rehearsed, the actors worked and worked until they made the words their own. This resulted in the performance becoming believable, beautiful, and sensuous as the actors reached the very heart of the play. Samuel Beckett looked me straight in the eyes and his gaze went straight through me. He nodded quietly with a warm smile. 'Why did you only perform the first act?' he asked. 'Did they not like the second act? Was there something wrong with it?' I answered that they loved the play, but that we did not have the money to pay for the rights to perform it all. 'So, the whole problem is financial, is it?' Sam asked. I answered that this was indeed the case. Then he quickly took a serviette from the table next to us, folded it out and wrote in his beautiful hand that he gave me the rights to set up the production of the whole play. Tenderly he folded the serviette and gave it to me, saying 'Take care of this serviette. Go back to these people . . . do the whole play . . . take them on the road . . . then come back to me and tell me what happened . . .'!

Extremely pleased I returned to Kumla prison to meet my brothers and, with strength renewed, we began work on the whole play. This time it was easier to get to its heart. We had been there before. There was a new tour; we were to visit three places, with a première at the Stadsteatern in Gothenburg. After a press conference, four of the five actors, quietly and unnoticed, left through the stage exit, and quickly made their way across Europe! Chaos broke out at the theatre and there was a national alarm about what had happened. All the tickets were sold out, the audience were waiting in their seats, oblivious to what had happened. With a cool head but a body in turmoil, hungry, thirsty and almost blind without my spectacles, I went on to the stage, with a chair in one hand and a Perrier in the other and blurted out, 'Welcome to the Gothenburg theatre. I'm sorry we will not be performing *Waiting for Godot* tonight. Four of the five actors are at this moment not in the building.'

It seemed as if the audience had stopped breathing. An elderly man on the first row with thick spectacles and a hearing-aid got up from his seat and asked me, 'I'm sorry . . . what is it that is not here?' 'THE ACTORS!' I shouted back at him. I stayed on stage, between the stone and the tree on Beckett's country road, and told the story of my time at Kumla prison to the shocked audience.

Soon I was sitting in front of Mr Beckett again in Paris. He took one look at my face before asking me softly, 'Whatever happened?' I answered in a low voice, 'Six hours before curtain-up all of them except Pozzo escaped . . .' For a short moment Sam held his breath, then he burst out laughing and said softly, 'That's the best thing that has ever happened to my play since I wrote it!'

News of my production in Kumla reached the management at San Quentin state prison in California and, after a preliminary meeting, Jim Carlsson, who was the chief of the 'Arts in Correction' at the prison, became my contact person to work with me in giving Sam Beckett's play to a group of inmates there to see what would happen.

I returned to Sam in Paris, and with great enthusiasm told him about it. I told him that the inmates at this prison are sentenced to live the rest of their entire lives there. He answered, 'If they ask you to stay there and set up a production of my play, please do me a favour. Go for it! Find out again what happens when the play is given to people who have no hope of being pardoned'.

I returned to San Francisco and to the gigantic place that is San Quentin. There I met hundreds of inmates desperately seeking some form of self-expression, some way of bearing their existence in their small cells. After months of intensive conversations and readings, I finally found four people whom I identified with the play's characters. I found everyone apart from Pozzo, so I used to read his lines. One day, there were about ten of us sitting round a table when the door to the room slowly opened. No one in the room noticed this, everyone was looking at his script. Slowly a face appeared, partially hidden by the doorframe, a face behind a pair of big sunglasses, filled with silence and deep concentration. I felt as if the room stood still. I felt that this was my Pozzo. I began reading Pozzo's lines, looking occasionally at the face and I saw something happening in the man. He listened intensely to what Pozzo was saying. It was as if the text was shooting out of my mouth, spearing across the room and hitting the man right in the heart. Carefully I wrote a note to Jim Carlsson, beside me, folded it and slowly gave it to him. I wrote, 'Jim, do you see the man in the doorway? I want him as Pozzo'. He wrote back, 'You can't use the man in the doorway. He is not talking. He has nothing more to say. Nobody in the prison has heard his voice for the last three years'. I wrote in return, 'I still want him as Pozzo'.

The following day, about half an hour after we resumed our reading, the door opened once more, and the same man came in and positioned himself wide-legged, filling the doorway with his entire body, smoking and concentrating as before on what I was conveying to him through Pozzo's text. The next day he appeared again with the same attitude in the doorway. The next day he entered the room. Throughout the week he came further and further into the room. The seventh day he appeared with a newly lit cigarette in his mouth and carrying a chair on his shoulder. He sat down behind Jim and me, finished his cigarette, put it out, came over to me and placed the back of his chair against the back of mine taking great care to ensure that the two chairs were touching each other. He sat down on his chair, and stared straight into the brick wall in front of him and

Spoon Jackson (*left*) as 'Pozzo' and Twin James (*right*)
as Vladimir in *Waiting for Godot*, San Quentin Prison.

stayed silent. I interrupted the men's reading and quickly found a part with Pozzo's lines. I read the following out loud, 'They give birth astride of a grave, the light gleams an instant, then it's night once more'. Quietly and firmly, the man pressed his chair against mine in such a way that my chair moved forwards a few millimetres. Quickly we both got up and moved our chairs to the side and faced each other in silence. Legs wide apart he stared at me from behind his shades, lit another cigarette and smoked it slowly. He has all the time in the world. Time is not rushing him. Then he put out the cigarette, took off his shades, put them in his pocket and looked me straight in the eyes for a while. Suddenly he put out his hand and we shook hands.

'My name is Spoon Jackson,' he said. 'Are you coming back to this prison to do this play?' I answered, 'Yes, I am.' Spoon continued, 'Can you do me a favour? Can you give me the part of Pozzo and help me express myself? Can you give me my life back?' I answered, 'I would love to help you express yourself, and give you your life back.' Spoon asked, 'Can I trust you?' 'Yes!' I answered. Proudly he took a script, put it under his arm, put his shades back on and lit another cigarette, exclaiming, 'All right! Have a nice weekend. I'll see you on Monday morning!' Jim asked me, 'How in Christ's name did you do that?!' I answered I did not know, the feeling was overwhelming. On Monday morning Spoon Jackson was back. He had somehow opened his door onto the world. He sat down and began to read the role of Pozzo as if he had written it himself.

We had been given a beautiful redbrick room for our rehearsals. But not far from there was 'Death Row' and the gas chamber. Heavily armed guards were everywhere and outside among the lush, trimmed lawns were gun towers from which faces would follow every step taken, every move made, through powerful binoculars. Posters declared *No Warning Shots*. This was the setting for our beautiful mission – to set up a production of Samuel Beckett's play *Waiting for Godot*.

During our work I frequently travelled to Paris to see Beckett and keep him informed about our progress. I told him that the men were now communicating with each other through his words, but with a rhythm and a way of listening that they had grown up with. I told him that sometimes they would finish their lines by saying, 'You dig what I'm saying?' And, after finishing a dialogue, they would sometimes 'give each other five'.

Proudly we built our stage in the prison's large sports hall. The costumes and props were loaned to us by the ACT theatre in San Francisco. Everything was falling into place. The prison management believed in this project, and with their support and Jim Carlsson's presence we reached the première. The men's family members were seated on the first row. The men got to tell their stories to their mothers, the women who had given birth to them, and who probably were the only ones to love them unconditionally. 'Happy', who performed the part of Estragon, opened the play by sitting still on a stone, looking his mother straight in the eyes and saying in a calm voice, 'Nothing to be done'.

Barney Rosset, Sam's publisher in America, came to see our production. At Sam's request, our three performances were filmed, not by professionals but by other inmates engaged in the prison's 'Arts in Correction' programme, people whom the actors could trust. Barney Rosset made sure that Sam got to see these films.

Eventually I dragged myself away from San Quentin. Once more I found myself in Paris, sitting in front of Sam. He held up a bottle of Jameson's, looked me in the eyes and said, 'Help yourself!' Then he asked me, 'Why have you done all this?' I answered, 'Because I love the silence in your work. I even love the silence in your face.' We got up and Sam kissed me on my forehead and said, 'I saw that you have got to the heart of my play. Do me a favour; go back to these people, taking my *Endgame* with you.'

Anthony Minghella

Anthony Minghella (1954–). Writer and film director. His films include *Truly Madly Deeply*, *Mr Wonderful*, the Oscar-winning *The English Patient*, *The Talented Mr Ripley*, *Cold Mountain*, and, most recently, *Breaking and Entering*. He directed Beckett's *Play* for the series *Beckett on Film*. Contribution revised in 2005 especially for this volume from an original text by Anthony Minghella.

I was the worst kind of Beckett anorak. I began reading his plays and novels when I arrived at university. I was at my most porous and, for the next four or five years, my thinking, my aspirations, even my handwriting was somehow defined by Beckett. I became obsessed with his writing – its mixture of austerity and romance. He's like Bach for me. And if there are two artists who have provided a lifelong compass it would be Beckett and Bach. Both are noted for their severity of line, the dry surface, but underneath there's a volcano, there's lava.

My unfinished doctoral thesis was on Beckett. *Play* was the first play I ever directed in the theatre, in a double bill with *Happy Days*. For several years, I read Beckett almost on a daily basis.

Ironically, when it came to make the film of *Play*, the way I worked with the actors was antithetical to everything I believe in when directing my own writing. Generally, I don't have much interest in being a martinet. The most pleasure from making drama comes from collaboration, from empowering the actors. But with *Play*, I found myself invading their process and trying to annihilate psychology, annihilate the organic creation of the moment. *Play* is not about psychology – it's a score in some way. And we're all hostage to it.

If you are making a film of *Play*, you have to find a cinematic correlative to the interrogative light, which the stage directions specify as prompting every speech; otherwise the only alternative is to lock off the camera and record a live performance. You can't have a light moving and a camera moving – one has to be still.

When I was teaching dramatic literature, I would sometimes say to students: look at the last page of Beckett's *Play* and the stage direction 'Repeat play'. There's no way you can experience that on the page; nobody's going to return to the first page and read again. In a novel the reader can fully experience the author's intention by reading, but with a play or with a screenplay, a core element of the dramatist's art comes from the manipulation of time and space. Time is experienced in a very specific and pungent way when you're sitting in front of a play which repeats itself. And obviously the Dantesque idea of Beckett's is that in purgatory we'll be forced to revisit the same trivial episodes of our lives again and again, in some kind of ironic rehearsing of life.

The interesting thing here is that the process of making a film mirrors Beckett's conceit for *Play*. Film employs repetition; actors repeat their lines and actions until they are correctly captured on film. Often the camera angle will change and the same sequence will be photographed from this new position, again requiring the actors to perform their lines and movements correctly before the next position. Essentially this is what the characters in *Play* are doing: they're saying things again and again, hoping they might be allowed to move on and, like actors, fearing that this might never happen.

My technique for shooting *Play* was not simply repeating the first iteration of the text, looping the same piece of edited film. The repeat comprises a different version of the same words, but with some recognizable and formal choreographies to allow the viewer to engage with the repetition, perceive it, experience it. The text remains exactly as it's written, but I'm looking to get a layered quality to the film, not just pressing the rewind button. I'm trying to find a film correlative to actors repeating the piece twice. In the theatre, a black-out can be used as a powerful form of punctuation, and this is what Beckett asks for, but you can't do that in film. Black in film means nothing. Instead, I've tried to use run-outs, lead-ins, fogging, clapperboards and other methods for the filmic equivalent of punctuation. They are the same kind of distancing devices.

It's bleak, but what I think is healing in Beckett is laughter. There's a constant movement towards farce in his plays – the frozen grin of farce. It's farce from repetition – first time round, you laugh, and next time round it's harder to laugh. I assume if it kept repeating the experience would get more and more terrifying. When the actors have been trapped in urns for two or three days, you start to sense their growing claustrophobia. It becomes very clear that the governing idea of this writing is terrifying and remorseless. I think the healing gradually disappeared from his writing.

Everybody who loves Beckett will say the same thing: no matter how miserable or dark or cruel it appears, his work is also profoundly uplifting. It's honest, naked, leavened with mischief. And full of pity.

10

In Brief

In this chapter we have assembled a few brief extracts from previously published tributes by several writers, a philosopher, a theatre director and a medical scientist.

Eugène Ionesco

Question: Among your contemporaries whom do you consider the best dramatist in France?
Answer: Samuel Beckett. We see each other rarely, but we're good friends. Beckett is a fine fellow. He lives in the country [his cottage at Ussy-sur-Marne] with his wife, but we see each other when he comes in, at the theatre, in cafés, in *brasseries*. We don't talk about anything much. He is a very generous man, very loyal. Those are rare qualities. I was told that for a long time his principal pre-occupation was to play chess with himself. [From *The Playwrights Speak*, ed. Walter Wager, London/Harlow, Longmans, Green and Co., 1969, p. 131.]

Tom Stoppard

There's stuff I've written I can't bear to watch. They get rotten like fruit and the softest get rotten first. They're not like ashtrays. You make an ashtray and come back next year and it's the same ashtray. Beckett and Pinter have a lot more chance of writing ashtrays because they've thrown out all the potentially soft stuff. I think Beckett has redefined the minima of what theatre could be . . . In 1956 when *Waiting for Godot* was done in Bristol, Peter O'Toole was in the company. I was immobilized for weeks after I saw it. Historically, people had assumed that in order to have a valid theatrical event you had to have x. Beckett did it with x minus 5. And it was intensely theatrical. He's now doing it with x minus 25. I think Pinter did something equally important and significant. He changed the ground rules. [From Mel Gussow, *Conversations with Stoppard*, interview with Tom Stoppard recorded in April 1972, London, Nick Hern Books, 1995, p. 6.]

B. S. Johnson

A lot of the trouble [in understanding him] begins with a failure to place Samuel Beckett in his tradition: in spirit he belongs with Petronius, Rabelais, Cervantes, Nashe, Burton, and Sterne. As with the latter, admiration or loathing of him is an indication of whether the reader is really interested in the novel as a form, or merely in being told a story. Thus to try to understand Beckett in terms of 'the great tradition' or of a main contemporary one which would include Graham Greene, Iris Murdoch, and Elias Canetti, for example, is as useless as to try to compare *Tristam Shandy* with *Clarissa Harlowe*. [*The Spectator*, 23 November 1962, quoted by Jonathan Coe in his outstanding biography, *Like a Fiery Elephant. The Story of B.S. Johnson*, London/Basingstoke/Oxford, Picador, 2004, p. 127.]

Robert Pinget

Generosity, humour, intelligence, superb erudition. It didn't matter what came up, he knew it all. An elephant's memory, he said of himself. I should stress too his horror of lies. As for his generosity, he shared the Nobel prize money out among his needy friends. With the cheque to Roger Blin he tucked in this note 'Neither thanks nor "no".'

He pursued his work right up to the end, trying to remove all trace of rhetoric, until he reached the threshold of silence with *Stirrings Still* [Beckett's last prose work]. As for his despair, it was the very [main]spring of his art. 'Hold tight to your despair and make it sing for us', he wrote to me when we were just getting to be friends. His despair hid something which he wanted to keep for ever quiet and which had to do with his great compassion for human suffering. He expressed it in such a way that everyone can interpret it as he sees fit. Open revolt or humble submission. That paradox was and remains his noblest and best-kept secret. [From *Eonta* I, 1991, pp. 9–10.]

E. M. Cioran

9 September 1968. The other day I noticed Beckett along one of the footpaths in the Luxembourg Gardens, reading a newspaper in a way that reminded me of one of his characters. He was seated in a chair, lost in thought, as he usually is. He looked rather unwell. I didn't dare approach him. What would I say? I like him so much but it's better that we not speak. He is so *discreet*! Conversation is a form of play-acting that requires a certain lack of restraint. It's a game which Beckett wasn't made for. Everything about him bespeaks a silent monologue.

21 April 1969. Beckett wrote to me about my book, *Démiurge*, 'In your ruins I find shelter'.

18 May 1970. At a rehearsal of *La dernière bande*, when I said to Mme. B [Beckett] that Sam was truly despairing and that I was surprised that he was able to continue, to 'live', etc., she replied, 'There's another side to him.'
  This answer applies, on a lesser scale to be sure, to myself as well.

21 August 1970. Last night, Suzanne B. told me that Sam wasted a ridiculous amount of time with second-rate people, whom he helped with their problems. When I asked where this peculiar solicitude could have come from, she told me that it was from his mother, who loved to comfort the sick and to care for hopeless wretches, but who turned away from them when they had recovered or were out of trouble. [Three entries from Cioran's *Cahiers* 1957–1972, translated by Thomas Cousineau. First appeared in *The Beckett Circle*, Spring 2005, vol. 28, no. 1, p. 5.)

Even if he were like his heroes, even if he had never known success, he would still have been exactly the same. He gives the impression of never wanting to assert himself at all, of being equally estranged from notions of success and failure . . . Amenity does not exclude exasperation. At dinner with some friends, while they showered him with futilely erudite questions about himself and his work, he took refuge in complete silence. The dinner was not yet over when he rose and left, preoccupied and gloomy . . . What he cannot tolerate are questions like: do you think this or that work is destined to last? That this or that one deserves its reputation? Of X and Y, which one will survive, which is the greater? All evaluations of this sort tax his patience and depress him. 'What's the point of all that?' he said to me after a particularly unpleasant evening, when the discussion at dinner had resembled a grotesque version of the Last Judgment. [From *Partisan Review*, 43, 2, 1976.]

Edna O'Brien

He has the reputation of being austere and hermetic, but those who have met him always attest to the mildness and courtesy of the man. On his face, though, you see evidence that must have wrestled for every second of its waking life with the cruelty, crassness and barbarity of mankind. His body by comparison is young, lithe, as if by some happy chance it was freed from the torments of the upstairs department. He is as straight and unassuming as an ash plant and the blue eyes have the particular gaze of an eagle in that they convey both hurt and fury. His searching disposition unwittingly cautions you not to talk cant, not to humiliate him or yourself with intemperate drivel, in fact not to talk at all unless you have something of import to say. But he cannot be called austere, having that particular charm and receptivity that makes you recognize that here at last is a born listener. [From the *Sunday Times* Magazine, 6 April 1986.]

John Montague

[Montague writes of Beckett's silences in his early meetings with him, yet his capacity in the right company for wild enjoyment.] I remember very little of what we said, except our seemingly mutual embarrassment. Mr Beckett was painfully shy, shy as an adolescent, twitching, touching things, rearranging objects on the table, a nervous habit of my own, so that it began to look like a game of phantom chess . . . Since I was not involved in the theatre, I had little or no Green Room gossip. Besides, I stammered, so we found ourselves in the absurd situation of someone who found it hard to speak engaging someone who did not believe in conversation, and certainly not in small talk. Sometimes there were long silences between us, as though we were gazing together down some deep well. [Then, speaking of the transformation effected in Beckett by the presence in Paris of his old Dublin friend A. J. 'Con' Leventhal and other Irish friends, Montague writes] . . . This was a different Beckett, the cockatoo hairdo flaring as he ran excited hands over or through it, the brandy or whiskey flowing (you could not pay for a drink in his company), the severe face crinkling with laughter . . . There was also his uneasiness at his increasing fame: after the Formentor prize that he shared with Borges, loomed the Nobel, and in some weird way he wanted to be reassured that the home ground was still there, and liked the fellow feeling that our little Irish group [Leventhal, Montague, Peter Lennon, Beckett] provided, where local references did not have to be explained. [From John Montague's memoirs, *Company. A Chosen Life*, London, Duckworth, 2001, pp. 127–8 and 130–1.]

Peter Brook

Beckett at his finest seems to have the power of casting a stage picture, a stage relationship, a stage machine from his most intense experiences that in a flash, inspired, exists, stands there complete in itself, not telling, not dictating, symbolic without symbolism. For Beckett's symbols are powerful just because we cannot quite grasp them: they are not signposts, they are not textbooks nor blueprints – they are literally creations . . .

Can we define a work of art as something that brings a new 'thing' into the world – something we may like or reject, but which annoyingly continues to be, and so for better or for worse becomes part of our field of reference? If so, this brings us back to Beckett. He did just this with two tramps under a tree. The whole world found something vague made visible in that absurd and awful picture. And those parents in the dustbin. [Peter Brook, *The Shifting*

Jay Levy (*left*), Samuel Beckett (*centre*), Stuart Levy (*right*).

Point: Forty Years of Theatrical Exploration 1946–1987, London, Methuen, 1988, p. 31.]

Jay Levy*

Stuart [Jay's brother, also a scientist] asks Beckett how he decided to write: 'When there was nothing else left for me to do . . . I had no money, so I started to write' is his reply. He does not regard himself as a professional writer, but as a French '*homme de lettres* [a man of letters]'; 'I write *comme ça*,' he says. Stuart gives him several articles on science, but Beckett doesn't have his glasses with him so it is difficult for him to read them. Nevertheless, showing a lot of charm and humility, he inquires about experiments in the laboratory. They are both amused by the interchange of their interests in science and

---

* Dr Jay A. Levy (1938–) Professor in the Department of Medicine and Research Associate at the Cancer Research Institute at the University of California, San Francisco, and a leading AIDS researcher.

the theatre. Beckett offers an explanation for this. The laboratory, he says, is like the theatre. The scientist is the director and the test-tubes are the players: 'you may predict what will happen, but you do not know exactly how it is going to turn out.'

From time to time, over the years, he would engross me in conversations about my research in France or in the United States. When I first met him in 1961, I was working with Professor Lender at the Faculté de Sciences in Orsay on the regeneration of planaria. When this freshwater flatworm is cut in half, it regenerates its tail or its head, whichever is missing. I kept thinking that Beckett might use this biologic event as some theme for a future literary piece of the 'absurd' – but he never surprised me with that. Our discussions on cancer, and later on AIDS, always reflected his great interest in the subjects and his concern for finding solutions to these human diseases. But, most of all, I appreciated him remembering certain details of my scientific work that I had discussed with him even years before. He was able to conceptualize areas of scientific study and to ask provocative questions. [Revised version of an extract from Jay Levy, 'Conversations with Beckett', *The American Scholar*, Winter 1992, pp. 124–31.]

11

And Finally . . .

In this chapter, three people whom Beckett knew fairly well – his Polish translator Antoni Libera, the American director and academic Robert Scanlan, and the bilingual writer Raymond Federman – write about the impact that Beckett's death in 1989 (after a lengthy period of ill health with emphysema) had upon them.

Antoni Libera: Beckett's Blessing

Antoni Libera (1949–). Literary critic, translator and theatre director. He translated many of Beckett's plays and prose works into Polish. He also directed many of the plays in Poland, England and the USA. His novel, *Madame*, published in Polish in 1998, which he refers to here had a great critical success when it was published in 2000 by Farrar, Straus and Giroux. Beckett's many kindnesses to him during the political upheavals in Poland in the late 1970s and early 1980s are described in *Damned to Fame*, pp. 639–41. He still lives and works in Warsaw. Contribution written especially for this volume.

It was early May 1986, in Paris. I had gone there for a literary symposium organized to celebrate the eightieth birthday of Samuel Beckett, for me the most important modern writer, whose work I have translated, annotated and staged in the theatre for many years and with whom I had been in regular contact since the mid-1970s.

According to established tradition, we arranged to meet after the symposium. As usual, Beckett suggested the Café Français at the Hotel PLM, which stood opposite his home on the boulevard St Jacques. I arrived slightly early and sat down at the table we had occupied the last time we'd met there, a few years before. Beckett arrived with his typical punctuality, at 12.00 on the dot, not a second later. To a meeting that wasn't connected with any creative plans or projects he usually came 'empty-handed', as he liked to put it. This time he was holding a small book, which turned out to be an old, very well-thumbed copy of *Effi Briest* by Teodor Fontane.

Beckett's close friends and those who are experts on his work will know that it was one of his favourite novels, which he often went back to and which he also referred to in his writing. 'Let us hasten home', says Mr Rooney to his old wife in the radio play *All That Fall*, 'and sit before the fire. We shall draw the blinds. You will read to me. I think Effi is going to commit adultery with the Major.' And in *Krapp's Last Tape*, as he's making his recording, old Krapp muses: 'Effi . . . Could have been happy with her, up there on the Baltic, and the pines, and the dunes' – because the action of the novel takes place near Stettin – a city which now, as Szczecin, belongs to Poland.

I too was aware of all these references, and so towards the end of the conversation, when the legendary silence, which anyone who ever met the writer may well have encountered, had descended on the little café table, I asked timidly:

'Are you reading *Effi* again?'

Paraphrasing a line of Krapp's he answered:

'Yes . . . a page a day, scalding the eyes out of me.'

'With tears again?' I said, picking up the thread of the quotation. He gave a wan smile.

'No, I wouldn't go so far as to say that.'

I plucked up the courage to ask the vital question:

'Why do you like that novel so much?'

There was a long pause before I got an answer.

'I used to dream of writing something like it. And I still have a bit of that dream left. But I never did. I never did write it . . .' He broke off.

'You never did write it . . .' I brazenly tried to drag the words out of him.

Another wan smile, and then, unfolding his hands, he said:

'For . . . I was born too late. No one writes like that nowadays. Nowadays one writes much worse.' He glanced at me and added jokingly: 'But don't worry. The world is changing. Perhaps you'll manage it.'

That was my last meeting with Beckett. After that we only spoke on the phone. He died in December 1989.

When a few years later I decided to write my own novel, I never planned to follow in the footsteps of my master. My aspirations were far more modest than that. However, I did want him to appear in some way within my book (like Hitchcock in his own films), and I already had a few ideas on how to create such a phantom appearance. And then suddenly I remembered that final meeting in Paris and the words he'd spoken towards the end. But of course! I thought. That's exactly how I should start!

And that indeed is the origin of the first line of my novel.

When in 1999 the novel was being translated into English, I added one more touch.

Beckett had an extraordinary ear for music and poetry, and retained in his memory all sorts of phrases and entire poems that were notable for their special beauty and metre. One of these quotations was the famous line from Joyce's *Finnegans Wake* (an extract of which he had translated into French in his youth), describing the circular Vico Road in Dalkey, south of Dublin.* It is written in iambic metre and goes like this: '*The Vico road goes round and round to meet where terms begin.*'

I told my English translator about this, quoted the line from Joyce and asked her to try to render the first line of my novel in the same metre. And so she did. The first line reads: '*For many years I used to think I had been born too late.*'

I am sure, when I think about it now, that I owe *Madame*'s success to a large extent to Beckett's 'blessing' and to his spirit, which was watching over everything.

---

* The Vico Road, named because of Giambattista Vico and his different 'cycles', winds its way from the coastal village of Dalkey down the coast to Killiney. It is also alluded to by James Joyce in Episode 2, 'Nestor', of *Ulysses*. 'Welloff people, proud that their eldest son was in the navy. Vico road, Dalkey'.

Robert Scanlan: Indeflectible Courtesy

Robert Scanlan (1943–) is currently Professor of the Practice of Theatre at Harvard University. He has specialized throughout his directing career in the work of Samuel Beckett. In 1995, he won the Boston Theatre Award for Outstanding Director for his production of three Beckett plays at the American Repertory Theatre, where for many years he was the Literary Director and where he headed the Dramaturgy and the Playwriting Programs for the Institute for Advanced Theatre Training. He is a past president of both the Samuel Beckett Society and the Poets' Theatre in Cambridge, Massachusetts, and a current member of its board of directors. Contribution written especially for this volume.

It was Samuel Beckett who first clued me in about Bushmill's. It is not typical in Paris to drink hard liquor, but he cared for the ceremony of offering whiskey, and he knew I enjoyed it. Beckett also pointed out to me that Bushmill's – in contradistinction to Jameson's – was 'protestant whiskey' – neither here nor there in any of our subsequent discussions, but a fact that he must have figured might account for my unfamiliarity with the mark. 'Orange in the bottle, you see.' I gathered he distinctly preferred it, and I drink it still *in memoriam*. I am raising a glass to him here, in spirit, for what I am writing is nothing but a wistful gesture of salutation anticipating the occasion that would have been his hundredth birthday . . . hundredth birthday! 'Spared that', 'tender mercies', *und so weiter* . . .

Reaching eighty-three was a long enough journey for him. By the time I met him, he had long since come to terms with Arnold Geulincx's second ethical obligation 'Not to go – leave one's station – until bidden', and he was a profound adept of the difficult precept of the seventh: 'To accept being here.' This last requires – in anyone – a certain *kind* of humility: *contemptus negativus sui ipsius*, according to Geulincx. Beckett led a lot of us to pay a lot more attention to the obscure (and forgotten) seventeenth-century theologian (and disciple of Descartes) than he probably meant to. But the whole latter half of the twentieth century has been following assiduously one or another of Beckett's ingenious leads into the *contemptus negativus*, in innumerable fields. The precept is not as bad as it sounds. Factoring down to essentials is a survival skill of our times, when authenticity and truthful courage are everywhere under siege. You don't have to throw rocks at yourself to achieve the leverage the precept delivers, and it is a *necessary* attribute for enduring 'it *all*'. Astonishing ambition, really – to endure it all to the last. Beckett's late work is all constructed around this patient outlasting, eyes wide open. Many have sensed (and said aloud) that Beckett's serenity towards the end resembled the patience of a saint. He certainly grew infallible in striking off masterpieces, and those are still with us and will outlast *us*, as they have him. Yet as I recall and revisit my precious face-to-face sessions with Samuel Beckett – fewer than one a year during the abbreviated decade of the 1980s – I perceive how vastly I learned in his presence (the Swedenborgian term 'vastations' comes to mind . . . the visitation of vasts). The essence of that learning was in the ineffable aura of his calm, his patient, persistent leads, his shared silences and his infinite kindness. How he cared that we get the plays right! And how he loved the persistent, systematic work of getting things firmly understood. But it seems strange to recall how I felt, above all, vastly at peace near him. We were focused and discoursed freely, even volubly at times (he could be charmingly funny), but his indeflectible courtesy carries the day in my recollections now.

Beckett was closing on seventy-five when I first met him in January of 1981. I had just turned thirty-three – ominous year to a *lecteur du Dante* – and I was spending a leave of absence in Paris. My first direct contact with Beckett was via telephone – he called me, unexpectedly. I had just moved myself into a studio apartment on the Ile Saint Louis and, jealous of my solitude, I had emphatically not given my telephone number to anyone. He knew the Polish bookshop (Librairie Libella) behind which I lived, and called the owner for my number. When the phone rang, I was frying potatoes for my dinner, and I assumed it was a wrong number, intended for the previous tenant. I answered rather brusquely in French, expecting to be off the line in seconds: 'Allo?' 'Hello, Robert Scanlan?' a very polite, somewhat high-pitched voice said at the other end. 'Yes?' I switched to English, puzzled. 'This is Samuel Beckett' . . . and I fumbled the phone and my spatula at the same time. Skillet a-sizzle, I had little choice over my first spoken words to Samuel Beckett: '. . . could you excuse me a minute . . . I have potatoes on the stove.'

At our first meeting, a few days later, I brought up a puzzle I encountered in close-reading *Company*. The heartbeat calculation on page 40 of the Grove Press hardback edition yielded an age for the protagonist of 2,220 years . . . what was I missing? 'He's in his twenties.' Beckett answered. I protested this was incompatible with the 'seventy American billion' of the text, and he proposed we work it out. I pulled out the little pocket calculator I used to convert francs to dollar equivalents, and Beckett started dictating numbers to me . . . 'My heart beats at roughly sixty per minute . . . times sixty, times twenty-four . . .' I entered the figures in the calculator as he spoke. 'Times 365, times twenty-two.' I pressed the 'equals' key and my hand-held went berserk, flashing a long string of capital E's, for 'error' presumably. We had a good laugh. Even this young age was too much for a modern calculator . . . if so few thumps exceeded the capacities of my pathetic little instrument, what were we to make of our respective thumps now? Then Beckett and I got serious over bits of paper, and – sure enough – the printed text was in error. It was to be the beginning of many subsequent discussions of numeration, and it was an invaluable first lesson in 'doing the math' – an injunction Beckett urged with wry irony each time I prepared to do another of his plays. When I staged *A Piece of Monologue* several years later, we pored over the numbers on that occasion, too. It became a habit I associated with Beckett: at his death, he had measured out (if you start counting only at his birth) exactly 30,568 nights and one more half day; 5,516 more days without Beckett have elapsed to the moment of this writing. In thumps, that's a grand total for him of roughly two-and-a-half American billion – 2,641,118,400 heartbeats (not counting his gestation) and 476,582,400 more we've all laboured through without him to this moment of lifting the glass in remembrance . . . but who's counting?

A middle meeting. We were at the Petit Café in springtime this time, and – after almost an hour of talk on many topics (chiefly my upcoming 'Undone Beckett Done' evening, as I closed on finishing a *tutti Beckett* sweep) – I asked Beckett what new work might be coming. He announced he was leaving next day to film *Quadrat* in a television studio in Stuttgart. It was a novel idea, and he sketched it on a café napkin. He showed the square he had drawn with crossing diagonals. Then he added arrows to explain the 'ever leftwards' path that he had envisioned as a trajectory for a 'creature' who would pace off all the sides and both diagonals (each diagonal in both directions) without once repeating any of the 'legs,' until a full 'circuit' had been exhaustively traced. It seemed odd to me to call the zig-zaggy trajectory a 'circuit' but I remember marvelling at the stark simplicity of its principle of generation. The whole geometry resulted from the single instruction ever to turn left whenever a corner was reached. From this one injunction – oh perfect Beckett pensum! – the endless tracing of the eight legs of an intricate circuit, a dogged duty-march leaving after each circuit no leg untravelled and no leg travelled twice (except each diagonal in opposite directions). Each time the full pattern is completed, the creature is in position for an identical repetition. O pointless geometric perfection! O heartbreaking wordless image! Once explained and drawn (with arrows) Beckett let me appreciate the plan, and I borrowed his pen to retrace on the napkin the eight sequential legs of one full circuit thus: side 1, diagonal A, side 2, diagonal B, side 3, diagonal A″, side 4, diagonal B′ – with the primes of A and B representing opposite directions along the same diagonal. It was ingenious as hell. I marvelled and Beckett remained impeccably still, quiet, contemplative, like a satisfied opponent at chess. Then he slowly crumpled the napkin and put it in the pocket of his jacket. 'I'm not sure how it will work in practice.' Again, silence. I was conscious of residing – we both were – in a hushed still point inside the very *nature* of our medium as theatre artists. We both remained silent for some time more. Finally, Beckett proposed a walk.

My last meeting with him was in 1989 – a month or so before what would turn out to be his 83rd and last birthday. I was planning (roughly for that date) one of my periodic 'Beckett Evenings' in Boston. Once I had arrived in Paris, he called me and gave me over the phone careful instructions for finding my way to his tiny room at his new quarters in the old-age home on rue Rémy-Dumoncel. He urged strict secrecy about his whereabouts. Whiskey – Bushmill's – had already been poured for me by the time I arrived, and we started our (last) conversation by shuddering over the ghastly circumstances of Thomas Bernhard's recently discovered death. The event we were planning for the Poets' Theatre in Boston was to be built around David Warrilow, an actor Beckett and I both admired greatly. We also both knew Warrilow to be dying. Beckett showed me a typescript of *Stirrings Still*. After I had glanced over it, he asked me to take a copy across Paris to Warrilow. He was releasing it to us for a public reading, the finale of this evening of ours, that was to include several other pieces. We spoke in our usual way about the other pieces. The planned solo reading of *Ohio Impromptu* troubled Beckett, and he insisted we place Warrilow carefully, fretting that his reading light, if onstage, would create an image that would obviate the text. It was our usual go-around before production, the ostensible purpose of all my visits to his side.

I paused at parting at his threshold and for some reason called him Sam for the first time, 'Sam, I don't know when I'll see you again . . .' Then, on impulse, I crossed the room back to him – he looked very wistful and frail in his drab plaid housecoat – and I enveloped him – most uncharacteristically – in a farewell hug. He spoke distinctly and deliberately to me, his eagle eyes intently fixed on mine, as I backed away again to the door. 'God bless you, Bob Scanlan.' We stared at each other across the tiny room. It was clear what was at stake, and – indeed – as things worked out, that was our last sight of each other.

I read the four loose sheets of *Stirrings Still* carefully just minutes later, on the Métro. It was the first time I fully absorbed what was written there – his own imagination of the end, the final term of the wearying series. I started weeping at what I had been given, and at the thought of who I was taking it to. And then at the fact that we are all heading for the same rendezvous. Some of us have a few more circuits to perform, some less, some of us are done, excused finally from the ongoing. The thumps, the thumps. Here's to you, Sam Beckett. God rest and bless your sweet and patient soul.

Raymond Federman: Sam's Gift of Words

Raymond Federman (1928–). Raymond Federman is a bilingual novelist, poet and translator, who is also a critic and scholar. He has written eight novels in French and English including *Double or Nothing*, *Amer Eldorado* (written in French and nominated for the Prix Médicis), *Take It or Leave It*, *The Voice in the Closet*, *The Twofold Vibration*, *Smiles on Washington Square* (Winner of the 1985 American Book Award), *To Whom It May Concern* and *La Fourrure de ma Tante Rachel*. A friend of Samuel Beckett for many years, he also wrote *Journey to Chaos: Samuel Beckett's Early Fiction* and was the co-author of the bibliography, *Samuel Beckett: His Works and His Critics*. Contribution first published in *Fiction International*, 19:1, 1990. Copyright © Raymond Federman, 2005.

Those who knew Sam, as his friends called him – and I was privileged to be one of them – knew that in the last few months he was ill, and alone, by choice, in that barren room of the nursing home where he spent his last days. A collective sadness was circulating among his friends. There was little to say or do. In conversation, in letters, one simply said 'Sam is ill', that's all. Finally, when the news of his death came, no one was surprised, but the sadness lingers. Yes, there is sadness now and a deep sense of loss. Sam is no longer in Paris, no longer writing another text for us. There will be no more books by Samuel Beckett.

But even though Samuel Beckett has now changed tense, as a friend wrote to me upon learning of his death, what remains is that immense *oeuvre* he has left behind. That incredible landscape of words. For this we are all deeply indebted to him. Personally, however, what Beckett left with me is the remembrance of a few phrases spoken or written each time we met or wrote to each other. Yes, each time I would leave him, holding on to the few precious words he had given me like a fragile gift.

Soon after we first met, more than forty years ago, I told Beckett that I too wanted to devote my life to writing fiction and poetry, and he said to me: 'Raymond, whatever you write, never compromise your work, and if you plan to write for money or for fame, do something else.' I have cherished these words, and hope that I have not betrayed them.

Years later, sitting in Sam's study in Paris, he showed me a text he had just finished. I read it while he sat there in silence, the kind of silence only Beckett could make comfortable. It was a short text, only a few pages, as all his later texts were – short but precise, without any superfluity of words – and I commented on it, saying how beautiful, how powerful, how moving it was. It was called *Company*. Sam replied (in French, we always spoke French to-gether): '*Oui, c'est pas mal, mais c'est pas ça encore.*' ['Yes, it's not bad, but it's not there yet.'] After all these years (Sam was in his seventies then), after the millions and millions of words he had scribbled, in English, in French, he was still not satisfied. 'It's not there yet'. I felt so humble that day as I wondered if he would ever be satisfied. Or tried to *fail better*.

Another time in Paris, again in his apartment on boulevard St Jacques. He had just finished the translation of *Comment c'est* into English. I read a dozen pages of *How It Is* while we both smoked cigarettes – Gitanes in those days – and then I marvelled at the music of his words, at the unusual syntax he had achieved in English, at the dislocation of the language, at this fantastic quaqua, this 'rumour transmissible ad infinitum in either direction', but Sam shook his head: 'No, Raymond [he had a particular way of pronouncing my name, his voice dragging with affection on the first syllable], 'I failed again. The English language resisted me'.

In 1971, Sam took my wife and I to the dress rehearsal of the revival of *En attendant Godot*, almost twenty years after the original production in Paris. Roger Blin was again the director, and except for the actor who played Lucky [Jean Martin, who had another commitment], the same actors who had created the roles of Gogo, Didi and Pozzo were there too, but of course all of them now twenty years older, and that made them even more tragicomic. I thought it was an interesting performance. Blin had deliberately slowed down the movement of the actors and the delivery of their lines, which made for a kind of play in slow motion, but as a result the symbolism became too obvious, even though, perhaps, there were *no symbols where none intended*. Later, in a restaurant with the cast, Roger Blin and Sam, I asked him what he thought of this new production. 'It's good, it's good. Unusual', Sam said. Then he hesitated a moment and added, quickly and softly: 'I only wish they would stop making me say more than I want to say'.

On the occasion of his seventieth birthday, I tried to convince Sam by letter to come and visit us in Buffalo, incognito, and even offered to take him to see Niagara Falls, only twenty minutes by car from my house. (Beckett once told me, half-jokingly, that he had almost won a literary prize which was an all-expenses-paid trip to Niagara Falls.) He wrote back: '*Cher Raymond, merde, j'en ai marre de toujours dire non, mais ces jours-ci je ne suis pas sortable . . .*' ['Dear Raymond, Damn it, I'm tired of always having to say no. But these days I'm not fit to be seen']. (This was written at the time when Sam was about to undergo cataract surgery, and he was wearing thick glasses as he groped his way.) The letter went on with a sentence which for me contains Beckett's endless and relentless struggle with words: '*Et puis tant à faire encore et si peu de quoi.*' ['And then so much still to do and so little to do it with.']

One day, George Plimpton, the editor of *The Paris Review* in New York, approached me to do an interview with Beckett for the series 'Writers at Work'. He offered to send me to Paris. I told Plimpton that Beckett never gave interviews, and besides I would not want to impose on him with such a request. But the next day I wrote to Sam saying that even though I knew he would say no, I could not resist asking him since *The Paris Review* would pay all my expenses for one week in Paris, this way we could have a couple of good expensive meals with excellent wine at his favourite restaurant, and pretend to do an interview. Sam's answer was only one line: 'Dear Raymond, Sorry, I have no views to inter'.

In 1974, I published a novel in Paris entitled *Amer Eldorado*. The book carried this dedication: *Pour Sam* . . . When Beckett received the copy I sent him he wrote back: 'Si la dédicace est bien pour celui à qui je pense il te remercie de tout coeur.' ['If the dedication is for the one I think it is, he thanks you from the bottom of his heart.'] All of Beckett is contained in that sentence – his generosity, his humility, his humour. Of course, he knew that the book was dedicated to him, but the next time I saw him he suggested that perhaps the dedication was for Uncle Sam, or else for my Dalmatian whose name was Samuel Beckett. Sam knew that.

The last time I saw Sam, two or three months before he changed tense, we were having lunch together in a café across the street from his apartment building. Sam had already moved to *Le Tiers Temps* (a medical retirement home not far from where he lived) but when he felt well he would go out for a walk or to check his mail. I was sitting by the window when I saw him walk across the street. He looked frail, and seemed to limp slightly. He held my hand a long time as he greeted me. We sat in silence for a while. Then he asked about Erica (my wife), about Simone (my daughter), who had met him when she was twenty, who now directs Beckettian plays in New York, about my stepson, Steve, the photographer, who took photos of Sam that appear on book covers. I asked him if he was writing anything. He answered that he was trying to translate *Worstward Ho* into French, but that he was stuck. 'I don't seem to be able to translate the title', he said. 'Why don't you skip the title and go on with the text?' I suggested. Sam smiled, the kind of smile that showed both hesitation and affection. 'That would be cheating', he replied. Though *Worstward Ho* was not translated by Sam, I am convinced that he invented the French title, *Cap au pire.** It's too good not to be by Sam.

---

* He suggested the French title to Edith Fournier, who translated the text. It was published by Les Editions de Minuit in 1991.

We finished lunch, and as I was walking with Sam to the nursing home, he suddenly stopped, placed his hand on my shoulder and asked: 'Do you remember that poem by Mallarmé, '*Le vierge, le vivace et le bel aujourd'hui* . . .?' I nodded. And then, right there in the middle of the street, Sam recited the entire poem to me. I didn't say anything, but it became clear at last, as I had suspected all along, that each day he faced the sheet of paper Beckett endured the same *blanche agonie* [white agony] Mallarmé reveals in that poem:

> Le vierge, le vivace et le bel aujourd'hui
> Va-t-il nous déchirer avec un coup d'aile ivre
> Ce lac dur oublié que hante sous le givre
> Le transparent glacier des vols qui n'ont pas fui!
>
> Un cygne d'autrefois se souvient que c'est lui
> Magnifique mais qui sans espoir se délivre
> Pour n'avoir pas chanté la région où vivre
> Quand du stérile hiver a resplendi l'ennui.
>
> Tout son col secouera cette *blanche agonie*
> Par l'espace infligée à l'oiseau qui le nie,
> Mais non l'horreur du sol où le plumage est pris.
> Fantôme qu'à ce lieu son pur éclat assigne,
> Il s'immobilise au songe froid de mépris
> Que vêt parmi l'exil inutile le Cygne.

I shall never forget Sam standing there in the middle of the street reciting these lines to me, and pausing imperceptibly on the *blanche agonie*. The greatest gift I have ever received. And then as we parted he said: '*Parfois tu sais, Raymond, c'est pire de ne pas écrire que d'écrire.*' ['Sometimes you know, Raymond, it is worse not to write than to write'].

We embraced. And I watched the door close behind him. My nose was running. My eyes were running, too. I wiped my face with the sleeve of my coat. I didn't have a handkerchief. It was windy that day.

Samuel Beckett in 1985.

Beckett on Racine

Beckett's Professor at Trinity College, Dublin, Thomas Brown Rudmose-Brown, loved the theatre of Jean Racine (1639–99) and lectured on most of Racine's plays to the young Samuel Beckett, who in turn became a firm devotee. So, when Beckett returned from the Ecole Normale to become Lecturer in French and assistant to Rudmose-Brown in 1930, it represented a tremendous gift of confidence for the professor to hand over his favourite lectures on *Andromaque, Phèdre* and *Bérénice* to his young protégé. This began an enduring and intimate relationship between Beckett and the seventeenth-century French dramatist's theatre that, although pointed out by Vivian Mercier, has yet to be fully explored and assessed by scholars. For if the impact and the influence of Racine on Beckett began when he was a student and can be seen in allusions to all of the above plays on which he lectured in his first novel, *Dream of Fair to Middling Women* (written just after he quit his lectureship), it extended well into his middle period as a dramatist, when he reread the entire theatre of Racine in the early 1960s, relating them directly to 'the chances of the theatre today'.

It may be partly as a result of this total re-immersion in Racine's drama that Beckett came to focus on inner worlds and adopt the monologue in his later plays as his dominant theatrical form, unlike Racine who integrated monologue and dialogue or played one off against the other. Beckett's concern with light and dark contrasts in his late plays also seems to echo the psychological oppositions and their physical manifestations in the stage lighting that he saw in *Phèdre*, as well as his fascination with the tradition of spotlight painting in art. But, above all, as his comments on the second act of *Andromaque* below reveal ('The precipitation of the mind towards a point where there is no longer more than one consideration, a precipitation towards a stasis. In this act the minds of all the characters make a leap towards this stasis') he was impressed by how Racine could depict over-all mental as well as physical stasis, conditions that he himself was keen to explore in the wider terms of their relations with being. If Beckett's views on Racine were then highly idiosyncratic, they are illuminating and revealing of how he himself approached the theatre in his late work seeking out its minima.

The Unpublished Lecture Notes of Grace McKinley, 1931*

Grace West (née McKinley), *c.* 1930.

Racine: *Andromaque*   *Mr Beckett*

For the first time in the Fr[ench] theatre we have no heroic love. Sexuality is rep[resented] at last, and treated realistically. None of the fine Cornelian phrases. The word hate is more frequent than love. We have the cruelty of sexuality stated. There is the pagan tiger of Lawrence with a dreadful Christian awareness. It chases its own tail. This is the tragic position.

---

* These notes are held in the Beckett International Foundation's Archive in the Library of the University of Reading where they reside with other notes taken by Leslie Daiken on Beckett's lectures on Racine. In Trinity College Library, Dublin, there are the notes of Rachel Burrows, some of which are on Racine and which are so far unpublished. We are most grateful to Mrs Grace West (née McKinley) for kindly giving us permission to use material from her notes in a letter to James Knowlson dated 1 September 1998 and to her son, Terence, for confirming that permission and for providing the photograph of his mother.

Andromaque is the most terrible and cruel play of Racine. No
gaiety as in *Phèdre* in the person of Hippolyte – with his youthful
gaiety, the person of Theseus with his blustering. Every cruelty in
Andromaque. There is the madness of desire: with one using the other
as a lever. The play is an explicit statement of Sadism: and even the
mother complex which occupies us so much to-day, (c.f. descrip[tion]
of Andromaque in Astyanax's nursery.) There is the hate impulse
applied to Andromaque and Hermione: There is every cruelty.
What A = P. = P = H = H : O = Astyanax: A
The whole time there is a desperate attempt to impact, to impinge.
We cannot take A at her face value. Her last speech reminds us very
much of Athalie: (see speech of Oreste's(?)).

Self-consciousness in this play is not self-criticism.

Here there is no possibility of the mind finding a solution. It is not
Andromaque's mind that finds her solution but a consultation of
the Oracle of Hector.

At what point of the self-consciousness does the play come to an
end?

When the mind has an integral awareness of the facts as opposed
to a fragmentary awareness. To explain: – the dialogue is really a
monologue. It is the exp[ression] of a fragmentary consciousness.

Pylade etc. are the fragments of the divided minds of Orestes etc.
Their function is to express the vision in the minds of their
protagonists. It is when all these fragments are blended into a
whole that the play comes to an end, e.g. when Hermione realises
after Pyrrhus has been murdered that her love for him is the greatest
thing, and not the soothing of her vanity – out she passes – suicide.

In the mind of Pyrrhus, the two emotions are hint for vengeance
and hint for possession. In Hermione, it is the conflict between fury
at being spurned and her furious need for Pyrrhus.

When these are merged into an integral cerebral state the catastrophe takes place.

The only freedom of mind is the capability of the mind to modify
from fragmentary to united state. (Tragedy of clairvoyance in the
end. Racine lived at a time when an artist could be an artist, and he
expressed his beliefs in art.)

An interesting point is to note how far Racine is present to modern
prose writers.

Background in Racine

Note the discretion with which Racine grades his background: provides reader with a depth of perspective, or plane; e.g. in *Andromaque*: we have: Troy, (smoke, blood, walls of Troy, Hector, Priam). Then the palace of Pyrrhus himself separated from Troy by the sea, all of which is given by the lines:–

Je sais de ce palais tous les détours [I know every corner of this Palace]

N.B. *Three depths of perspective*:
1 Palace
2 Sea
3 Unextinguished flames of Troy.

Racine's background is for the artist, not for the psychologist.
He does not want to explain Andromaque by Troy etc. as Balzac would have done. In Racine the work of background is to give substance to the characters – to give them overtones: it is worth more than its face-value.

The description of Andromaque's first encounter with Pyrrhus gives tone to all the others. Phyrrus covered with blood etc. – and this plays its part in future encounters.

Racine does not want to explain it. Blood, fire etc. are there as so many accretions of character.

Stress on background has nothing whatever to do with the phylogenesis of Balzac. This phylogenetic position of Balzac is to be distinguished from the ontogenetic position of Racine.

The interesting part of the background is the suggestion of the place where the unknotting will take place. Prospective as opposed to perspective:

All the light in Racine is on the front of the stage. The background is only a recurrent menace in the shadow behind. Quite the contrary in Balzac whose background was a devouring thing to his characters.

We find that the great interest in Racine is the Etat[?] dialogue.

When Céphise talks it is Andromaque's thoughts being exposed. Each of Racine's characters has two poles. It is only when these two poles become one that the dialogue will cease.

With Andromaque the two poles are a very real affection for

Astyanax on the one hand and on the other the necessity for keeping him alive (and therefore marrying Pyrrhus).

With Hermione the poles are her vanity and her very real love for Pyrrhus.

With Pyrrhus the poles are love for Andromaque and hate for Andromaque. N.B. that politics never provide a pole for his antagonism, although they provide the whole situation. Thus the play ends when the minds become depolarised, when it becomes a oneness of consciousness, an awareness. This is what the critics mean when they talk of the growth of lucidity in Racine's characters. A gradual invasion by one mental sphere of another.

Act III, sc.2. Oreste's speech gives us the key to his character. Andromaque herself is rather Cornelian: she is not the merely cerebral polarisation that we have in Oreste, who with Hermione is the most interesting character. We get the peculiar relations between Astyanax and Andromaque repeated in *Britannicus* and again in *Athalie* with Eliacin (Joas). The same might be said of Hippolyte (and Phèdre) though she is not his mother.

N.B. Act II of *Andromaque* is the best bit of dramatic construction ever made. The precipitation of the mind towards a point where there is no longer more than one consideration, a precipitation towards a stasis. In this act the minds of all the characters make a leap towards this stasis.

Andromaque is structurally perfect. Note the 5 scenes [acts?]. Not a word too much. Utility of everything.

III 1675–77 Between *Mithridate* and *Phèdre* something happens to Racine. *Phèdre* is the first play of Racine to bring in the sense of sin. Hermione has none, Britannicus has none. The moral issue never arose in the plays before this. Perhaps there is none in Phèdre, but there appears to be.

From 1675 on, Racine was losing his place in the court, so he may have gone back to Jansenism – *faute de mieux* – knowing the precarious faith of the King. Phèdre is the final statement of the Racinian invariable. Obsession of Phèdre.

In Phèdre R[acine] states not a simple position but a false awareness. She thinks she has sinful relations with H[ippolyte] but she has not. She has this false awareness, and Racine deals with that.

Phèdre is almost a pathological study – everything passes in her mind.

We can reduce everything in Racine to a cerebral position. We cannot over-estimate the importance of this. Racine is only concerned with the passion that is refoulée, repressed. He only can see it when it has been forced underground. Not interested in any simple relations between a man and a woman. If the relations receive no interference they do not interest him.

In *Bajazet* his interest is in the relations between Bajazet and Roxane.

Up to the time of Racine in the *théâtre galant* the *objet* had been easily obtained. In Racine, however, we have this great originality that the *objet* is not merely unobtainable but unaware.

The importance of Aricie in *Phèdre* is merely, that without her Phèdre would not be jealous. Her only function is to clarify one aspect of Phèdre. Aricie and Hippolyte are quite without interest.

In *Athalie* what undoes Athalie is pity. The *veuve* [widow] Scarron thought it such a nice play for *jeunes filles* [young ladies]. But she is quite wrong! The play is not at all for *jeunes filles*.

Brittanicus is a study of the mutual relations between Julie and Britannicus. But Racine is only interested in the irretrievable position: i.e. Agrippine and Britannicus.

State of mind cannot be concealed in Racine.

In *Britannicus* we have the scene in which the hero is behind a curtain when he has advised Julie to be standoffish with Brit[annicus]. But she says what is the use since he will see everything in her face.

We have the sense of the involuntary revelation in the features.

We get the same in *Andromaque* between Pyrrhus and Hermione. By her speech she reveals that he is not even looking at her.

Racine develops from chiaroscuro to chiaro.

In *Andromaque* Racine accepts the inapproachability of the mind – the person of Oreste whose mind defies analysis. It is left as a complex, contrary to most of Racine's characters.

Oreste is stated by Racine as *indisponible*, inaccessible.

*   *   *

'Influence of painting and sculpture on Racine. *Andromaque.*
Notice in all Racine the way he can call up pictures. This is
especially seen in *Andromaque*, Act I scene 2: a picture of Troy
before and after the war – also note the description on page 112.
'Songe, songe . . .' In *Bérénice* this is not so much [i.e. pronounced]
– it is more statuary. Picture nevertheless of imperial grandeur.
Phèdre standing in marble white gown in front of marble pictures –
tall and slim with grey eyes with corn coloured hair twisted in ropes
round her head – 'all bathed in white light.'

Bérénice: the most Cornelian play of Racine. Cornelian in the
sense that Bérénice sacrifices what she thinks is her passion to what
she also considers her duty and so leaves Titus. There is something
far milder than in *Athalie, Andromaque,* or *Phèdre*. Racine is not an
idealist – he is a psychologist. No writing is less humble than
Racine's – see irony at end of Preface to *Bérénice* . . . Phèdre and
Hermione are stationary. *Bérénice*: conclusion of the play is an
intensification not modification of the opening. Unbearable clarity.
'Dark with excessive light'. Movement within a piétinement sur
place [a marching on the spot]. Gradual conquest of character by
light of her own character. Bérénice has denied herself – end of B. is
negation of the beginning. Antiochus is a Racinian character who
ends in grief and speaks the most beautiful lines in the play: 'Hélas!'
Titus and Bérénice are non Racinian. Racine is treating a subject of
duty and will, in which as a psychologist he could not have been
interested. Yet Bérénice contains some of his finest writing . . .
What bothered Racine was not the rules (unities etc.) of classical
theatre, but the extraordinary exigencies of his own requirements.
Racine did not waste anything – by pictorial beauty of his treatment
he achieved something. Poetical beauty is not all. His mind recoils
from what is remote to what is actual and present and we are
involved in the crisis. Direct expression brutal with Racine. Invisible
milieu in *Phèdre* – light in the play. Racine unlike Corneille was not
interested in local colour, David's temple as as historian and as
dramatist. Racine interested in non-historical. All rules of theatre,
bare stage etc. suited Racine.

In the dialogues between the confid[a]nt and antagonist what is
really taking place is a monologue. Last floundering of the character's credulity and vulgarity. Racine as modern as any of the

moderns. See treatment of subconscious – all his characters evolve beneath the conscious in the shadow of the 'infraconscient'. Athalie is aware that confusion and darkness are in her own mind – same with Antiochus – but for this Antiochus would be ridiculous and comic. His dramatic function is to serve as a hyphen between Titus and Bérénice – to reveal the feelings of B. for T. and vice versa. Rather comic at the end – the whimper which is not Racinian. Racine's plays do not end with a bang as a rule but with an adequate explosion and fatigue and weariness form the end of the play. If it is not Racinian neither is it Cornelian. The Cornelian triumph of victory. Bérénice shrugs her shoulders at the end – that is not the Cornelian gesture. The Cornelian gesture is the energetic affirmation of the human will – the will always works in Stendhal. The voluntary act is victorious but not necessary – no question of will in Racine – apprehension that is the subconscious is the only thing that has any validity in Racine. Racine endows B. and T. with a will. Yet the play collapses in fatigue and this is not Racinian. There is always a collapse at end of Rac. play but it is a collapse of inanition, when character has been consumed in 'clairvoyance'.

Again [in the fact that] Bérénice evolves and she moves[,] the play is not Racinian. Every dialogue a soliloquy and results in the elimination of so much shadow.

A NOTE ON THE EDITORS

James Knowlson is Emeritus Professor of French at the
University of Reading where he founded the Beckett
Archive (now the Beckett International Foundation). He
was a friend of Samuel Beckett for twenty years and is
his authorised biographer, publishing *Damned to Fame:
The Life of Samuel Beckett* with Bloomsbury in 1996.
He has written and edited many other books and essays
on Beckett and modern drama, including most recently
Images of Beckett with theatre photographer
John Haynes.

Dr Elizabeth Knowlson lectured in French at the
University of Glasgow and later worked in the Centre for
Applied Language Studies at the University of Reading.
She assisted her husband with his biography of
Beckett and his later books and essays.

A NOTE ON THE TYPE

The text of this book is set in Linotype Sabon, named
after the type founder, Jacques Sabon. It was designed by
Jan Tschichold and jointly developed by Linotype,
Monotype and Stempel, in response to a need for
a typeface to be available in identical form for
mechanical hot metal composition and hand
composition using foundry type.

Tschichold based his design for Sabon roman on a
font engraved by Garamond, and Sabon italic on a font
by Granjon. It was first used in 1966 and has proved
an enduring modern classic.